DISCOVER WASHINGTON WITH KIDS

THIRD EDITION

Rosanne Cohn & Larry Kahn

JOHNSTON
ASSOCIATES
INTERNATIONAL

P.O. BOX 313
MEDINA, WASHINGTON 98039
(425) 454-7333 • FAX (425) 462-1335
ONLINE ADDRESS: jasibooks@aol.com

Discover Washington with Kids, Third Edition

ISBN: 1-881409-29-5

Cover photos courtesy Tacoma Children's Museum, The City of Kennewick, Tiger
Mountain Photography, Spokane Chamber/dominic az bonuccelli (az foto.com), and
Tillicum Village.

All entries in this book have been included at the decision of the authors and
publisher. No advertising is accepted for *Discover Washington with Kids*.

Although diligent efforts have been made to confirm the accuracy of information
contained in this work, neither the publisher nor the author is responsible for errors
or inaccuracies or for changes occuring after publication. This work was not prepared
under the sponsorship, license, or authorization of any business, attraction, park,
person, or organization described, depicted, or discussed herein.

First printing January 2005

Book production by Mike Jaynes

JASI
Post Office Box 313
Medina, Washington 98039 U.S.A.
(425) 454-7333

Printed in the United States of America

Library of Congress Cataloging-in-Publication Data

Cohn, Rosanne.
    Discover Washington with kids / Rosanne Cohn & Larry Kahn–3rd ed.
        p. cm.
    Includes index.
    ISBN 1-881409-29-5
    1. Washington (State)–Guidebooks. 2. Family recreation–Washington
(State)–Guidebooks. I. Kahn, Larry, 1926-II. Title.

F889.3.C58 2004
917.9704'44–dc22

                                                                      2004062497

Dedication

To Kit, Joel, Marnie and Marissa: the lights of our life.

Acknowledgements

Our deep appreciation for extraordinary help and support from the directors of chambers of commerce throughout Washington state.

Many thanks to Tracy Schneider, Gayle Picken, Theresa Metzger and Stephanie Cleveland for hints, ideas and parenting insights.

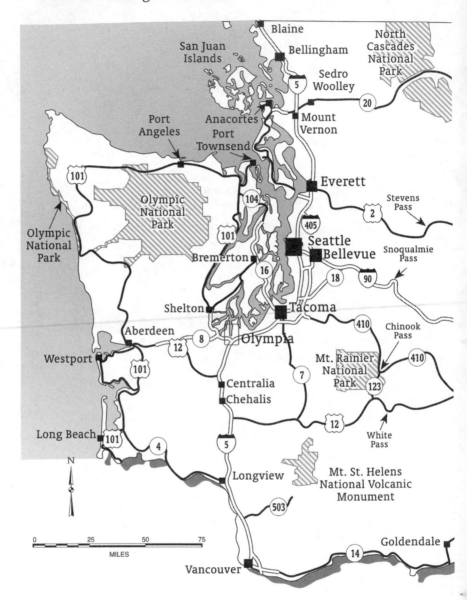

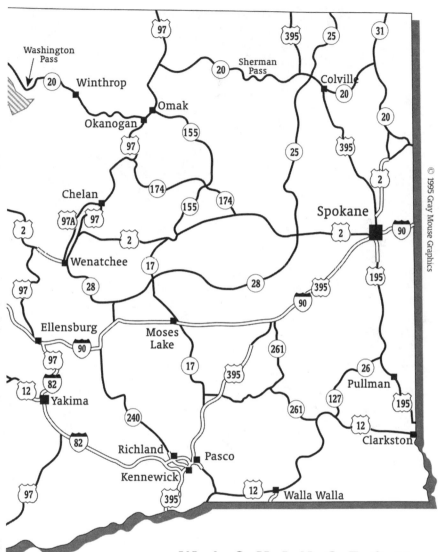

W A S H I N G T O N

Foreword

You are holding in your hand, MEMORIES.

Think back on a wonderful sunny summer day at the beach, or a crisp winter afternoon sledding at Snoqualmie Pass. The time with family that everybody talks about at Thanksgiving or on birthdays. They say, "remember when we went to…"

Sometimes those excursions are planned, but more often than not, they are serendipitous accidents, when everything somehow turned out just right. Outings where there is something for the toddlers to do, the teenagers are busy and even grandparents find a wonderful place for dinner with a nice view. With this book, you don't have to rely on serendipitous accidents any more.

Rosanne Cohn and Larry Kahn have done the research and the legwork for you. You'll know before you pack the car if there are video games waiting for the teenagers at your destination and whether you can get the stroller from the car to the park.

And what's really nice is that you'll come to the realization that you don't have to take out a second mortgage to create a memorable day. We are lucky in the State of Washington. We live in the most beautiful playground in the world. This book will help you get the most out of it. Enjoy all there is and cherish the memories.

Bill Yeend

Morning Host, KOMO AM RADIO

Tips for Travelling with Kids

BE PREPARED! This motto certainly works for families. Getting ready for a family trip can involve everyone, especially when planning the trip. Planning can be the key to preventing or being ready for those small crises or misadventures that are bound to happen. Here are some suggestions:

Have a family conference to plan the trip. Let everyone share his or her ideas about where to go so that everyone has some "say" in the planning.

For longer trips, one mom suggests a rotating "planner of the day" ritual. Every day one of the kids gets to choose the fun activity for that day, be it swimming or going to the arcade. Everyone knows their turn will eventually come around.

If you can't come to an agreement about something, have a lottery.

After you've decided "when" and "where," mark those dates on a calendar—a BIG calendar! The kids get a sense of when it will happen, and anticipation builds as the days go by. They can mark off the days, too. It also helps when you're prioritizing tasks to get ready for the big day.

Involve the younger members in making the plans. After the age of 7 or 8, children can make some of the phone calls to request information, maps, prices, availability, etc. You, of course, can do some role-playing in helping them prepare to make the call. Be sure to stand by in case of confusion or puzzlement. Encourage them to use the Internet to gather information.

Pack a travel bag with all the items you might possibly need, especially those that can forestall a crisis. Let the kids help plan what goes into the bag, then keep it handy for any occasion that involves leaving the house. Suggested items: clean plastic bags, aspirin or other pain-relievers, a complete first aid kit, extra toys and books, CDs or tapes for the tape or CD player, blankets or towels (even a pillow), canned food, snacks and juices, toilet paper and paper towels, change of clothing (old jeans are good), disposable camera, quarters for pay phones, extra batteries for anything—you get the idea!

Ask each child to pack a toy or "entertainment" bag with their most portable play items.

Encourage your kids to start a scrapbook and show them how to collect memorabilia and photos and write entries to record their memories.

And last but not least, remember to stay flexible; preparing a back-up plan in case of bad weather or road-delays will help.

Whatever you can do to create consensus to make your family trip truly a family event contributes to everyone's enjoyment, Planning ahead helps to avoid situations that might spoil this wonderful occasion. These good memories last a lifetime.

Table of Contents

In and Around Seattle

At the Whale's Tail in the Neototems Children's Garden at the Seattle Center
Photo courtesy of Seattle Center

MAGNOLIA, north of downtown, was named by early settlers who mistook the elegant madrona trees for magnolias. The stroll along Magnolia Blvd. is most appealing for its view of the Sound and of the ships and ferries that ply the waters. Nearby Queen Anne was named for the architectural style favored by early residents in the neighborhood.

BALLARD, WALLINGFORD, FREMONT, GREEN LAKE, GREENWOOD, SHORELINE and several other neighborhoods are north of Lake Union and the ship canal. Public art is a distinctive feature here, especially the great Viking Statue on

Ballard's Shilshole Ave. and "Waiting for the Interurban," a sculpture of bus riders in Fremont. The Troll emerges from under the north end of the Aurora Bridge between Wallingford and Fremont.

UNIVERSITY DISTRICT and SAND POINT are also north but separated from Lake Union by I-5. Here you'll find much of the University of Washington community with picturesque neighborhoods to walk through. Second-guessing the Montlake Bridge's raising and lowering has become an art form.

In season, you'll see hordes of people lining the bridge to watch the shells (and rowers) come racing across Lake Washington and under the bridge.

LAKE CITY, BOTHELL and KENMORE (home to the Kenmore Air Harbor seaplanes) lie northeast, connected to much of the Greater Seattle area by the Burke-Gilman trail.

MADISON PARK, CAPITOL HILL, MONTLAKE and MADRONA are east of the city center. At the foot of Madison Street, on your way to Lake Washington, the Washington Park Arboretum is one of the city's most popular and scenic focal points, home to walking trails, athletic fields and the lovely Japanese Garden. Capitol Hill's Broadway district can be a cosmopolitan twenty-four hour bustle of activity; Madison Park is much more sedate. Driving through Washington Park, you'll see some of the city's oldest, most elegant homes.

MOUNT BAKER, SEWARD PARK, BEACON HILL and RAINIER VALLEY are considered South Seattle melting pots, housing much of the city's diverse ethnic mix. In summer, Seward Park is humming with walkers, bikers and swimmers, and literally enveloped by Seafair crowds in early August.

WEST SEATTLE, west of the downtown area, has both the new and the old to commend it. The Fauntleroy ferry (to Vashon Island) is sequestered in this neighborhood; industrial growth sprawls along the water. One of the city's most magnificent views can be seen from Alki Beach (or at the end of a gravel road off WeSt. Marginal Way at Dakota St.). Alki is one of the most popular meeting and greeting places, with multitudes coming to fly kites and walk the shores, picnic and swim. It was here at Alki that the Arthur Denny party arrived in 1851 with some of the first white women to live in Seattle.

Magnolia and Queen Anne

Places to Go

BHY KRACKE PARK
Location: 1215 5th Ave. N on Queen Anne at Bigelow Ave. N and Comstock Pl.
Web Site: www.cityofseattle.net/parks
Days/Hours: 4:00am–11:30pm
Wheelchair/Stroller Access: Yes

Neighborhood children love this playground, and parents enjoy watching them. There's a bike rack, and climbing equipment, and a most extraordinary view. In the spring, the steep, ivy-covered hillside is lush with azaleas and rhododendron. Some visitors come here at night to enjoy the city's lights. (Yes, it's pronounced "by cracky.")

DAYBREAK STAR ART CENTER/UNITED INDIANS   206-285-4425
Location: North side of Discovery Park
Web Site: www.unitedindians.com
Days/Hours: Monday-Saturday, 10am-5pm; Sunday, noon-5pm
Tours: $5/visitors; group must be at least fifteen people ($3.50/per visitor over fifteen); reservations needed prior to visit; discount rates available for children.
Wheelchair/Stroller Access: Yes

The upper level of this Native American center houses a collection of artwork from many North American Native American tribes. You'll find Seminole and Miccosukee dolls, plus major collections of contemporary works by Native American artists featuring large murals and sculpted pieces. On the second Saturday of the month, November through April, organizers host an Indian Art Mart between 10am and 4 pm. Daybreak Star Art Center is administered by the United Indians of All Tribe Foundation.

DISCOVERY PARK   206-386-4236
Location: 3801 West Government Way, Magnolia
Web Site: www.discoverypark.org
Days/Hours: Daily, 6am-11pm. Visitors Center, Tuesday–Sunday, 8:30am–5pm; closed major holidays
Tours: Supervised walks available; reservations necessary. Call for information.
Wheelchair/Stroller Access: Yes

With five hundred acres and four parks in one—cliffs, beach, meadows and forest—Discovery is the largest park in Seattle's Parks and Recreation System and there's always something to explore here. Visit the Wolf Tree Nature Trail, a self-guided educational quarter-mile walk; there's a brochure at the Visitors Center near the park's entrance. The Visitors Center has a small exhibit space for exploration with small children, and there's a playground near the Center as well.

Discovery Park has a diversity of wildlife and nesting birds; tide pool exploration is popular, too. Children under 5 years old qualify for parking permits at the beach (obtainable at the Visitor Center on a first come/first serve basis). Call for a schedule of modestly priced group programs about polliwogs, spiders and snakes planned for preschoolers through eighth graders.

INTERBAY FAMILY GOLF CENTER'S GARDEN GOLF   **206-285-2200**
    Location: West side of 15th Ave. W, near Wheeler St.
    Web Site: www.interbaygolf.com
    Days/Hours: These vary; best to call ahead
    Wheelchair/Stroller Access: Strollers are easy to maneuver on the
        course; wheelchairs are difficult. Pro shop is accessible to both.

Not your traditional miniature golf course, this garden golf layout appeals to golfers eager to improve their putting skills. The lighted eighteen-hole course offers natural contours and hills with no artificial obstacles; landscaping is exceptional. Each hole features a par, and the course is designed with two eight- to ten-foot-high waterfalls, with streams, ponds or water cascading down rocks near every green. Course designers hope that golfing parents will teach their children putting skills here. An adjacent full-size par three nine-hole course is also available, (plus a fully equipped driving range). They do offer junior programs during the summer months; call for current schedules.

Places to Eat

CHINOOK'S AT SALMON BAY   **206-283-HOOK (4665)**
    Location: 1900 W Nickerson St; At Fisherman's Terminal, just south of
        Ballard Bridge
    Web Site: www.anthonys.com/restaurants/info/chinooks.html
    Days/Hours: Sunday, 7:30am–10pm; Monday–Thursday, 11am–10pm;
        Friday, 11am–11pm; Saturday, 7:30am–11pm
    Wheelchair/Stroller Access: Yes

Their great view of the Seattle Fishing Terminal is a drawing card, plus the popular menu specializing in seafood. Young visitors get a placemat menu with crayons and a choice of fish and chips, prawns, burgers or grilled cheese sandwich. Breakfast scones are a favorite and the scrumptious blackberry cobbler (in season) or the hot fudge sundaes. Be prepared, it can be noisy.

After dining, you can walk the docks and do some boat-watching; there are fishing boats of all description with some pretty unusual (and interesting) names.

Northwest Neighborhoods

Fremont, Wallingford, Green Lake, Bitter Lake, Ballard, Carkeek, Shoreline and Phinney Ridge

Places to Go

SHORELINE REGIONAL LIBRARY BRANCH　　　　　　　　**206-362-7550**
　　Location: 3435 NE 175TH St., Shoreline
　　Days/Hours: Monday–Thursday, 10am–9pm; Friday, 10am–6pm; Satur-
　　　　day, 10am–5pm; Sunday, 1–5pm.
　　Wheelchair/Stroller Access: Yes

Shoreline is the third busiest branch in the system, circulating more than 700,000 items annually. Midday readings for toddlers and preschoolers are very popular here, providing a wonderful opportunity for moms (or dads or grandparents) to spend time in the library with the young ones. The branch's summer reading program awards prizes in age groups for those reaching their goals.

BITTER LAKE COMMUNITY CENTER WADING POOL　　　　**206-684-7524**
　　Location: 13035 Linden Ave. N
　　Days/Hours: Varies; usually open daily June through Labor Day
　　Wheelchair/Stroller Access: Yes

Located just off NE 130th St. and open most summer days when it's not rain-ing, this splash-around pool is hot weather heaven for toddlers. It's emptied at night and refilled daily with chlorinated water. You'll find parking and play-climbing equipment, too.

CARKEEK PARK　　　　　　　　**206-684-0877 (for information)**
　　Location: 950 NW Carkeek Park Rd. (North of Greenwood at NW Car-
　　　　keek Park Rd. and Ninth Ave. NW, near NW 100th St.)
　　Web Site: www.cityofseattle.parks.net/parks
　　Days/Hours: Daily, 6am–10pm; Environmental Learning Center, Mon-
　　　　day–Friday, 10am–4pm,
　　Wheelchair/Stroller Access: Difficult

Thanks to a lot of hard work by concerned volunteers, the salmon are back in Pipers Creek at Carkeek. A wilderness park of 180 forested acres, Carkeek rests on a hill above its Puget Sound beach. European-style playground equipment attracts young children. The swings near the picnic shelter are among the most popular; on a clear day they offer incredible views of the Olympic Mountains. A hiking trail with a mountain view runs to the hill's edge. Just inside the main gate is an Archery Range; bring your own bows and arrows. Model airplanes are welcome on the grassy area. Permanent fire pits are located on the beach for park-sponsored events. Dangerous railroad tracks running through this park have been fenced off, but be aware of them. A pedestrian bridge links the beach and park land. The Carkeek Environmental Learning Center, built from environmentally friendly materials to set an example for the public, offers year-round nature and environmental education classes.

GAS WORKS PARK   206-584-4075 (for information)
Location: 2101 N Northlake Way (near Wallingford at Northlake Way and Meridian).Take Northlake Way east and follow Lake Union's north shore
Web Site: www.cityofseattle.net.parks/
Days/Hours: Park is open, 4am–11:30pm; parking lot, 6am–9pm
Wheelchair/Stroller Access: Yes

Gas Works Parks is one of Seattle's favorite play places for kids and parents. Outside, children can climb up the park's highest hill to study the sundial, then roll down the grassy mound to the bottom. In the play barn they can scale the wheels and gears of some old gas works' plant equipment. Breezes off the north shore of Lake Union make this one of the best kite-flying destinations in the city. It's also THE place to be to catch the annual July 4th fireworks show. Gas Works is also the beginning of the Burke-Gilman Trail, a much-used, much-enjoyed recreational pathway for bicyclists, joggers, pedestrians and in-line skaters. The Seattle portion (twelve and a half miles) of the trail goes to Kirkland's Log Boom Park and then hooks up to the 16-mile Sammamish River Trail. Changes are coming to Gas Works–watch for them!

GREEN LAKE   206-684-4075 (for information)
Location: 7201 E Green Lake Dr.
Web Site: www.cityofseattle.net/parks/
Days/Hours: Open 24 hours
Wheelchair/Stroller Access: Absolutely

The tree-lined lakefront park is the city's busiest meeting place for active Seattleites of all ages. If you were to compare it to another destination, Vancouver's Stanley Park walkway comes to mind. Seattleites come from all over to skate, bike, walk, jog and stroll the meandering three-mile asphalt path that encircles the lake (joggers have a slightly longer trail). A line down the middle of the path dictates pedestrians on one side, skaters and cyclists on the other.

This works, most of the time. On the northeast side are tennis and basketball courts, playfields, an indoor swimming pool, gymnasium, canoe rentals, a sandy beach, and a community center. Behind the community center is a playground with swimming and climbing equipment and slides.

The northwest side of the park offers an island game preserve and fishing piers where anglers reel in trout, stocked here annually. Picnic tables, the Green Lake Small Craft Center, lawn bowling, horseshoes and a pitch-and putt course take up the park's south side. One of the most beautiful winter holiday events here is the "Pathway of Lights," held the first or second week of December. Literally hundreds of luminaria — candles sheltered within paper bags — line the path around the lake and carolers fill the night air with holiday music. People of all persuasions enjoy this evening.

GREENLAKE BOAT RENTAL   **206-527-0171**
   Location: 7351 E Greenlake Dr. N
   Days/Hours: Vary seasonally; usually open from
      April–September
   Wheelchair/Stroller Access: Yes

If the urge to hit the water at Green Lake in a canoe, pedalboat, kayak or rowboat is irresistible, rent one here. Teens as young as 14 with experience may rent their own boats, perhaps for a trip to the lake's island; younger children less experienced are advised to try it with an adult in the boat. Pedalboats, rowboats and canoes rent for $8 an hour; kayaks are $10 an hour. Wind surf boards and sailboats are $12 an hour. Life jackets are provided, but parents of children weighing less than 25 pounds will want to bring their own for the best fit.

GREEN LAKE WADING POOL   **206-684-7796**
                                             (Seattle wading pool hotline)
   Location: N 73rd St. and W Green Lake Way
   Days/Hours: Vary, but typically open June–Labor Day:
   Wheelchair/Stroller Access: Yes

Parking is not easy here—the closest is on-street along W Green Lake Way. But when the weather is warm, this pool is filled daily with warm, chlorinated water for lots of splashing. There's little shade for shelter during midday sun, so many families often show up later in the day (or bring umbrellas).

LAKE WASHINGTON SHIP CANAL AND HIRAM M. CHITTENDEN LOCKS
(also known as the Ballard Locks) 206-783-7001; 206-783-7059
(Visitor Center/tours)
   Location: In Ballard at 3015 NW 54th St.
   Web Site: www.nws.usace.army.mil/PublicMenu/Menu.cfm
   Days/Hours: Daily, 7am–9pm. Visitors Center: May–September, daily

from 11am–7pm. October–May, Thursday–Monday, 10am–4pm.
Admission: Free
Tours: Yes; appointments are required for group tours, which last
about an hour.
Summer tours are daily at 1pm and 3 pm. From October–May, tours
are Saturdays and Sundays at 2pm.
Age Minimum: 5 years old
Wheelchair/Stroller Access: Yes, there are ramps to the fish ladder to
assist physically challenged visitors
Driving Directions: From Elliott Ave., cross the Ballard Bridge to 15th
Ave. NW; turn west on Market St. and drive about fifteen blocks.
(Detailed instructions available on their Web site)

It looks as though you could reach out and grab the fish as they migrate
through the fish ladders at these boating locks. The locks are easily one of our
city's most popular tourist attractions. Tours begin in the Visitors Center with
a history of the locks, then move through the immaculately landscaped gardens and, finally, to the locks. You'll learn about the fish cycle at the fish ladder,
which has underwater viewing designed to let you watch salmon returning to
their spawning grounds. It's quite exciting at the height of the season (June–
October); more than 1.5 million people visit the locks annually.

Thousands of boats pass between Lake Washington and Puget Sound via these
locks; watching them rise and fall with the water levels is an interesting experience. Commodore Park, adjacent to the locks on the south side, is a delightful
park setting. Public access at the Locks is from 7am–9pm daily. Grounds adjacent to the Locks are well-lit, with convenient restrooms and bike racks. It's a
good walk; best to wear comfortable shoes and warm outer clothing in cool
weather.

NORDIC HERITAGE MUSEUM   206-789-5707
Location: 3014 NW 67th St. in Ballard
Web Site: www.nordicmuseum.com
Days/Hours: Tuesday–Saturday, 10am–4pm; Sunday, noon–4 pm
Admission: $6/adults; $5/seniors and college students; $4/students
6–17; Free/children 5 and younger
Tours: Yes; self-guided
Wheelchair/Stroller Access: Yes

Scandinavian Americans take great pride in the story of the immigration that
brought their families to this county. Displays cover Sweden, Denmark, Norway, Finland and Iceland; exhibits retrace local Scandinavians' journey across
the Atlantic to Ellis Island. Each nationality has its own display room on the
second floor. Exhibits highlight the fishing, farming and logging work immigrants performed when they arrived in the U.S. Lively holiday celebrations,

including Christmas and summer Tivoli events, are hosted here, with hands-on activities and crafts for children. During tours and special children's events, docents share fascinating history-come-to-life lessons. Watch local papers for weekend performances and art and music demonstrations, check the Web site or call ahead for a current schedule.

NORTHWEST OUTDOOR CENTER   206-281-9694
   Location: 2100 Westlake N
   Web Site: www.nwoc.com
   Days/Hours: Vary; call for a schedule
   Wheelchair/Stroller Access: Yes

Weather willing, children strong enough to paddle a two-person kayak can team up with an adult at this Lake Union boating facility. Rates vary with different trips, so it's wise to call ahead. For many families with children 10 years or older, the guided "full moon paddles" during the summer are a big hit.

STONE GARDENS   206-781-9828
   Location: 2839 NW Market St. in Ballard
   Web Site: www.stonegardens.com
   Days/Hours: Monday and Friday, 6am–10pm; Saturday and Sunday,
      10am–10pm; Tuesday, Wednesday, Thursday, 6am–10pm
   Admission: Varies with class or program
   Wheelchair/Stroller Access: Yes

The kids who drove you crazy climbing up to places from which they couldn't get down will love the challenges at this indoor rock climbing center. Instructors provide equipment and safety instruction as they teach the proper ways to climb. Programs and classes are geared to kids from 5 years old and up; they plan for a ratio of one instructor to four students. Activities include top roping, bouldering, crack climbing, leading (for experienced climbers). Now that's intimidating! Novel idea for a birthday party–plan a two-hour class with three to four children per instructor; all gear is provided. Prices are about $20 per session per child. Most parents have to peel their kids off the wall after a session.

THE TROLL
   Location: Under the north end of the Aurora Bridge, between Walling-
      ford and Fremont
   Wheelchair/Stroller Access: Up to the base on the city sidewalk

Tots like to play "Three Billy Goats Gruff" with this oddball sculpture tucked under the base of the Aurora Bridge. Scope out the Troll before letting the kids start their climbing. Unfortunately, some visitors leave garbage on this whimsical guy.

WOODLAND PARK
Location: Aurora Ave N and N 59th St.
Web Site: www.cityofseattle.net/park
Days/Hours: 4:30am–11pm
Wheelchair/Stroller Access: yes

There's more here than just the city's zoo. You can play tennis, soccer, softball, or just let the kids run within the greenbelt, which is as large as the zoo. The park's upper and lower sections, on the east side of Aurora Ave., are linked by three pedestrian bridges. Wooded trails and pleasant picnic areas with grassy hills overlooking Green Lake are accessible from parking lots off Aurora Ave. and from N 50th St.

WOODLAND PARK ZOO   206-684-4800 (recorded information)
Location: Between Green Lake and Ballard at N 50th St. and Fremont Ave.
Web Site: www.zoo.org
Days/Hours: Open daily year-round. March 15–April 30, 9:30am–5pm; May 1–September 14, 9:30am–6pm; September 15–October 14, 9:30am–5pm; October 15–March 14, 9:30am–4pm
Admission: $10/adults, 13 and older; $7/children 3–12; $9/seniors; Free/toddlers 7 and younger. Groups: Twenty or more receive a 10% discount; all members of the group must enter together.
Wheelchair/Stroller Access: Yes.

Everyone loves to visit the Woodland Park Zoo again and again because there's always something new. Kids still go buggy over the indoor Bug World, featuring 19 fascinating species of arthropods (including insects and spiders), from those in your own backyard to those from the temperate forest, desert, savanna, and tropics. Other enticing exhibits (to name a few) include the Trail of Vines, the six-acre Northern Trail of Alaska (with river otters, brown bears, wolves and elk), and the Family Farm. Here 3–10 year olds can burn off energy climbing on the "spider web," inside the "turtle shells" or on some of the animal-style toys. They can also try their hand at milking a life-size cow, climb aboard a circa 1941 tractor or wiggle their way through a Worm Crawl.

Nationally renowned for its cutting-edge exhibits and animal care, Woodland Park Zoo has created realistic habitats for its creatures. A specially designed and nationally acclaimed Asian tropical forest houses elephants and orangutans; ask about schedules for the elephant baths and programs. Bats and other night creatures live in the Night Exhibit. Giraffes, African wild dogs and zebras roam in the Africa-like savanna, and jumbo hippopotami lurk under water. One of Seattle's most popular celebrities was–and still is–Hansa, the baby elephant born in 2000. New in June of 2003 was the Jaguar Cove. A two and a half acre Tropical Rain Forest (the natural habit of jaguars) with simulated limestone cliffs and a four and a half foot pool fed by a waterfall are all part of this very authentic environment. We can't resist telling you about the gardener's delight–Zoo Doo, the most excellent compost you can find, available through the zoo's Fecal Fests program by calling their hotline, 206-625-POOP.

Stores to Browse

ARCHIE McPHEE AND CO.   **206-297-0240**
Location: 2428 NW Market St. in Ballard
Web Site: www.mcphee.com
Days/Hours: Monday–Saturday, 9am–7pm; Sunday, 10am–6pm
Wheelchair/Stroller Access: Yes, but some aisles are narrow.

This gag gift shop is a magnet for practical jokers – and anyone with a corny sense of humor. It's so popular that the Store's mail-order catalog has thousands of customers around the world. For a few dollars, kids can buy fake eyeballs, Groucho Marx glasses-and-nose, glow-in-the-dark plastic bugs, and hundreds of other goofy things. One of the new items is a J.P. Patches patch. If you don't want to visit the store, you can join the "cult" and order online.

THE SECRET GARDEN (bookstore)   **206-789-5006**
Location: 2214 NW Market St. in Ballard
Web Site: www.secretgardenbooks.com
Days/Hours: Monday–Friday, 10am–8pm; Saturday, 10am–6pm; Sunday, noon – 5pm
Wheelchair/Stroller Access: Yes

Some parents began visiting this cozy bookstore when its home was near Green Lake. Now in Ballard in a much bigger location, they carry books for all ages but still concentrate on titles for the younger readers.

THE CENTER FOR WOODEN BOATS   **206-382-2628**
Location: 1010 Valley St.

Web Site: www.cwb.org
Days/Hours: Summer: May–Labor Day; open daily, noon–8pm. Winter, September 29–April 4, boat rental and boathouse, 11am–5pm.
Admission: Free; boat rental rates vary, ranging from $12–$20 per hour for members, slightly more for nonmembers. Call for info.

The Center for Wooden Boats is a nonprofit organization founded to promote the rich history, lore and romance of wooden boats, their construction and operation. They provide hands-on instruction for the boats in sailing, boat building, navigation and other historical maritime skills. You can ride in rowboats, pedalboats and a steamboat. You'll learn how to tie ropes, knots and "gilhikies." (Ask any sailor you know about that!) The boats here are considered museum exhibits, and they ask that visitors treat them with respect. There are some pretty specific guidelines to be followed; once in a boat, you can "wander" around Lake Union, staying between the bridges. If you're renting a sailboat, you'll be "checked out" by the staff first (this takes about half-hour and costs $5). Why, you're thinking? Because these are traditional small boats, often quite different from the sailing craft you're familiar with–and they are concerned for your safety. On Sunday afternoons at 2pm they offer a free sail on Lake Union–bring the family! The Center offers several youth and family programs as well (including a sailboat-building class for youngsters). During summer months you may see and tour historic sailing and power vessels (such as Lady Washington–Admiral Vancouver's flagship).

Places to Eat

GREAT HARVEST BREAD COMPANY   206-706-3434
   Location: 2218 NW Market St.
   Days/Hours: Monday–Saturday, 6am–7pm; Sunday, 10am–5pm
   Wheelchair/Stroller Access: Yes

There's something here to snack on. See the Lake Forest Park Towne Centre entry (in North King County) for complete write-up.

University District, Montlake, Sand Point

THE BURKE MUSEUM OF NATURAL HISTORY   206-543-5590
   Location: At the University of Washington, at NE 45th St. and 17th Ave
   NE
   Web Site: www.burkemuseum.org; www.washington.edu/burkemu-
   seum/
   Days/Hours: Daily, 10am–5pm; first Thursday of every month is free,
   10am–8pm
   Admission: $6.50/adults; $5/seniors; $3/students; Free/children 5 and
   younger.
   Tours: Yes, self-guided, but you can request a docent by calling at least
   two weeks in advance.
   Wheelchair/Stroller Access: Yes

You'll walk through a 20-foot rumbling, glowing volcano in this remodeled family museum on the University of Washington campus. Most of the exhibits on the top floor of this two-story center are interactive. In the Discovery Center, kids can use a working seismograph and periscope, or touch real fossils. The museum boasts exhibits spanning 545 million years, from the region's earliest dinosaurs to a thousand bugs that call Washington home. In the Pacific Voices exhibits, visitors can learn about seventeen different Pacific Rim cultures, experiment with authentic mask replicas, or learn a few words in an international language. Exhibits are designed for children 5 and older, and best suited to older grade-school and middle-school-age kids (but kids are never too young to visit a museum). Check the Web site for special Family Events throughout the year. If time allows, stop at the Burke Museum Café on the ground floor for a light snack; lots of campus characters for people-watching. Outside, the museum is bordered on two sides by gardens of native Washington plants.

BURKE-GILMAN PLAYGROUNDPARK
Location: North of Laurelhurst at NE 52nd St. and Sand Point Way NE
Days/Hours: Dawn till dusk
Wheelchair/Stroller Access: Yes

This playground near Children's Hospital and Regional Medical Center is totally accessible to the physically challenged. Look for the innovative water-play equipment; there are picnic tables and restrooms also. The park is a stop along the Burke-Gilman Trail.

BURKE-GILMAN/SAMMAMISH RIVER TRAIL
Location: From the north side of the ship canal in Fremont, to Redmond
Web Site: www.metrokc.gov/parks; www.cityofseattle.net/parks
Days/Hours: Open year-round, dawn till dusk
Wheelchair/Stroller Access: Yes

The 28-mile Burke-Gilman/Sammamish River Trail is the second most used urban recreation trail in the country. It's a flat, paved route for bicycling, in-line skating, walking, jogging and stroller-pushing. Ten to twelve feet wide in most places, it attracts active families. The trail officially begins in Fremont on the north side of the ship canal, extends along the north shore of Lake Union, then continues along the abandoned Burlington-Northern Railroad route for twelve and a half miles to Kenmore's Tracey Owen Station (previously called Log Boom Park). The trail then meanders another six miles along the Sammamish Slough to northeast of Bothell; here it meets the Sammamish River Trail and continues into Redmond. One of the favorite pauses is the extensive under-cover scenic playground area in Woodinville (good restroom stop). Maps are available from the City of Seattle's Bicycle and Pedestrian program; call 206-684-7583.

CIVIC LIGHT OPERA 206-363-2809
Location: Performances at the Shoreline Center Auditorium
Web Site: www.clo-online.org
Days/Hours: Box Office: Monday and Wednesday, 1pm–5pm
Admission: $20–$30; depends on the production
Wheelchair/Stroller Access: Yes

These premium musical productions are terrific entertainment for children 6 and older—or those who can sit through a two-hour show. Performers are all local talent. The CLO offers summer workshops for children in grades 2 through 12 in acting, dancing and singing. Call for class listings. The CLO has built quite a loyal following over the years.

GEORGE POCOCK MEMORIAL ROWING CENTER 206-328-0778
Location: 3320 Fuhrman Ave. E
Days/Hours: Monday–Friday, 10am–6pm
Wheelchair/Stroller Access: Yes

The Center was built in memory of Pocock, who was a master builder of racing shells, used by rowers of all ages. If anyone in the family has an interest in rowing, the artwork and photos here will be exciting. There are many photographs of rowing celebrities, teams and events that have made history in Washington State, some shot by nationally known photographers. Their "Learn to Row" classes will teach you the basics, or get you ready for the serious stuff. Anyone completing the Beginner and Intermediate classes gets a free one-month membership to the Center. Rowing and sculling are highly prized skills in the Puget Sound area.

HENRY ART GALLERY/FAYE G. ALLEN CENTER FOR THE VISUAL ARTS 206-543-2280; 206-543-2281 (for tour guides)
Location: University of Washington campus; 15th Ave. NE at NE Campus Parkway
Web Site: www.henryart.org
Days/Hours: Tuesday and Friday–Sunday, 11am–5pm; Thursday, 11am–8pm.
Admission: $8/adults; $6/seniors; Free/UW and high school students with student ID and students 13 and younger. Thursdays from 5–8pm by donation. Ask about group discounts.
Tours: Guides available; see number above. Allow at least one adult to each group of ten children.
Wheelchair/Stroller Access: Yes

After a long closure for remodeling, the revamped Henry Art Gallery has greater opportunities for children. Best suited for older children, the gallery specializes in modern and contemporary art and is noted for featuring new work by local artists as well as important exhibitions of national scope. The underground addition creates even more space to exhibit American paintings and sculptures and the new Skyspace is particularly magical. Please note: some exhibitions are not suitable for all audiences. Best to preview yourself or ask at the front desk. Parking fees are sometimes charged in the underground garage next to the museum; parking is always free on Sundays.

LAURELHURST COMMUNITY CENTER
Location: 4554 NE 41St St.
Days/Hours: Dawn till dusk
Wheelchair/Stroller Access: Yes

The big play structure here is a barrel of fun. It has tire swings, two slides, arch climbers, trapeze rings and climbing platforms installed over a safe bed of sand.

SAND POINT MAGNUSON PARK   206-684-4946
Location: 7400 Sand Point Way NE (at NE 65th)
Web Site: www.cityofseattle.net/parks
Days/Hours: May 1–Labor Day, 4am–11:30pm; Labor Day–April 30, 4am–10pm
Wheelchair/Stroller Access: Yes

The paved paths at this park near Lake Washington attract families who enjoy bicycling and in-line skating. Part of the former Sand Point Naval Air Base, the site features tennis courts, softball fields, picnic tables, restrooms, barbecue sites, a boat launch and more. Young children are mesmerized by the Sound Garden, a sculpture of pipes that makes music in the wind. It's a favorite attraction here; look for it next door in the National Oceanographic and Atmospheric Administration (NOAA) campus. There's a life guarded beach and wading pool open during summer months.

MATTHEWS BEACH
Location: NE 93rd St. at Sand Point Way NE
Web Site: www.seattleparks.gov
Days/Hours: Dawn till dusk
Wheelchair/Stroller Access: Yes

Many north-end families consider this their favorite playground because of the innovative bridges and climbing equipment for toddlers, and challenging play equipment for older children. This park also boasts Seattle's largest freshwater beach; lifeguards usually are on duty here during the period when Seattle public schools are out for the summer. During warm weather months, families on bicycles make this their picnic destination via the Burke-Gilman Trail, which runs through the park.

MEDICINAL HERB GARDEN   206-543-1126
Location: University of Washington campus (on Stevens Way across from the Botany greenhouse). From I-5, take the NE 45th St. exit (#169); travel east to the campus.
Web Site: www//nnlm.gov/pnr/uwmhg
Days/Hours: Daily during daylight hours
Admission: Free
Tours: Free guided tours on the second and fourth Sundays at noon during the growing season; special tours by arrangement for a small free.
Wheelchair/Stroller Access: Limited

This fascinating little garden was established in 1911 on one acre. It has expanded and retracted over the years, due to university expansion, but today almost 600 species of medicinal herbs and shrubs are grown on two acres, making it the largest such garden in both North and South America. Many of the plants have been grown from seeds gathered from around the world; it is maintained by the Friends of the Medicinal Herb Garden. While you're there, look for the Cascara Circle, a circular garden with a raised pool and charming wooden monkeys perched on pillars. Early summer is the best time to visit.

NORTH ACRES PARK WADING POOL 206-684-7796
Location: 12800 First Ave. NE
Web Site: www.seattleparks.gov
Days/Hours: Varies, but usually open daily from June–Labor Day
Wheelchair/Stroller Access: Yes

Tots may splash around in this shallow pool on warm weather days. The pool is filled daily with clean water.

NORTHWEST. PUPPET CENTER   206-523-2579
Location: 9123 15th Ave. NE
Web Site: www.nwpuppet.org
Days/Hours: Varies, depending on scheduled weekend performances
Admission: $7.50/adults; $5.50/children 16 and younger
Wheelchair/Stroller Access: Yes

Enchanting puppets and marionettes from all over the world come alive on this stage. Some shows are performed by Seattle's own Carter Family Marionettes; other performers come from as far away as Tashkent (in the former Soviet Republic, Uzbekistan) and China. Before or after a show, visit the center's puppet museum, featuring rotating international exhibits. The first Saturday matinee in each series is signed for the hearing-impaired. For $7.50/child and $9.50/adult, you can reserve a birthday party here. Each guest receives admission to a puppet play and a puppet to take home; the birthday kid gets a crown.

SEATTLE YOUTH SYMPHONY   206-362-2300
Location: 11065 5th Ave. NE, Suite E (box office)
Web Site: www.syso.org
Days/Hours: Box Office, Monday–Friday, 9am–5pm
Admission: $7–$35
Wheelchair/Stroller Access: Depends on the location of
   the concert

For families who enjoy listening to music together, these concerts are a good introduction to classical music. The young musicians (ages 7–23) play a fairly sophisticated repertoire and have gained a reputation for very professional performances. SYSO's goal is to provide outstanding music education and performance opportunities for Pacific Northwest youth, regardless of financial capability; they administrate and operate five full orchestras, three summer music festivals, concerto competitions, public school programs and scholarships. The recommended age for concert-goers is 7 and older, as many performances can be up to ninety minutes long.

UNIVERSITY OF WASHINGTON   206-543-2100
Location: 15th Ave. NE and 45th Ave.
Web Site: www.washington.edu
Days/Hours: Call for a brochure.
Tours: Self-guided tours only; guided tours are for prospective stu-
   dents
Wheelchair/Stroller Access: Yes

The U.W. campus is worth a stroll, especially on autumn afternoons when the fall colors are brilliant, or spring when the cherry blossoms in the Quad are bursting out. Pick up a map from the Visitors Information Center at 4014 University Way NE and a brochure on the university's history, and you're on your way. You can stop for a snack at the HUB (the student union building, also known as the Husky Union Building) or wander down to Drumheller Fountain. Include the Burke Museum or the Henry Art Gallery on your tour, if time allows.

UNIVERSITY OF WASHINGTON WATERFRONT
ACTIVITY CENTER   206-543-9433
Location: Behind Husky Football Stadium off Montlake Blvd.
Web Site: http://depts/washington.edu/ima
Days/Hours: Daily in February, March, April. February, 10am–6pm;
   March, 10am–7pm; April, 10am–8pm. February–October: Monday–
   Friday, 10am–dusk; Saturday and Sunday, 9am–dusk. No boat rental
   November, December, January.

Admission: For canoes and rowboats: $4/UW students; $5.50/UW faculty and staff; $7/UW alumni; $7.50/general public. Prices quotes for one-hour rental. Valid ID required. Cash or check only.
Wheelchair/Stroller Access: Yes

A great place for families, especially on a sunny afternoon! The rental is modest and you can go exploring through the waterways around Foster Island and through the arboretum. You'll find water lilies, cattails, weeping willows and lots of exuberant overgrowth. It can be very peaceful and relaxing. They don't take reservations, so you might want to plan for a wait with either a picnic or some activity that will keep the whole family involved. Life jackets are provided, but children must weigh at least 25 pounds to assure the tops of their life jackets don't cover their chins. Valid ID will be required for each boat rental.

Places to Eat

PAGLIACCI'S   206-632-0421
Location: 4529 University Way NE (other locations throughout the city)
Days/Hours: Sunday–Thursday, 11am–11pm; Friday–Saturday, 11am–
    midnight
Wheelchair/Stroller Access: Yes

From the front of the restaurant you can watch pizza makers toss dough high above their heads as they spin it out for pies to be laden with sauces, cheese, and dozens of other toppings. Buy pizza by the pie or the slice; the menu features salads, too. Strolling through the restaurant, see how many cinema posters tacked to the walls your child can recognize. The posters are printed in Italian with many familiar words and pictures.

Stores to Browse

DISPLAY AND COSTUME SUPPLY   206-362-4810 (Seattle);
                                                     425-535-3364 (Everett)
Location:11201 Roosevelt Way NE, Seattle; 5209 Evergreen Way, Everett
Web Site: www.displaycostume.com
Days/Hours: Monday–Friday, 8:30am–8:30pm; Saturday, 9:30am–6pm;
    Sunday, 10am–5pm
Wheelchair/Stroller Access: Yes

Not only are they on the Web, they're into webs—especially at Halloween. Everything is here but the invitations; they have a full line of party accessories and costumes for all occasions. In past years Batman Forever, Robin and Cat Woman were "hot"—recently it's been Harry Potter (of course!), Lord of the Rings and Spiderman. Witches, policemen and firemen are old favorites – who knows what the future brings! Face painting and makeup, tiaras and crowns (even in toddler sizes), and plenty of free parking available here. They also rent helium tanks; you'll need them for the balloons.

Madison Park and Capitol Hill

Places to Go

CORNISH COLLEGE OF THE ARTS   206-726-5066
   Location: On Capitol Hill at 710 E Roy St..
   Web Site: www.cornish.edu
   Days/Hours: Monday–Friday, 9am–4pm
   Wheelchair/Stroller Access: Yes

At Cornish, student artists and performers offer several presentations each year that are wonderful attractions for children interested in the creative arts. Ask about Cornish Junior dance company performances and the school's Fisher Gallery, which hosts visual art exhibits Monday through Friday, noon – 5pm. Admission is free. Works on display are by professional artists, with occasional student shows.

MUSEUM OF HISTORY AND INDUSTRY (MOHAI)   206-324-1126
   Location: 2700 24th Ave. E; near the Arboretum, off Lake Washington
      Blvd.
   Web Site: www.seattlehistory.org
   Days/Hours: Daily, 10am–5pm
   Admission: $6.50/adults; $5/seniors; $4/youth 5–17 and students; Free/4
      years and under, UW students and members.
   Wheelchair/Stroller Access: Yes

Dedicated to the history of Seattle and King County, MOHAI features various programs for families. There are interactive games and hands-on activities for kids throughout the year, and each December the museum highlights international holiday traditions with an exhibition and activities. Outside the Museum, two lakeside nature trails (bordering Portage Bay and the Montlake Cut) belonging to the arboretum offer pleasant places to observe nesting birds, ducks, geese and fish. Or you can drift through in a canoe with a picnic lunch (see UW Waterfront Activities Center). One trail winds under the Montlake Bridge and meanders before ending at the Seattle Yacht Club. Another trail goes to little Marsh Island, crosses a bridge and continues to Foster Island. The walk around Foster Island is long for most small children. The trails have no restrooms, and the path can be muddy (it's wise to bring boots).

PEPPI'S PLAYGROUND   206-684-4075 (Seattle parks info)
Location: 3233 E Spruce St.
Web Site: www.cityofseattle.net/parks
Days/Hours: Daily, 4:30am–11pm,
Wheelchair/Stroller Access: Yes

Named by Leschi schoolchildren for a first grader who was killed in an auto accident, Peppi's is a lovely playground, with a wading pool and excellent play equipment. During summer months it is a popular supervised recreational site.

ROANOKE PARK   206-684-4075
Location: 950 E Roanoke St. (follow 10th Ave. E; it will end at Roanoke)
Web Site: www.cityofseattle.net/parks
Days/Hours: Daily, 4:30am–11pm,
Wheelchair/Stroller Access: Yes

Here's a nice place to spread a blanket and relax over a picnic lunch (or brunch if you prefer). It's especially pretty in spring when the flowering trees are in bloom.

SEATTLE ASIAN ART MUSEUM   206-654-3100
Location: In Volunteer Park at 14th Ave. E and E Prospect St. (on Capitol
    Hill's north end)
Web Site: www.seattleartmuseum.org
Days/Hours: Closed Mondays and Tuesdays. Open Wednesday–Sunday,
    10am–5; Thursdays, 10am–9pm. Closed on Christmas and New Year's
    Day and holidays that fall on a Monday.
Admission: $3/general admission; children 12 and under free when ac-
    companied by an adult. Free on the first Thursday and Saturday of the
    month; first Fridays free for seniors 62 and over.
Tours: Group tours available through their Adult Program; discounted
    admission for groups of 10 or more; advance reservations necessary.
Wheelchair/Stroller Access: Yes

Formerly the site of the Seattle Art Museum (now downtown), this facility has been remodeled to showcase numerous galleries of Asian art. Six galleries are devoted to Chinese works; another six feature Japanese pieces. Look for masterpieces from the Himalayas, India, Korea and Southeast Asia. Your ticket for this museum is also good for the Seattle Art Museum within one week of purchase.

SEATTLE MIME THEATER   206-324-8788
Location: 915 E Pine St., Studio 419 (administration)
Web Site: www.seattlemime.org

Days/Hours: Box office; Monday–Friday, 9am–5pm
Wheelchair/Stroller Access: Yes

Seattle Mime is a troupe with unique talent, enchanting to their audiences. The group usually tours to different locations, spending quite a bit of time in schools, but they do perform in their own space as well. These performers are not silent all the time; they are actors who speak, use sound effects and music, in addition to the movements and gestures that "make the invisible real and the imagination soar." In one of their most successful assembly programs, monkeys will spill off the stage and into the audience, bubblegum balloons pull people off the floor and into the air…and much more, giving each member of the audience something to think, talk and laugh about long after the performance is over.

VOLUNTEER PARK CONSERVATORY   206-684-4743
Location: 1400 E Galer St. (in Volunteer Park on Capitol Hill)
Web Site: www.cityofseattle.net/parks
Days/Hours: Open daily, including holidays. Memorial–Labor Day,
    10am–7pm. Otherwise, 10am–4pm.
Admission: Free, but large groups require an appointment. Donations
    are very welcome.
Wheelchair/Stroller Access: Yes, but some areas are narrow. Floor can
    be damp in places.

Just by using your imagination, you can travel from the desert to the tropics inside this Victorian-style greenhouse conservatory. The temperature in the Bromeliad House is 72 degrees and is home to just about every relative in the pineapple family. There are more than 2000 species. In the Fern House, you'll see a Sago Palm, a small pond (no coins, please; metal kills the fish) and many tropical and subtropical flowers. The Palm House is also tropical and has a permanent display of orchids that bloom year-round. The Seasonal Display House, at 65 degrees, is slighter cooler. Here, as the seasons change, you'll find begonias, coleus, fuchsia, geraniums, gardenias and poinsettias.

VOLUNTEER PARK WADING POOL   206-684-7796
                                              (Seattle wading pool hot-line)
Location: 1400 E Galer St.
Days/Hours: Park is open year-round from 6am–11pm; pool is usually
    11am–8pm from mid-June to Labor Day
Wheelchair/Stroller Access: Yes

When the weather is warm, this pool is filled daily with clean, chlorinated water, perfect for lots of splashing. You'll enjoy the tree shade during hot weather. Parking is limited; nearby 15th Ave. E is an option.

VOLUNTEER PARK WATER TOWER
Location: Volunteer Park
Web Site: www.cityofseattle.net/parks
Days/Hours: Daily, 8am–5:30pm
Admission: Free
Wheelchair/Stroller Access: No

Put those energetic legs to work climbing the 106 steps of the historic Olmsted-designed Water Tower to the top of the observation deck. When you reach the top, you'll find a beautiful view of the city. The park is a great place to visit during the day, but should be avoided after dark.

WASHINGTON PARK ARBORETUM   206-543-8800
Location: Park is located on Lake Washington Blvd. between E Madison St. and the State Rte. 520 Bridge. Graham Visitors Center is at 2300 Arboretum Dr. E.
Web Site: www.wparboretum.org
Days/Hours: Daily, dawn to dusk. Visitors Center: 10am–4pm daily.
Admission: Free
Tours: First Sundays at 1 pm; free; custom tours for a small fee (call to arrange)
Wheelchair/Stroller Access: Yes at the Visitors Center, but limited on the trails

Many Puget Sound families have a favorite time of year to visit this sprawling park. Autumn offers the brilliant colors of turning leaves, while winter displays a refreshing collection of camellia and witch hazel. During snowfall, the textures and landscapes are dramatic. Spring showcases the well-loved (and often photographed) azaleas, rhododendron and cherry trees. The arboretum is literally a living museum of woody plants, one of the finest collections in western North America, but all suitable for the Puget Sound region. There are over 5,000 species to admire and learn about here; the collections are well marked, but you can pick up a brochure at the Graham Visitors Center that will help you identify specimens. The Arboretum staff offers guided tours, all designed to include the most interesting areas for the particular time of year. It's important that children be able to walk the distance. The one- to two-hour tours may cover several acres; the Arboretum covers 230 acres in all.

WASHINGTON PARK ARBORETUM/JAPANESE GARDEN   206-684-4725
Location: Lake Washington Blvd., two blocks north of Madison St.
Days/Hours: From March 1–November 30, Tuesday–Sunday, 10am till closing (closing varies from 4pm–8pm, changes seasonally). Closed December–February. The Garden will open the last day of February

at 10am with a special "opening blessing ceremony" to which the public is invited.

Admission: $3/ages 19–65; $2/ages 6–18, 65 and over and college students; Free/5 & under

Tours: Group tours available with two weeks advance notice; appointment required; call number listed above.

Public Tea Ceremony: for observation only; held in the teahouse, third Saturday of each month, April – October.

Wheelchair/Stroller Access: Yes

This garden is beautiful year-round, but most colorful in April and May when the shrubs are in bloom. Especially lovely are the water irises in late spring and early summer. Children's Day in early May is an excellent time to visit with children. Japanese drums, storytelling, koi (carp) feeding, origami making, Japanese games and martial arts demonstrations are all part of the festivities.

Founded in 1960, the three-acre Japanese Tea Garden was designed and created by a Japanese landscape architect who was considered a national treasure in Japan. A fire destroyed the teahouse in the 1980s but local Japanese architects, artists and volunteers helped restore it. With a brochure available at the garden's gate, you can interpret this authentic garden by understanding how the various elements in the garden–mountains, water and fire- represent nature. Plantings in the garden are tended and pruned according to the original design. For children, one of the highlights here is the view from the small bridge where they can watch the elegant koi moving through the pond. If you visit the garden midafternoon, the staff often invites the children to help feed the koi. Turtles and frogs have a comfortable home here as well, threatened only by the large blue heron that visits from time to time. No smoking or food is permitted in the garden.

Wallingford

Shops to Browse

WALLINGFORD CENTER

1815 N 45th St. 206-517-7773 (Center office)

The building is—or was—a classic old schoolhouse in the Wallingford district. It's surrounded by small stores and a neighborhood of traditional houses and parks. The school was built in 1904 and renovated in the 1980s. It now houses a collection of small shops and restaurants. There are two floors to explore; wheelchair access at the service entrance on the south side of the building. For kids, you'll find:

SECOND STORY BOOKSTORE
Special section for kids; go up the stairs and sit on the carpet for a quiet, secluded story time.

IMAGINATION TOYS
Of course the kids will have fun browsing here!

Place to Eat

JULIA'S 206-633-1175
  Location: 440 Wallingford Ave.N (across the street from the Wallingford Center)
  Web Site: www.eatatjulias.com
  Days/Hours: Open daily. Monday, 7am–3pm; Tuesday, Wednesday, Thursday, 7am–9pm; Friday–Saturday, 7am–10pm; Sunday, 7:30am–9pm.
  Wheelchair/Stroller Access: Yes

It's funky and fun, with wooden tables and chairs, but good food reigns. Portions are ample and they specialize in healthy eating. Kids 8 and under can color and eat; there's also a small Julia's "lending library" (with one of our favorites, Goodnight Gorilla). Lunch is special; kids can order cheese and pasta, burger and fries, fish and chips, pb&j, or choose soup and salad and bread. Beverages include apple juice and hot chocolate. Boosters and high chairs available.

Other Julia's locations: 300 Broadway E, Seattle (206-860-1818); 375 Gilman Blvd., Issaquah (425-557-1919). Hours vary at each. Call for information.

South Seattle

BEER SHEVA PARK   **206-684-4075 (Seattle parks info)**
  Location: S Atlantic and Rainier Ave.
  Web Site: www.cityofseattle.net/parks
  Days/Hours: Daily; 4am–11:30pm
  Wheelchair/Stroller Access: Yes

This park's name honors Seattle's sister city in Israel, a site of great historical and religious significance. In the autumn it's a colorful place for a family stroll among the park's chestnut trees; some are more than 100 years old. For kids, there's a play area, plus picnic tables and restrooms

GOODWILL MEMORY LANE MUSEUM   **206-329-1000**
  Location: 1400 S Lane St. (near corner of Rainier Ave. S and S Dearborn St.)
  Web Site: www.seattlegoodwill.org

Days/Hours: Monday–Friday, 10am–5pm; Saturday, 9am–5pm; Sunday, 10am–5pm
Admission: Free
Tours: Monday–Friday by appointment only; tours last about forty-five minutes. Schedule one week ahead.
Wheelchair/Stroller Access: Yes

Located in the back of the huge Goodwill Store is the Memory Lane Museum, showcasing special donations reflecting Seattle's history between World War I and II. The items are not for sale, and the exhibits change periodically. Highlights include "Miss Bardahl," one of the favorite Seafair hydroplanes of the 1960s and an eleven-foot-tall grizzly bear named Bruce, a gift from retailer Eddie Bauer.

KUBOTA GARDEN   425-725-5060

Location: Renton Ave. S at 55th St. S
Web Site: www.cityofseattle.net/parks
Days/Hours: Daily, dawn to dusk
Admission: Free
Wheelchair/Stroller Access: Yes

Even in one of the busiest parts of the city, you will find a quiet place in this historical and cultural garden. Part of the city's open-space program, it covers 20 acres and features an exquisite display of plants, waterfalls, ponds and prayer stones tended by a local foundation. This is an environmental education site for the children's forest school program, also. Originally designed and created by Fujitaro Kubota, the garden was maintained by the Kubota family for many years and purchased by the City of Seattle in 1987. Today it is a lovely sanctuary showcasing the coalescing of Japanese and Northwest garden concepts.

MOUNT BAKER ROWING AND SAILING CENTER   206-386-1913

Location: Stan Sayres Park (between Seward Park and the I-90 floating bridge)
Web Site: www.mtbakercrew.com
Days/Hours: Monday–Thursday, 5:30am–9pm; Friday, 5:30am–6pm; Saturday, 7am–4pm; Sunday, noon–7pm. Closed July 4, July 29–August 4 (Seafair), May 25–27, and Labor Day. Call for additional information if needed.
Wheelchair/Stroller Access: Yes

Adult, child and family water classes at this center on Lake Washington are very popular, with summer the busiest time of year. The sailboard and sailing camps are for children 10 years or older. During the rest of the year, kids must be 13 to 18 to participate in the sailing, rowing, canoeing and kayaking lessons. Courses are six to twelve weeks long. Children who have not taken a class but have passed a float test (ten minutes floating in the water while fully dressed) may ride in a watercraft with an adult who has passed a class. At nearby Mount Baker Beach, lifeguards are on duty during the summer. During Seafair in late July through early August, this area serves as hydroplane pits for crews and media.

MUSEUM OF FLIGHT   **206-764-5720; 206-764-5712 (tours)**
>   **Location: 9404 E Marginal Way S**
>   **Web Site: www.museumofflight.org**
>   **Days/Hours: Open daily, 10am–5pm; first Thursday of each month from 10am–9pm. Closed Thanksgiving and Christmas.**
>   **Admission: Free of charge on the first Thursday evening of every month from 5:00–9:00pm. Other: $11/adults 18–64; $10/adult groups* and seniors 65 and older; $5.50/Youth group*; $6.50/youth 5–17; Free/4 and under. *Groups must be 10 or more paying in one transaction.**
>   **Tours: For group tours, call visitor reservation line: 206-764-5720, #384**
>   **Wheelchair/Stroller Access: Yes. Some wheelchairs available at the Admissions Desk; all restrooms are accessible.**
>   **Driving Directions: Take I-5 exit #158; turn right on E Marginal Way S and follow this road one-half mile.**

The Red Barn, formerly Boeing's first manufacturing plant, is now an integral part of the Museum of Flight. Two floors of exhibits in the Museum capture visitors' imagination with flight displays dating back to the replica of the Wright Brothers' 1902 glider. A new arrival in 2003 has caused enormous interest—a British Airways Concorde (retired). Donated to the Museum of Flight and the only Concorde on display on the West Coast, the jetliner is open to the general public daily from 11:00am to 3:30pm; the tour is free with Museum admission. Elsewhere in the Museum, a hands-on exhibit for kids called The Hanger includes a plane into which they can climb. The exhibit includes a life-size replica of an actual FAA control tower, with a control panel that leads you through all the stages of the FAA air traffic control system. The Museum is a wonderland for kids of all ages, but older kids are really captivated by the history and panorama of flight development. Fifty-four authentic airplanes in perfect condition entice them, plus Air Force One, America's first presidential jet. There's no lack of excitement here—allow plenty of time to enjoy the whole experience.

PRATT FINE ARTS CENTER   **206-328-2200**
>   **Location: 1902 S Main St.**
>   **Web Site: www.pratt.org**

Days/Hours: Offices open, 9am–5pm daily (reception only on weekends); Studios open Monday–Sunday, 9am–10pm. Closed most federal holidays.
Admission: Call for specific class fees.
Wheelchair/Stroller Access: Yes

Almost hidden behind the Wonder Bread plant in Pratt Park is the Pratt Fine Arts Center. Teachers here are professional artists offering classes in printmaking, jewelry casting, and all disciplines of glass-making. Elementary school-age youngsters can learn some of these skills in the Kids Artworks program offered each Saturday, September–November. There's a $10 registration fee. The school emphasizes artwork teams between artists and students. Pratt is one of the few nonacademic visual arts facilities in the country offering beginning and advanced classes and studio space.

PRATT WADING POOL   206-684-7796 (Seattle wading pool hotline)
Location: 1800 S Main St., near Yesler St. and 20th Ave.
Web Site: www.cityofseattle.net/parks
Days/Hours: Usually open June through the summer. Hours may vary.
Wheelchair/Stroller Access: Yes

This wading pool is shaped like the continent of Africa. The creative and innovative design attracts children like a magnet; they delight in playing in the water spraying from spouts that resemble a menagerie of African animals. This is unlike any other in the city and admired for its artistic imagery. Pool guidelines are important: among others, no glass containers allowed, and swim diapers or tight plastic pants on infants are required.

SEWARD PARK   206-684-4075 (Seattle parks info)
Location: 5902 Lake Washington Blvd. S
Web Site: www.cityofseattle.net/parks
Days/Hours: Daily, 4am–11:30pm
Wheelchair/Stroller Access: Yes

In the summer, this park (a peninsula jutting out into Lake Washington) pulsates with activities: music concerts in the amphitheater, kids running on the playground, families dining at picnic tables adjacent to the water, plus some environmental education opportunities in this outdoor classroom. A paved path runs through the park; bicycling families pedal around the lake, serious walkers, joggers and skaters move along very intent on their pace. Others come for the beach, where lifeguards are usually on duty during the summer. Lovely flowering cherry trees at the entrance were a gift from Seattle's Japanese community. There are some changes coming; watch for the new Seward Environmental and Audubon Center coming soon.

THE MUSEUM OF COMMUNICATIONS   206-767-3012
Location: 7000 E Marginal Way
Web Site: www.museumofcommunications.org
Days/Hours: Tuesdays only; 8:30am–2:30pm; by appointment other
    days
Admission: Free; donations gratefully accepted
Tours: Self-guided; guided tours available by request
Wheelchair/Stroller Access: Yes; both entrance ramp
    and elevator
Driving Directions: From I-5 take the Corson Ave. exit, turn left into
    the museum parking lot.

This small museum is a tribute to the energy and loyalty of the Telecom Pioneers (formerly the Telephone Pioneers), retirees who wanted to see their history preserved. There are three floors of antique telephone and telegraph gear, and everything works! You'll see a British Call Box from Derby, England, a piece from the Timbuktu Telephone Company, and a panel server test board which – when placed in service in 1923—marked the start of dial tone and dial service in the Seattle area. Visiting hours are limited; this is a great destination during a vacation or for a school-group field trip.

West Seattle

ALKI BEACH PARK   206-684-4075 (Seattle parks info)
Location: 1702 Alki Way
Web Site: www.cityofseattle.net
Days/Hours: Dawn till dusk
Wheelchair/Stroller Access: Yes

The waters of Elliott Bay may be chilly, but that doesn't discourage children playing on the shores of this two-mile, gently sloping stretch of beach (the walking path is approximately two and a half miles) On spring and summer evenings, it's a popular place for teens, but you'll find walkers, joggers, rollerbladers and strollers of all ages come here to enjoy the spectacular view. There's also volleyball, beachcombing, sunbathing, bicycling—and people-watching! Watch for the annual sand-sculpturing contest in August—a lively time to be here.

CAMP LONG   206-684-7434
Location: 5200 35th Ave. SW (West Seattle's Delridge
    neighborhood)
Web Site: www.cityofseattle.net
Days/Hours: Winter: December–February, Tuesday–Saturday, 10am–
    6pm. Summer: Tuesday–Sunday, 10am–6pm

Admission: Free
Tours: Choose a self-guided trail or a ninety-minute nature hike led by
   a Camp Long naturalist, Saturdays, 2pm. Call for reservations ahead
   or during the same week as the hike you want to attend. No age
   minimum, but they request that groups of children be accompanied
   by an adult.
Wheelchair/Stroller Access: Yes

Camp Long is a wilderness experience within the city limits. It's especially good for families who love the outdoors, but don't want to travel far to enjoy it. The tours are educational and the guides are quite knowledgeable.

Ten cabins provide overnight accommodations. Each has six double beds and can sleep as many as twelve people. Three cabins are wheelchair accessible. Cabin rentals are $30 per night.

Ask about the rock-climbing program for those 7 or older. Students learn how to scale a 25-foot artificial rock with safety harnesses and ropes. It was the first manmade climbing rock in the country. Rock climbing is free the fourth Saturday of each month; otherwise there's a small fee. Climbing rate for student groups of 15 or more is about $45 per group.

DELRIDGE WADING POOL
206-684-7796
(Seattle wading pool hotline)
Web Site: www.cityofseattle.net
Days/Hours: Varies; usually open 11am–4pm from late June–Labor Day
Admission: Free
Wheelchair/Stroller Access: Yes

When the weather is warm, this pool is filled daily with clean, chlorinated water for lots of splashing. Summer months bring lots of sunshine (we hope). The Delridge Community Center nearby brings lots of visitors to the area.

ED MUNRO – SEAHURST. PARK
206-684-4075
Location: 12th SW at SW 144th
Web Site: www.cityofseattle.net
Days/Hours: Dawn to dusk
Wheelchair/Stroller Access: Limited, but special parking
   is available
Driving Directions: Turn west off Ambaum Blvd to SW 144th St. Turn
   north on 13th St. SW; access road leads to beach.

At Seahurst, you'll find 185 acres of saltwater park land with lots of activities. The south part offers great beachcombing; the north end is both sand and grass. There are fire pits on the beach, picnic tables with individual grills, a Marine Skill Center at the north end, freshwater holding ponds and a fish ladder. As with all Seattle and King County parks, all pets must be leashed within the park. Parking near the beach is available only to the physically challenged.

LINCOLN PARK   206-684-4075
Location: 8011 Fauntleroy St. SW
Web Site: www.cityofseattle.net
Days/Hours: Daily, 4:30am–11pm. Parking lot: 6am–11pm.
Wheelchair/Stroller Access: Yes

In the summer, treat the kids to something great in Seattle—swimming in heated seawater at the Colman Pool at Point Williams, found only at Lincoln Park during summer months. This beautiful beachfront park stretches along the coast from southwest Webster St. to Trenton St. Playgrounds, a restroom, picnic tables and a few picnic shelters are located throughout the park. Paths wind through groves of madrona, fir and redwoods. Other activity areas include tennis courts, 11 acres of playfields, and horseshoe pitching pits. The beach has no lifeguard but does offer beachside barbecues, an Olympic Mountains view, and a vantage point for watching the Vashon-Southworth ferries. That's relaxing in itself.

For an added treat, take a short Puget Sound cruise at the adjacent Fauntleroy ferry terminal.

LOG HOUSE MUSEUM   206-938-5293
Location: 3003 61st Ave SW (corner of 61St SW
    and SW Stevens St.)
Web Site: www.loghousemuseum.org
Days/Hours: Thursdays, noon–6pm; Weekends, noon–3pm.
Admission: By donation
Wheelchair/Stroller Access: Yes

Known as the "birthplace of Seattle," Log House Museum is just a block from Alki Beach, and a few blocks from the historic marker at the beach memorializing the landing of the 1851 Denny Party at Duwamish Head. Initially the carriage house of the William Bernard family, the home is now under the guardianship of the Southwest Seattle Historical Society. In the early days, the ferry from downtown Seattle to West Seattle took eight minutes; nearby was an amusement park known as Luna Park—giving West Seattle the title "Coney Island of the West." The Log House Museum is an interesting collection of early Seattle memorabilia, especially to children studying our city's history. Kids are especially fascinated with the tales surrounding the 100-year-old carriage house, including items discovered during the restoration. Parking is limited.

SEACREST. BOATHOUSE   206-932-1050
   Location: 1660 Harbor Ave. SW
   Web Site: www.cityofseattle.net/parks
   Days/Hours: Monday–Friday, 5:30am–6pm; Saturday and Sunday,
      4:30am–7pm; closed Monday and Tuesdays during
      the winter
   Wheelchair/Stroller Access: Yes

You can putter around for about two hours on a tank of gas in one of their 14- or 16-foot Fiberglas boats. The six-or eight-horse-powered motor is strong enough to take you across Elliott Bay to a marina or the Fauntleroy ferry terminal. Boaters are discouraged from cruising up the Duwamish River, where more than one embarrassed parent has had to be rescued after running out of gas and beaching a boat. Rentals run $15 an hour. You must be 18 or older to rent a boat at Seacrest, but adults are welcome to bring children along. Life jackets and cushions provided. Put teenage muscles to work by renting a Seacrest boat with oars—but no motor—for $25 per day. In summer, boats are available from 5am until at least 6pm Sundays through Tuesdays, and until 8pm on Fridays and Saturdays.

HUSKY DELI AND ICE CREAM   206-937-2810
   Location: 4721 Californa St. SW
   Days/Hours: Monday, 9am–9pm; Tuesday–Friday, 9am–9pm; Satur-
      day–Sunday, 9am–7pm.
   Wheelchair/Stroller Access: Yes

You can sit-in or take-out at this sandwich deli and ice cream shop. It's so popular that people have been known to drive all the way from the University District when they crave Husky's ice cream. There are more than a dozen flavors to choose from; all are homemade, and they use real fruit (try the banana).

PEGASUS PIZZA   206-932-4849
   Location: 2758 Alki Ave. SW
   Days/Hours: Monday–Friday, 11:30am–11pm; Saturday–Sunday,
      noon–11pm.
   Wheelchair/Stroller Access: Yes

Pizza lovers who like a Greek flair to their pies should seek out this eatery, conveniently located across the street from Alki Park beach. Pegasus Pizza offers feta cheese, spinach, diced mushrooms, green peppers, mushrooms, olives, fresh garlic and sunflower seed toppings, plus some additional Italian varieties. Pizzas are available for take-out or dining-in.

SPUD FISH AND CHIPS   206-938-0606
  Location: 2666 Alki Ave. SW
  Days/Hours: Daily, 11am–9pm
  Wheelchair/Stroller Access: First floor only

A Seattle favorite, this place makes some of the best fish and chips around. Both are prepared in cholesterol-free oil, and the French fries are from fresh-not frozen-potatoes. Adults may order a single "fish with fries" or a heaping order of prawns, oysters, scallops or clams. Kids may prefer the children's meal for less than $4. Most families like to sit at the second-floor window tables for a great view of the water. High chairs and boosters available.

GREAT HARVEST. BREAD COMPANY   206-935-6882
  Location: 4709 California Ave. SW
  Web Site: www.greatharvestsea.com
  Days/Hours: Open Monday through Saturday
  Wheelchair/Stroller Access: Yes

Same treats as the other locations. See Lake Forest Park Towne Centre for complete information.

RESOURCES
King County Library System: 425-462-9600 (the "answer line"); 206-684-4494 (TDD); Web site: www.kcls.org

Downtown Seattle

Ice skating at Seattle Center's annual Winterfest. Look Mom! Almost no hands

Photo courtesy Seattle Center

Seattle has become an extraordinary city, celebrating its cultures, its nationalities, and its geographical beauty in so many ways. Our commanding skyline, fascinating shoreline and the myriad of outdoor and recreational opportunities...all have brought new faces to Seattle and Puget Sound. In spite of economic and corporate woes in 2001–2002, Seattle's downtown core has invested in a dramatic new rebuilding effort. The diversity of our neighborhoods and multiplicity of our retail sector has created an ever-changing kaleidoscope for families, indeed, everyone, to enjoy.

PIONEER SQUARE: The triangular park at First Ave. and Yesler Way marks Seattle's first settlement. Yesler Way was originally called "skid road" because logs were dragged down its steep slope to a steam–powered lumber mill (whose location is now occupied by Magic Mouse Toys). Pioneer Square is fascinating to explore but not a place to let children explore alone.

INTERNATIONAL DISTRICT: Once called Chinatown, this community now encompasses many Asian cultures. Restaurants of all sizes and types, shops with exotic and unusual merchandise, plus a museum and proximity to the ever-popular Safeco Field and Qwest Field brings tourists and visitors from everywhere. Watch the newspapers in spring and summer months for several wonderful festivals with authentic foods, traditional dancing and art. Don't miss Uwajimaya Village – it's a destination in and of itself.

PIKE PLACE MARKET: As the oldest continuously operating farmers' market in the country, the Market is one of Seattle's most popular destinations. With its eclectic mix of local farmers, specialty shops, artisans and street musicians, it's a great place to bring the family on weekends. Some have achieved national celebrity, such as Pike Place Fish Market, known for its entertaining "salmon-toss," especially when celebrities are on the receiving end. Open year-round, the Market is the perfect place to bring visitors, especially for the exuberant flowers, and grandparents love to bring their favorite charges here for a day's outing. A gentle reminder: Victor Steinbrueck Park is a lovely vantage point in daylight hours, but one to be avoided after dark.

SEATTLE CENTER: Once a Northwest Native American tribal gathering spot for festive ceremonial feasts, the center now serves a similar purpose for today's families. There is literally something for everyone here, from the huge annual festivals to the world-class Children's Museum. From science to culture to entertainment to sports, the center challenges your imagination, stimulates your mind and piques your curiosity.

THE WATERFRONT and ALASKAN WAY: In 1897, the waterfront was Seattle's primary working harbor. Most industry has moved south to Harbor Island, but Alaskan Way piers have been refurbished for various uses. At Pier 69, the high-speed catamaran Victoria Clipper sets sail between Seattle and British Columbia, harbor excursion boats depart from Pier 55, and Seattle's fireboats dock at Pier 53. Pier 51 is the point of departure for Washington State Ferries to Bremerton and Bainbridge Island. You can take the Waterfront Streetcar (for a modest charge) from the International District (5th Ave. at Jackson St.) or Pioneer Square (Main St. at Occidental St.) all the way to the north end of the waterfront for an overview, then stroll back along the bay. Call 206-553-3000 for details. At Pier 57, the bright lights and music on the vintage carousel inside the Bay Pavilion delight youngsters.

DOWNTOWN SEATTLE: The face of downtown Seattle keeps changing. December's holiday season is especially exciting. In Westlake Park, a nineteenth-century carousel of painted horses offers free rides for all ages. Across the street at Westlake Center, beginning the first Friday after Thanksgiving, a Christmas tree sparkling with more than 10,000 lights illuminates the square. Metro's tunnel station at Westlake Center provides an underground bus link between Seattle's leading department stores and beyond. The over-the-ground Monorail connects downtown with the Seattle Center.

Pioneer Square

Places to Go

AMTRAK/MOUNT BAKER INTERNATIONAL TRAIN 800-872-7245
  Location: King St. Station, one block northwest of Qwest Field
  Web Site: www.amtrak.com
  Days/Hours: Daily at least once, departing for Vancouver, British Columbia and Portland, Oregon
  Admission: Round-trip prices can vary; average is $50/adults, $30/children. Up to two children, ages 2–15, ride half-price with an adult. Under 2/free.
  Wheelchair/Stroller Access: Yes

Zoom from Seattle to Vancouver, B.C. or Portland, Oregon within four hours aboard this high-speed Spanish-made train. Its family-friendly design offers dome seating where riders can face each other for a board game or cards. The state-of-the-art system can travel up to 140 mph but goes slower to meet U.S. regulations. Aisles are wide enough for strollers; restrooms offer diaper-changing facilities. The Seattle-to-Vancouver run takes a scenic waterfront route most of the way, making brief stops in Edmonds, Everett, Mount Vernon and Bellingham. There is a dining car available.

KLONDIKE GOLD RUSH NATIONAL HISTORICAL PARK 206-553-7220
  Location: 117 S Main St.
  Web Site: www.npr.gov/nr/travel/seattle
  Days/Hours: Daily, 9am–5pm; closed Thanksgiving, Christmas and New Year's Day
  Admission: Free
  Wheelchair/Stroller Access: Yes

This storefront museum has been getting more attention since the 1997 centennial celebration of the 1897 Alaska Gold Rush. The smallest national park west of the Mississippi, the exhibits here show how early Seattle's economy boomed as nearly 100,000 miners shopped here on their way to pan for gold.

Films featured in the auditorium include Charlie Chaplin's The Gold Rush (3 pm, first Sunday of the month). Park rangers guide free one-hour walking tours of Pioneer Square Historic District at 1:30 pm on Saturdays, Memorial Day to Labor Day. Children younger than 12 must be accompanied by an adult; appointments required for large groups.

SEATTLE MARINERS   **206-622-HITS (tickets);**
206-346-4001 (general info)

Location: Safeco Field. 1st Ave S and S Atlantic St.

Web Site: www.seattlemariners.com; www.safeco.com/safeco/safeco-field

Days/Hours: Season is April – September; game times vary. Ticket Office open Monday Friday. 9am–5:30pm; gates open two hours prior to game time.

Admission: Single game tickets range from $7–$50.

Wheelchair/Stroller Access: Yes

With a line-up that includes All-Stars, top rookies and pitching aces, a Seattle Mariners ticket has become a very hot thing in this town. And there's more than just baseball happening during a Mariners home game at Safeco Field. The three-wheeling Mariner Moose mascot is always good for laughs. Families love to compete in the computerized games on the mega-screen. There are special areas for kids within the ballpark and LOTS to eat. Many games offer free promotions, including jerseys, posters and other give-aways; you have to get there early for these offers. When ordering tickets, ask about family packages and other special price discounts. Batting practice and infield activity give autograph hunters a chance to ask their favorite players for signatures. There are other special events during the off-season that kids and families enjoy, as well. Watch the papers for announcements, or check the Mariners' website.

SEATTLE SEAHAWKS   **888-635-4295 (ticket sales office)**

Location: Home games in Qwest Field

Web Site: www.seahawks.com

Days/Hours: Most games held on Sundays; game time will vary. Preseason games begin in early August; postseason playoffs possible in early January.

Tickets: Call or go online for current info.

Bone-crunching action kicks off in the Qwest Field when the Seattle Seahawks take on other National Football League competitors. During the summer months, the team trains in Cheney, Washington. Summer training camp practices are open to the public.The team's training field is in Kirkland, but those practices are closed to the public. Game tickets are not discounted for children, but those under three are admitted free if they sit on their parent's lap. If you want to put a birthday message up on the HawkVision scoreboard, call 206-381-7800. What a great surprise!

QWEST FIELD   **206-381-7582 (for tours)**
   Location: 800 Occidental Ave. S
   Web Site: www.seahawks.com/stadium
   Days/Hours: Tours on non-event days only: daily at 12:30 and 2:30pm.
      No tours on event days or major holidays. Call number above for tour
      availability. (Inclement weather can affect this).
   Admission: $7/adults; $5/youth under 12 and seniors 65 and over;
      Free/children under 3
   Tours: Group packages available; cost will vary according to group
      size.
   Wheelchair/Stroller Access: Yes, ramps and elevator

Qwest Field rarely sits empty. When the Hawks aren't playing there, the A-League Seattle Sounders are during spring and summer months. High school and college football, world-class soccer and even lacrosse – all take advantage of this excellent venue. The Stadium features 67,000 seats, a sweeping view of Puget Sound and lots of area to cover if you're taking a tour. Even if you're an avid fan and think you know the stadium well, or are just fascinated by the building, the guided tours take you places usually closed to the public. The tour begins at the Seahawks Pro Shop on the west side of the stadium (along Occidental Ave.) You'll see the press box, a luxury suite, the visitors' locker room and step on to the playing field. A tour lasts approximately an hour and half and is designed to entertain and educate. You'll be doing some walking, so comfortable shoes are advised.

UNDERGROUND TOUR
   Location: 610 First Ave., Doc Maynard's Public House
   Web Site: www.undergroundtour.com
   Days/Hours: Daily year-round, but schedule changes seasonally.
      Admission: $10/adult; $8/seniors and students; $5/children 7–12;
      Free/under 7
   Wheelchair/Stroller Access: Yes, for the lecture, but not the tour.

This is Seattle's "ghost town;" it lurks under the streets of Pioneer Square. The ghosts are part of Seattle's mystery and history – old Seattle after the fire of 1889. The town was rebuilt but the mystery under the streets lingers on. The tour starts at Doc Maynard's Public House with a twenty-minute presentation. From here you walk along sidewalks from the 1890s. It's five block of rough ground and steep flights of stairs; this is hard work for youngsters under 7. Guides on this amazing tour tell anecdotes, replete with details about the glue-pot fire and other city legends. Reservations are recommended; bring along a flashlight and good walking shoes. It gets damp and cool down there. Note: the only restroom stop on the tour is at Doc Maynard's. This is a great experience for teens and preteens, especially good for birthday parties. Light lunches are available before and after the tour.

WATERFALL PARK
   Locations: Main St. at Second Ave. S
   Wheelchair/Stroller Access: Partially

This park is a summer favorite, welcoming visitors with water cascading over massive rocks, drowning out all street noise. A glass-covered shelter with tables and chairs offers a serene place for a picnic. Privately built and maintained by the Annie E. Casey Foundation, the park commemorates the original offices of United Parcel Service.

Places to Eat

COW CHIP COOKIES   206-292-9808
   Location: 102 First Ave. S
   Days/Hours: Monday–Friday, 10am–6:15pm; Saturday, 9am–6:15pm.
   Closed Sunday.
   Wheelchair/Stroller Access: Yes

This is a good snack stop during your Pioneer Square outing. Cow Chip cookies means big crunchy ones, some with melt-in-your-mouth chocolate chips. Plan to bring some home. (Not a peanut-free zone.)

GRAND CENTRAL BAKING CO.   206-622-3644
   Location: 214 First Ave. S in the Grand Central Arcade
   Days/Hours: Open Monday–Friday. Summer Hours: Monday–Friday,
   7am–6pm; Saturday, 8am–4pm; Closed Sunday.
   Wheelchair/Stroller Access: Yes

Now a deli/restaurant, Grand Central has been a long-time favorite for their popular cinnamon rolls, great desserts, hearty sandwiches (including pb&j), home-made soups and breads. They do have half-orders for smaller appetites and chairs of varying heights (including high chairs) for youngsters. There's upper level and main floor; the wooden tables with benches are fun for kids. You can enter from the main entrance on First Ave. or from the plaza behind the building.

Shops to Browse

ELLIOTT BAY BOOK COMPANY — 206-624-6600

Location: 101 S. Main St
Web Site: www.elliottbaybook.com
Days/Hours: Open year-round, except Christmas and Thanksgiving.
  Monday – Friday, 9:30am–10pm; Saturday, 10am–10pm; Sunday,
  11am–7pm. Holidays: 11am–5pm.
Wheelchair/Stroller Access: First floor only

There is almost always a reading event or special program for children on Saturday mornings at this venerable and popular old bookstore. Kids love the wooden playhouse; parents love the bargain loft and well-stocked shelves. The café (which is not handicap-accessible) is quiet and diners usually have their noses in books or magazines. There's no children's menu, but soups and half-sandwiches can be had. There is a restroom upstairs with a baby-changing table. Watch the papers for celebrity readings and other happenings here, some well-suited for families.

GLASS HOUSE STUDIO — 206-682-9939

Location: 311 Occidental Ave. S
Days/Hours: Open daily, year round. Monday–Saturday, 10am–5pm;
  Sunday (May– December) 11am–4pm.
Tours: Free for groups of twenty or less. Please call ahead.
Wheelchair/Stroller Access: Yes

It's plenty hot here, and with good reason! The glassblower is at work from 10am – 3pm (lunch break is 11:30am – 12:30pm) in front of a gas furnace heated to 2,000 degrees. Blowers use the same procedure artisans have used for nearly 3,000 years. Amazingly, glass is little more than melted sand, but what exquisite shapes and pieces they produce. There are glass forms of all sizes here, from small perfume bottles to large sculptures. It's good idea to prepare the kids to be careful.

MAGIC MOUSE TOYS — 206-682-8097

Location: 603 First Ave.
Days/Hours: Open year-round. Winter: Monday–Saturday, 10am–9pm;
  Sunday, 10am – 6pm. Summer: Monday–Thursday, 10am – 7pm; Friday
  and Saturday, 10 am – 9pm; Sunday, 10am – 6pm
Wheelchair/Stroller Access: Yes, first floor only

A Pioneer Square fixture, Magic Mouse is a superb conglomeration of international games, puzzles and playthings. You'll find electric trains from Germany, a wide collection of museum-quality puzzles for all ages (including some from Germany, Holland, Spain and Italy), plus an eclectic selection of children's books and art products. Most visitors can't leave without hugging at least one of the furry stuffed animals. It's not limited to goodies for kids. Board games for serious competitors attract many adults to this store, too.

The International District

Places to Go

CHINATOWN DISCOVERY TOURS　　　　　　**425-885-3085 (reservations)**
  Location: Throughout the International District
  Web Site: www.seattlechinatowntour.com
  Days/Hours: Flexible schedule; usually starts by 10:00am; tours are
    ninety minutes to three and half hours. Evening dinner tours start
    at 6pm.
  Tours: By reservation only; PO Box 3406, Seattle, WA 98114; phone 425-
    885-3085; fax 425-869-9170; email: heking@juno.com.
  Admission: Adults/$14.95 to $39.95; Children/$9.94 to $22.95; price will
    depend on tour selected.
  Wheelchair/Stroller Access: Yes

Children will use and count with an abacus and watch how fortune cookies are made during one of several guided walking tours led by Seattle native Vi Mar. While the tour is best for children over 5, this knowledgeable guide tailors tours for families of all ages so they can discover the hidden treasures in Seattle's International District. Vi describes how Asian delicacies are prepared and shares the history of Seattle's Asian communities, including the Chinese, Cambodian, Vietnamese, Japanese, Filipino, Laotian, Thai, Pacific Islanders and Korean. There are four different tours to choose from; one includes a dim sum lunch. Teachers and other youth leaders may be interested in the Asian Cultural Youth Program tours designed for first- through sixth-grade students. There's no richer, more lively part of Seattle than the International District; it becomes much more interesting when you see it through Vi Mar's eyes.

INTERNATIONAL CHILDREN'S PARK
  Location: Seventh Ave. S at S Lane St.
  Wheelchair/Stroller Access: Yes

This little playground is among the most charming in the city. A slide spirals down a mound of rocks into a huge bed of sand while a delightful dragon stands guard.

WING LUKE ASIAN MUSEUM   206-623-5124
  Location: 407 Seventh Ave. S
  Web Site: www.wingluke.org
  Days/Hours: Tuesday–Friday, 11am–4:30pm; Saturday–Sunday, noon–
    4pm
  Admission: $4/adults; $3/students and seniors; $2/children 5–12
  Tours: Self-guided/free. Guided tours/these are docent-led for an ad-
    ditional cost; must have at least 10 or more in party; appointment
    required.
  Wheelchair/Stroller Access: Yes

Even young children enjoy this museum because there are so many things
they can handle and create. In fact, guided tours are the best for kids because
they're designed to include kid-friendly history. Children may explore the
trunks filled with colorful clothing brought by Seattle's earliest Asian settlers.
Seattle's Asian community dates back to 1860; its rich history is reflected in
many ways here. Especially interesting are the photo displays commemorating
those Asian Pacific Americans who built their communities and made generous
contributions in the Pacific Northwest. The museum tells its stories through
both special and permanent exhibitions.

TSUE CHONG COMPANY   206-623-0801
  Location: 800 S Weller St.
  Days/Hours: Tours offered year-round on Tuesday, Wednesday, Friday
    beginning at 10am.
  Admission: Free
  Tours: They can accommodate two groups a day; minimum group size is
    15 including adults; age limit is first grade and up; homeschoolers are
    welcome. Tour lasts about thirty minutes.
  Wheelchair/Stroller Access: Difficult

The Louie family has been making fortune cookies and noodles for four generations. Founded in 1917, the company has been family-owned and run since
then. Chinese egg noodles in 19 varieties and fortune cookies are the staples
here. On tour you'll get to sample a cookie and see the different styles of
Chinese noodles and how they're processed. When Tsue Chong first opened,
noodles were made by hand-cranked machines; today everything is automated.
The cookies are made from wheat flour, although sometimes rice flour is used
as well. The tour ends in the store; here you can buy a bag of fortune cookies
to take home. Did you know you can put your own fortunes (or sayings) into
the cookies? Ask about the procedure—you'll be surprised how easy it is. You'll
find Tsue Chong's cookies in most of the Chinese restaurants in Seattle; the Rose
Brand label on cookies and noodles is theirs as well.

UWAJIMAYA VILLAGE   206-624-6248
Location: 600 5th Ave. S
Web Site: www.uwajimaya.com
Days/Hours: Daily, 9am–10pm
Wheelchair/Stroller Access: Yes

From a quaint, strictly local Asian environment, Uwajimaya has developed into the major shopping destination in the International district. Hard to know where to put them – part of the store is a gift shop, the other a food court and grocery market. There are throngs during lunch hour. You can choose from Thai, Japanese, Saigon, Korean and Cantonese food. The Deli offers a wide variety of choices and portions are ample. They are still THE place to go when you're looking for the greatest selection of Asian foods in town.

HOUSE OF HONG   206-622-7997
Location: 409 Eighth Ave S
Days/Hours: Monday–Friday, 11am–5pm; Saturday–Sunday, 10:30am–
5pm
Wheelchair/Stroller Access: Yes

A restaurant with a slightly more formal décor, House of Hong offers seventy kinds of dishes of generous portions as well as dim sum. Lined with comfortable booths, they specialize in family gatherings.

KING CAFÉ   260-622-6373
Location: 7223 S King St.
Days/Hours: Thursday–Tuesday, 11am–5pm
Wheelchair/Stroller Access: No

Dim sum is served fresh and hot upstairs. Dishes come up on a dumbwaiter and are quickly distributed. Seating is limited, but tables open up quickly.

OCEAN CITY   206-623-2333
Location: 609 S Weller St.
Days/Hours: Dim sum served daily from 9am–3pm. "Hot Pot" dinner
Monday–Friday, 5pm–10pm; reservations not necessary.
Wheelchair/Stroller Access: Yes, by elevator through the garage

Dim sum is something of a Chinese smorgasbord. Ocean City offers over 30 dishes and provides high chairs and boosters for little ones. It gets crowded on weekends, but the food is worth waiting for. The wait staff pushes carts filled with small dishes of fried, steamed or baked beef, pork, fish and vegetables past your table, pausing while you make your selection. First timers may want to try fried Fun Gow, a crescent-shaped type of egg roll (also available steamed); Gin Dau, a sweetish sesame-covered dough filled with red-bean paste; or steamed Hum Bow, a white baked dough usually filled with a tangy barbecue sauce with bits of pork. Most dishes contain two to four portions, easily divided among a family. Kids get to take a bit of everything, and parents don't have to waste time with the old "clean your plate" routine. The restaurant can accommodate any size group here; the rooms are very large. You can also order regular dishes off the menu.

The Waterfront and Alaskan Way

Places to Eat and Explore

SIMPLY SEATTLE   **206-447-2628**
  Location: 1201 Alaskan Way
  Web Site: www.simplyseattle.com
  Days/Hours: Sunday–Thursday, 9:30am–6pm; Friday and Saturday,
    9:30am–8 pm
  Wheelchair/Stroller Access: Yes

More an adult store, but kids might find some good ideas for birthday and holiday gifts here. Seattle pot holders, for instance.

IVARS ACRES OF CLAMS   **206-624-6852**
  Location: Pier 54
  Web Site: www.ivars.net
  Days/Hours: Memorial Day–Labor Day, 11am–11pm. Remainder of year:
    Sunday–Thursday, 11am–10pm.
  Wheelchair/Stroller Access: Yes

Seagulls and children love Ivar Haglund's statue, which stands outside the restaurant. One of Seattle's most colorful and much beloved characters, Ivar is long gone but still invokes lots of nostalgia. In the restaurant, there's a children's menu with seafood and other choices for $4.25 and less. The chowder is great here, either red or white. Lots of menu choices for adults. At the street-side Fish Bar, chowder and fish and chips are a great sunny-day option; take your "feast" over to the adjoining outdoor picnic area and watch the water traffic. The cheeky seagulls will beg—they expect to be fed. The waterfront trolley stops across the street at "Clam Central Station."

STEAMER'S   **206-623-2066 (Pier 56); 206-624-0312 (Pier 59)**
  Location: Pier 56 and Pier 59
  Days/Hours: Sunday – Thursday, 10am–8pm; Friday and Saturday,
    10am–9pm
  Wheelchair/Stroller Access: Yes

Their Just For Kids menu has a chicken dinner with fries or fish and chips. Beverages include hot chocolate, apple juice, milk and orange juice. But over in the Ice Cream Corner there are soft drinks, lemonade and BIG waffle cones. Their Colossal Cone comes in five flavors plus whipping cream and a cherry.

Note: there are no nuts in their ice cream.

THE BAY PAVILION

1301 Alaskan Way

This collection of shops on the pier offers visitors plenty of "stuff" with which to remember their vacation.

PIRATES PLUNDER
Days/Hours: Open daily 9:30am–8:30pm
Wheelchair/Stroller Access: Yes

Definitely a tourist destination, but Seattleites would get a kick out of some of the items: Seattle-specific games, Washington Ferry salt and pepper shakers, and a Seattle skyline snow globe.

THE CRAB POT
Days/Hours: Sunday–Thursday, 11am–10pm; Friday & Saturday, 11am–11pm
Wheelchair/Stroller Access: Yes

SEATTLE SOURDOUGH BAKING COMPANY
Days/Hours: Monday – Friday, 9 am–5 pm; Saturday and Sunday, 8am–5pm
Wheelchair/Stroller Access: Yes

A good stopping point if you're ready for a snack. Great made-to-order sandwiches, with jumbo chocolate chip cookies and snicker doodles for dessert.

THE SPORTS DEN
Just what the name implies, lots of sports-related clothing and small items.

YUKON CANDY
Yes, candy galore, everything you could think of, plus some long, skinny lollypops.

MICHELANGELO'S BAKERY & CAFÉ
What's special here are their crocodile and turtle breads. Great for birthday parties, or any party, for that matter. Must order ahead; price is $3.50 at this writing.

THE FRANKFURTER   206-622-1748
    Location: Pier 55
    Days/Hours: Memorial Day–Labor Day; daily, 9am–9pm. Rest of the
        year: daily, 9am–5pm. (They may stay open later on weekends if
        they're busy.)
    Wheelchair/Stroller Access: Yes

Wieners, franks, hot dogs or foot-longs, no matter what you call them, this
place has them. Eat them plain or slap on anything from the condiment bar. In
summer months, their fresh-squeezed lemonade is very refreshing.

THE OLD SPAGHETTI FACTORY   206-441-7724
    Location: 2801 Elliott St. at Broad St.: across from Pier 70
    Days/Hours: Lunch served Monday Friday, 11:30am–2pm. Dinner
        served: Monday–Thursday, 4:30pm–10pm; Friday, 4:30pm–11pm;
        Saturday, noon–11pm; Sunday, noon–10pm. No reservations during
        summer months; during nonsummer months, reservations taken for
        groups of 15 or more from Monday–Thursday.
    Wheelchair/stroller Access: Yes

This pasta place is frequently crowded on weekends. It's a great favorite with
families, especially if they can be seated in the 1917 Birney Car. Diners enjoy spaghetti while relaxing on velvet-covered sofas under red Tiffany lamps. Crayons
and menus to color go a long way to keep restless spirits busy. Bring your own
cake if you're celebrating a birthday; the wait staff will sing to you. Spumoni ice
cream is served with all orders.

SANDPIPER GIFT SHOP   206-624-2835
    Location: Pier 59, next to the Aquarium
    Days/Hours: Labor Day–Memorial Day: daily, 10am–7pm; Memorial
        Day–Labor Day, daily, 10am–6pm.
    Wheelchair/Stroller Access: Yes

Kids on a budget can find affordable souvenirs for only a few dollars at this
Pacific Northwest specialty shop. Look for postcards, bookmarks, games and
puzzles in a child's price range.

WATERFRONT LANDMARK   206-622-3939
    Location: 1101 Alaskan Way, on Pier 55
    Days/Hours: Labor Day–Memorial Day; Monday–Thursday, 10am–6pm;
        Friday–Saturday, 9am–6pm. Memorial Day–Labor Day; daily,
        9am–9:30pm.
    Wheelchair/stroller Access: Yes

Admittedly a tourist destination, the Landmark still has some inviting things to see and buy. If you're looking for pink flamingoes, they're here! There's a myriad of shells, thousands of colored, tumbler-polished stones, and a Native American headdress on the wall. You can munch on 15 kinds of fudge, made right there on the premises, or admire a display of totems by Northwest carvers.

YE OLDE CURIOSITY SHOP   206-682-5844
Location: Pier 54
Web Site: www.yeoldecuriosityshop.com
Days/Hours: Summer: Monday–Sunday, 9am–9pm. Rest of the year:
   Monday–Thursday, 10am–6pm; Friday–Saturday 9am–9pm; Sunday;
   10am–6pm.
Wheelchair/stroller Access: Yes, although some aisles can be tight.

Part museum, part curio shop, part gift shop, this establishment has been in the Standley family since 1899. Four generations later, the family still scours the earth for the strange and unusual. Even those with perfect vision might need a magnifying glass to read the Lord's Prayer carved on a grain of rice. Hosts and chief residents are Sylvester and Sylvia, a pair of six-foot-tall mummies. You're sure to find many other things you think are amazing.

COAST GUARD MUSEUM   206-217-6993
Location:1519 Alaskan Way S, Pier 36
Days/Hours: Open Monday, Wednesday, Friday only; 9am–3pm (until
   further notice).
Admission: Free
Wheelchair/Stroller Access: Yes

This small but very interesting museum is dedicated to the work and history of the U.S. Coast Guard. There are thousands of Coast Guard-related items on display, including navigational aids such as a magnetic compass, ship models, Arctic ivory (no longer available on the open market), and a four-foot-high Fresnel lens made in France. A Lighthouse Service clock from 1860, early uniforms, ship's wheels, lots to see here.

SEATTLE IMAX DOME THEATER   206-622-1868
Location: Pier 59 at Waterfront Park, next to the Seattle Aquarium
Web Site: www.seattleimaxdome.com
Days/Hours: Open year-round except Christmas; shows begin at 10am.
   Admission: $7/adults; $6/youth 6–12; Free/children 5 and under; $2/
   Additional (same day) film
Wheelchair/Stroller Access: Yes

Formerly known as the Omnidome, you get your entertainment on the BIG screen here. Waves of sights and sound flood your senses; movies shown here have a nature theme, but they are exciting and almost larger than life. Showing in 2004 are the Eruption of Mount St. Helens, Ocean Oasis and The Living Sea. Best to call ahead for schedules as shows, times and prices do change. You do feel like you're face to face with the creatures swimming on the screen. Fun to make this part of a day at the waterfront. Ride the trolley, do the Aquarium, browse the shops and, of course, take some time to perch on a bench and watch the water traffic.

PIER 70

Built in 1901 by Elton Ainsworth and Arthur Dunn, Pier 70 was a full-fledged ocean terminal for steamship lines until 1910. The Coast Guard leased it until 1954, and since then it has become a place to browse and explore. The ambiance is dim and cavern-like, but there are number of interesting dining places and shops that capture the Pacific Northwest flavor. Don't miss the main level restrooms with their nostalgic flush chains.

SEATTLE AQUARIUM

**206-386-4300; 206-386-4353
(group rates and registration)**

Location: 1483 Alaskan Way, Pier 59
Web Site: www.seattleaquarium.org
Days/Hours: Open year-round. September–March, 10am–5pm. April–May, 9:30am–5pm. Summer; Memorial Day–Labor Day, 9:30am–7pm. Holiday hours will vary.
Admission: Aquarium only: $11.50/13 and up; $7.50/6–12; $5.25/ages 3–5; Free/2 and under. There are combo packages available, such as Aquarium/Seattle Imax Dome or the Odyssey Maritime Discovery Center. Call for specific information. Group rates also available. Call 206-386-4353 or email aquarium.programs@seattle.gov for more information.
City Passes: $42/adults, $29/ages 4–13. Please remember all prices are subject to change.
Wheelchair/Stroller Access: Yes

Since the ocean never closes, neither does the Aquarium. They just alter hours seasonally. Pacific Northwest sea life is at its best here, easily one of Seattle's most popular rainy day outings. From behind the safety of viewing glass, children can go nose to nose with sharks, rays, eels and more. Even the outdoor exhibits, featuring lively sea otters, playful seals and chipper sea birds are under overhead cover; these are especially popular in summer months. Older children enjoy looking under the microscope at the tiniest creatures which start the food chain. Note: the restrooms are nearby if your child is eager to reach into the touch tank to stroke the starfish. Don't miss the domed aquarium, surrounded on all side and overhead by a 400,000 gallon tank filled with other large sea creatures. When you first arrive, check to see what time divers are in the dome to feed the fish. Self-guided tours take anywhere from one to several hours. Treat your child to a "sea-themed" birthday party. That's one they won't forget.

TILLICUM VILLAGE ON BLAKE ISLAND   800-426-1205; 206-933-8600
   Location: Sailing from Pier 55
   Web Site: www.tillicumvillage.com
   Days/Hours: Most tours take place from February to early December; call for specific information.
   Admission: Varies seasonally; call or go online for current info.
   Wheelchair/Stroller Access: Yes

This is a nice opportunity to sample Native American hospitality. You'll cruise across Elliott Bay to Tillicum Village on Blake Island where your welcome includes a bowl of clams, a typical Northwest delicacy. It's a four-hour outing and no matter what the age, children take something special away with them from this experience. After eating the clams, children learn to crush the white shells into the beach to recycle them. The main course includes a Native-American-style salmon dinner, tribal dancing, and forty-five minutes of free time to explore the pristine island's totem poles, masks and carvings. If the timing is right, a tribal artist will be designing a new piece during your visit. The artists enjoy taking time to tell you about their works. Tillicum Village is also accessible from Port Orchard. Reservations are recommended.

WASHINGTON STATE FERRIES   206-464-6400; 800-84-FERRY
   Location: Pier 52
   Web Site: www.wsdot.wa.gov/ferries
   Days/Hours: Schedules vary; call ahead or check the Web site.
   Wheelchair/Stroller Access: Yes

Riding a Washington State ferry is a never-ending adventure for kids. Whether it's the bellow of the ship's horn as it nears the dock or pulls away, the seagulls diving for handouts, or the rush of spray in your face—any of the three Sound routes is worth the trip. The one-hour ride to Bremerton allows time to explore the ship, watch the skyline disappear, or enjoy an on-board picnic (by this writing, on-board ferry food might again be available). If you're going to Bainbridge (or Bremerton), you can walk on and leave the car behind. With or without kids, the evening ferries are romantic as the city lights begin to sparkle. The Tacoma carries 2,500 passengers, 500 more than the next largest ferry. Fares vary according to the season and destination, but summer rates are usually higher. For answers to questions, call the numbers above. They'll also mail you a brochure, which is available at the Public Information Desk at Pier 52, too. When calling for information, be forewarned that working your way through the system can be tedious. Have paper and pencil ready and allow lots of time. The agents are very helpful and patient.

PIKE PLACE MARKET
  Location: First Ave. and Pike St.
  Web Site: www.pikeplacemarket.org
  Days/Hours: Market is open daily; Monday–Saturday, 9am–6pm; Sunday, 11am–5pm
  Wheelchair/Stroller Access: Yes, but with precautions; floors are uneven and can be slippery in places.

Tours: Tours are offered from Wednesday – Sunday at 11am and 2pm; cost is $7/adults; $5/seniors 60 and up and youth under 18. Tours are available at 9 am, Wednesday–Saturday by special arrangement; advance payment required. For tours, call Wendy at 206-774-5262 or email wendyc@pikeplacemarket.org.

Tours of the market take about one hour and give you a totally different perspective, rather than walking it on your own. History, anecdotes and familiarity all make it a delightful experience. One of the most entertaining parts of your visit will be watching the "flying fish." When someone buys a salmon or any other large fish at the seafood shop under the big clock (at the foot of Pike St.), the fish will take to the air (propelled by skilled hands) before it's wrapped for purchase. The main entrance at First Ave. and Pike St. is the gateway to stands run by dozens of local farmers selling the finest in fruits and vegetables, and more than 250 shops and restaurants and nearly 200 artisans. Don't miss the market pig; she loves to be photographed. Strolling down through the stalls, the flowers, both dried and fresh, are a major attraction here. Gorgeous bouquets "walk out" by the hundreds. Many Seattleites make shopping here part of their weekly schedule.

Places to Eat

CHOCOLATE AND ICE CREAM DELIGHT 206-441-8877
  Location: Soames Dunn Bldg.
  Days/Hours: Market hours
  Wheelchair/Stroller Access: Yes

Just the place on a warm summer day. They sell delicious ice cream treats by the cone or dish, plus sodas, sundaes and floats. Check the case for enticing chocolates.

THE CRUMPET SHOP   206-682-1598
  Location: 1503 First Ave. Corner Market Bldg.
  Days/Hours: Monday–Friday, 7am–4pm; Saturday, 7:30am–4pm. Closed Sundays.
  Wheelchair/Stroller Access: Difficult; stairs will hamper your entrance.

If you show up between 7:30am and noon, you can watch from the sidewalk as the baker pours the batter into the ring molds. The crumpets are cooked right there on a griddle. Good for a mid-morning or mid-afternoon tea or coffee stop. They have crumpets in almost ANY form or flavor, as well as old fashioned English sandwiches. For kids there is hot chocolate.

PROCOPIO GELATERIA ITALIAN ICE CREAM   206-622-4280
Location: On the HillClimb
Days/Hours: Monday–Friday, 10am–5pm; Saturday, 11am–6pm. Closed Sundays
Wheelchair/Stroller Access: Take the elevator from Western Ave.

Another good warm-weather stopping point. The gelato is good; they have other desserts and coffee, also.

THE SHY GIANT 206-622-1988
Location: Corner Market Building
Days/Hours: Monday–Saturday, 10am–5:30pm; Sunday, 11am–5pm
(best to call ahead on Sunday; opening can be seasonal.)
Wheelchair/Stroller Access: Yes

A long-time market favorite for yogurt, waffle cones and ice cream. They also do fruit smoothies and shakes. Kid-sized cones are $1 for either yogurt or ice cream.

THREE GIRLS SANDWICH SHOP AND BAKERY   206-622-1045
Location: Sanitary Market
Days/Hours: Open daily; 6am–5:30pm in the deli; until 6pm in the bakery
Wheelchair/Stroller Access: Yes

If you're on a casual swing through the market, you'll find a delicious array of baked goods here. They have a consistent clientele—you may have trouble finding a stool to perch on! You can eat there or take it out. Five kinds of bread to choose from, flavorful homemade soups and for kids, pb&j, egg salad, tuna and chicken salad sandwiches.

DAILY DOZEN DOUGHNUT CO.   206-467-7769
Location: 93 Pike St.
Days/Hours: Market hours
Wheelchair/Stroller Access: Yes

You can stand right there and watch the doughnut mixer (or robot) plunk the balls of dough into the hot (!) fat. They plump as they cook, browning as they move along on the belt to be (unceremoniously) frosted or coated with powdered sugar, or left plain, and piled on the display shelf waiting for you to buy.

SOUND VIEW CAFÉ   206-623-5700
  Location: From Western Ave., on Floor 6, or walk in through the market
  Days/Hours: Market hours
  Wheelchair/Stroller Access: On the main floor, not upstairs

You come here for the view, although the food is fine. The only kid-friendly item for lunch is the toasted cheese sandwich, but portions are ample and you can always "split." Lots of choices for sandwiches and soup; buy salad by the plate (small, $3.95, large, $4.95).

Shops to Browse

GOLDEN AGE COLLECTABLES   206-622-9799
  Location: 401 Level
  Days/Hours: Monday–Saturday, 10am–6pm; Sunday, 11am–5pm
  Wheelchair/Stroller Access: Take the elevator from Western Ave.

If comic books, posters or baseball cards are your passion, this is the place. You can always tell what's "hot" in the entertainment field by looking at their shelves. At this writing, the Lord of the Rings was taking up lots of space! Popular among the comic books, the Japanese "Manga," translated into English. There are many bobbing heads in assorted sizes and styles, collectable lunch boxes, and if you're planning a major birthday party, their assortment of full-size cardboard figures will add to the ambiance.

MINIATURE CAR DEALER   206-624-7799
  Location: Leland Mezzanine
  Web Site: www.Theminiaturecardealer.com
  Days/Hours: Open daily from 9:30am–5:30pm except Tuesdays and Sundays when they close at 3:00 pm.
  Wheelchair/Stroller Access: Yes

With over 250 models in the store to choose from, no miniature car fancier could leave empty-handed. On the shelves are cars, bikes, buses, trucks, motorcycles and planes of every conceivable style and vintage. New models, very old models…it's a treasure trove. There are Kenworth trucks, a '49 Buick, a '31 Peerless, a '34 Packard, a '67 Corvette Stingray, plus some little action figures to complete the picture. And if you can't find what you want, they'll order it for you.

THE GREAT WIND-UP   206-621-9370
   Location: Economy Market (at the Pike Place Market)
   Website: www.greatwindup.com
   Days/Hours: Monday–Saturday, 10am–5pm; Sunday, 11am–4pm
   Wheelchair/Stroller Access: Yes, although the aisles are not very wide

It's a compact little shop and they've been here in the market for 18 years. You don't have to be a kid to be mesmerized by the myriad of wind-up, blow-up, animated, stuffed and movable toys that surround you. There are also waterproof toys for the bathtub, and lots of stocking stuffers when you're Christmas shopping.

THE PIKE PLACE MAGIC SHOP   206-624-4271
   Location: #427 at the market
   Web Site: www.speakeasy.org/magic
   Days/Hours: Market hours
   Wheelchair/Stroller Access: Yes

Before you can say "abracadabra," you'll be drawn into this shop of prestidigitation. There's everything imaginable for the magician; for youngsters just venturing into the world of magic, this is a good starting place. They're very helpful and eager to see you succeed. They'll demonstrate ALMOST anything (the magic word for a demonstration is "please"). From juggling balls to balloon animals, it's here, so ask about their classes.

Downtown Seattle

SMITH TOWER 206-622-4004
   Location: 506 Second Ave.
   Web Site: www.smithtower.com
   Days/Hours: April–October; daily, 11am–sunset. Year-round; weekends,
      10am–sunset
   Admission: $6/adults; $5/seniors over 60; $4/students with ID, children
      6–12; Free/children under 6
   Wheelchair/Stroller Access: Yes

Built in 1914, the 42-story Smith tower was the tallest building west of the Mississippi River until the early 1930s. It was built by the family whose name is synonymous with typewriters. Unlike today's high-rises, the Smith Tower's elevators are still run manually, a novelty that appeals to the visitor. In the lobby on the first floor, look for art depicting Chief Seattle and other Native Americans important to Seattle's history. In 2000, the Tower enjoyed a major restoration, including a complete seismic retrofit. That's significant to Seattle-ites. Soaring to the 35th floor, you'll watch the floors go by through the glass doors. When you arrive, you'll find an observatory that offers a 360-degree view of the city, Elliott Bay and Puget Sound. When the Chinese Room is open, glance inside at antique furniture presented to L.C. Smith by the Empress of China during the 1910s, and look for the Wishing Chair. It has a very romantic significance.

FREEWAY PARK
   Location: Seneca at Sixth Ave., next to the Convention Center
   Wheelchair/Stroller Access: Yes

This garden-style park was designed to restore pedestrian access between First Hill and the downtown area, but children may think it was built just for them. That's because 27,000 gallons of recycled water rushes over the fountains each day, providing a splash of fun for youngsters. A peaceful place by day, it's not considered safe in early morning hours or after dark. At the park's east end, children may romp in the grassy area known as Freedom Plaza. During the summer, watch for weekly noon concerts.

SEATTLE ART MUSEUM
206-654-3100
(recorded information and operator)
206-654-3137 (TDD)
   Location: 100 University St. between First and Second Avenues
   Web Site: www.sam.tripl.org
   Days/Hours: Tuesday, Wednesday and Friday–Sunday, 10am–5pm;
      Thursday, 10am–9pm; closed most Mondays except Labor Day, July
      4th, Presidents Day, Memorial Day and Martin Luther King Jr. holi-
      days; closed Thanksgiving, Christmas and New Year's Day.
      Admission: $6/13 and older; $4/seniors; Free/children under 12 when
      accompanied by an adult. The Boeing Company provides free admis-
      sion to all visitors the first Thursday of each month. SAM admission
      tickets are good for the Seattle Asian Art Museum if used within
      one week.
   Tours: Guided; Tuesday–Saturday, 2pm; Sunday, 2:30pm; Thursday,
      7pm
   Wheelchair/Stroller Access: Yes, from the First Ave. entrance; NOT from
      the museum entrance

Comfortably known around town as SAM, there is a vast world of art waiting for visitors to this four-story treasure. A good way to view the exhibits with kids is with a family guidebook, available in the lobby. Probably best for 6 to 10 years old, the guide suggests museum routes, using photographs of the displays that will be of interest to children. Other pages recommend activities children can complete at home or as they're strolling the museum. Often there are hands-on activities available for children in areas of the museum. The museum store is located on the first floor; special exhibits on the second floor. The third floor is dedicated to art from Asia, the Near East, Africa and the Americas; European and U.S. art is on the fourth floor. The fine collection of Northwest Coast Native American pieces on the third floor is outstanding, and the masks on display usually fascinate youngsters. And, of course, don't miss Hammering Man–a daunting sculpture just outside the museum entrance. There is a café on the mezzanine when you need a bit of refreshment.

SAM offers a sign language program the first Sunday of each month. Sign language interpreters are available for other programs with two weeks' notice. The Seattle Asian Art Museum is housed in the former SAM site at Volunteer Park.

SEATTLE PUBLIC LIBRARY   **206-386-4636 (quick information)**
206-386-4190 (circulation information)
206-386-4675 (children's department)

Location: 1000 Fourth Ave.
Web Site: www.spl.org
Days/Hours: Monday–Wednesday, 10am–8pm; Thursday–Saturday,
    10am–6pm; Sunday, 1–5pm.

Seattleites check out over 3 million books, audio selections (including cassettes and DVDs) and other materials from the Seattle Public Library annually. The Children's Department alone circulates over one million children's books, and provides many other services for school-age children. Check their Web site for updated information regarding summer reading programs; these are always excellent (making vacation much more bearable). The library's recently designed Web site is also a great place to apply for a library card; it will be mailed to your house! Use the Quick Information line when you have a pressing question to which you can't find an answer. The staff is amazing at uncovering all kinds of information—we speak from personal experience!

FAIRMONT OLYMPIC   **HOTEL 206-621-1700**

Location: 411 University St.
Wheelchair/Stroller Access: Yes
Tours: Yes, by request only

For a stroll or a stay, there's an elegant world inside the hotel. For many families, a year-round favorite is the Children's Afternoon Tea in the Garden Court restaurant, held daily between 3 and 5 pm. It features a selection of petit fours, fruit breads, scones with Devonshire cream and strawberry preserves, and a pot of brewed tea for $8.75 per person. Before the Christmas holidays, walk the lobby to see festive Yuletide trees, each adorned with decorations marking the names of patients at Children's Hospital and Regional Medical Center.

Another December favorite is the annual Teddy Bear Suite. The concierge will direct you to this room decorated with a multitude of bears, bear ornaments, a tea table with cookies and other delightful holiday décor. Sneak a peak inside the bathroom. Teddies are even in the tub!

Overnight guests will find everything from popular video games to infant bathtubs. Cribs arrive with teddy bears ready for hugging. Guests may also ask for special hotel tours for children, including a peek inside the pastry kitchen.

THE WESTIN SEATTLE   206-728-1000
Location: 1900 Fifth Ave.
Days/Hours: Times vary per restaurant.
Wheelchair/Stroller Access: Yes

Located in the heart of the city, The Westin Seattle may be a posh hotel but they definitely welcome kids as visitors and guests. Upon arrival kids will receive an age appropriate Westin KidsClub goody bag, along with special courtesies during their stay. These will include express meal service by advance request, children's menus, lock-out service on in-room movies, special laundry prices for children's clothing, jogging strollers and emergency diapers. A complimentary room safety kit is available by request (includes band aids and outlet covers). Families can even bring their dogs; the pets get to sleep on a Heavenly Dog Bed and receive an amenity bag that includes a Westin dog collar tag. Roy's is the main restaurant at the hotel; for lunch they do offer a pb&j and banana sandwich and other junior foods. For quicker meals, the Fifth Avenue Corner Café (open daily, 6am–8pm) has breakfast, lunch and dinner choices, plus a long list of smoothies and juices. Would you believe Fresh Wheat Grass Juice?

EXPERIENCE MUSIC PROJECT   206-EMPLIVE
Location: At the Seattle Center
Web Site: www.emplive.com
Days/Hours: Summer: Sunday–Thursday, 9am–6pm; Friday–Saturday, 9am–9pm. Fall/Winter/Spring: Sunday–Thursday, 10am–5pm; Friday–Saturday, 10am–9pm; closed Mondays, Thanksgiving and Christmas. Note: hours are subject to change.
Admission: $19.95/18–64; $15.95/seniors, military with ID, 13–17 with ID; $14.95/7–12; Free/6 and under.

Not only is the building itself startling and amazing, the opportunities inside are just as amazing. Experience Music delights in the unusual; there are interactive exhibits, rare artifacts and educational programming on a grand scale. Plan to spend a good part of your day exploring everything available to you. Of special interest, the Museum, the JBL Theater and the Digital Lab. Entrance to the Turntable Restaurant and EMP Store are open to the public and do not require an admission fee. If you live in Seattle and you haven't been here yet, you've got some catching up to do!

REI (RECREATIONAL REQUIPMENT, INC.)   206-223-1944
    Location: 222 Yale Ave. N
    Web Site: www.rei.com
    Days/Hours: Monday–Friday, 10am–9pm; Saturday, 9am–9pm; Sunday,
    9am–6pm
    Wheelchair/Stroller Access: Yes, in most places

Outdoorsy persons come here to hide for hours. Although indoors, it's make-believe outdoors, with lots of opportunities to try out equipment in relatively real situations. Small ones can slide down a mountain, crawl through a cave, or wade through an imaginary river. Older kids can test hiking boots by trekking across an indoor path or scale a three-story boulder simulating rock-climbing lessons. There's even an outside bicycling path (around the store's perimeter) if you're bike-shopping. If you become an REI member, you'll become aware of many other values as well. There are REI stores in other Washington cities that may not have all these accoutrements, but you can be assured they are usually well supplied with whatever you're looking for.

SEATTLE SYMPHONY AT BENAROYA HALL

206-215-4700 (ticket office);
206-336-6600 (Soundbridge)

    Location: 200 University St.
    Web Site: www.seattlesymphony.org
    Days/Hours: The Symphony season runs from September to July,
        including educational activities and classes in Soundbridge (Seattle
        Symphony Music Discover Center in Benaroya Hall).
        Admission: Varies with concert and/or event
    Wheelchair/Stroller Access: Yes

Recognizing that music is–and should be–an integral part of a child's life, the Seattle Symphony offers parents a marvelous opportunity. The five-part Tiny Tots series, called the "Rhythms of the Season," is offered on Tuesday and Saturday mornings, at 9:30am, 10:30am and 11:30am, with pre-concert activities in the lobby beginning a half-hour earlier. The series is designed for little ones up to five years of age (with an adult). Everyone is invited to dance, wiggle, clap – whatever moves them–in time to the music, which ranges from folk to symphonic. It's a forty-minute concert, one worth making time for. Other musical opportunities are offered in the Soundbridge Seattle Symphony Music Discover Center in Benaroya Hall, Tuesday through Sunday from 10am–4pm. For novices to experts of all ages, these include Musical Storytelling, Early Childhood and Early Preschool Music Classes, Meet the Musician sessions, Workshops and Symposia, Instrument Demonstrations and Student Recitals. Call for more information on time and costs. For older children, the Pops Series could be another excellent introduction to the Symphony.

The Seattle Center

Playing in the water at the International Fountain

Photo courtesy Seattle Center

SEATTLE CENTER

Location: Denny Way and Fifth Ave. N
Events Line: 206-674-8582; 206-684-7200
Web Site: www.seattlecenter.com

Seattle Center is an 87-acre entertainment and sports complex, open year-round with over 5,400 free performances every year, but some exhibits and areas operate seasonally. Daily information is available by calling the events line listed above; this is a wise way to decide on your parking options. Watch the newspapers for the popular annual festivals that take place here; almost all have something to attract families. In early May, more than 70,000 people flock to the annual Seattle International Children's Festival. This week-long cultural arts event is the largest of its kind in the country, with nearly 300 performances from almost a dozen countries. Dance, theatre and musical productions with young and adult performers are geared to children and their families. Tickets range from $5–$125, depending on the performance. Other large family events include Whirligig (an indoor children's festival that runs five weeks during March and April spring breaks), Festival Sundiata (an African-American cele-bration), Northwest Folklife Festival (music of all kinds) and Bumbershoot (a multifaceted "umbrella" event). Some of Seattle's major entertainment and cul-tural facilities are on the Center grounds, including KeyArena, Seattle Repertory Theatre, Intiman Theater and McCaw Hall, (home to Pacific Northwest Ballet), and Seattle Opera. As you stroll the grounds, be sure to stop by the International fountain, a lighted, musically synchronized waterworks extravaganza. In sum-mer months, kids delight in running in and out of the water spray.

Places to Go

BOEING IMAX THEATER   206-443-IMAX
  Location: Pacific Science Center
  Web Site: www.pacsci.org
  Days/Hours: Monday–Friday, 10–5pm; Saturday, Sunday and holidays,
    10–6pm.
  Admission: From $7–$22.50; varies with show
  Wheelchair/Stroller Access: Yes

On a screen three and a half stories high and 60 feet wide, viewers are nearly engulfed in the nature and science films shown here. Shows change periodically and most are an hour long; best to call for a current schedule. Three-dimen-sional technology is very exciting here.

FUN FOREST   206-728-1585
  Location: Seattle Center Grounds
  Web Site: www.funforest.com
  Days/Hours: Memorial Day through Labor Day; daily, 11–midnight. Pa-
    vilion open year-round but outside attractions open weekends only
    in spring and fall. Outside rides are typically closed during winter
    months.
  Admission: Free, but tickets to rides will vary.
  Wheelchair/Stroller Access: Yes

The Center's facelift provides a new layout for family games and activities.

Amusement rides for preschoolers and younger tots are separated from the head-spinning, stomach-turning, thrill rides for older children and adults. Inside the Entertainment Pavilion (open year-round) are rides, laser tag and a video arcade plus mini-golf. This facility has some open-air walls, ideal for our varying climate.

LASER SHOW   206-443-2850
   Location: Pacific Science Center at the Seattle Center
   Web Site: www.pacsci.org/laser
   Days/Hours: Thursday–Sunday. No shows on Monday, Tuesday,
      Wednesday
   Admission: $5–$7.50
   Wheelchair/Stroller Access: Yes

Most shows here are geared for teens and adults. Many visitors bypass the reclining chairs and opt for a seat on the floor to get the full view of the ceiling production set to 14,000 watts of digital sound. For a few more dollars, laser show admission is included in the price of a Pacific Science Center ticket. Note: No late seating here.

SEATTLE CENTER MONORAIL
   Location: Terminals at Fifth Ave. and Pine St. at the third floor of West-
      lake Center, and at Seattle Center near the Space Needle
   Web Site: www.theseattlemonorail.com
   Days/Hours: Monday through Friday, 7:30–11pm; Saturday and Sunday,
      9–11pm.
   Admission: Round-trip tickets: $3/adults; $1.50/youth, seniors and dis-
      abled; Free/4 and under. One-way tickets are half the price.
   Wheelchair/Stroller Access: Yes

Originally created for the 1962 World's Fair, this quick, two-minute connection between Seattle Center and Westlake Center is fast, but not too fast for the small set. The cars accommodate up to 400 passengers on the one-mile route; large windows on the glass cars give children a peek at the city as they rush past on their way to the downtown retail shopping area.

PACIFIC SCIENCE CENTER   206-443-2001
   Location: 200 2nd Ave. N at the Center; under the white arches
   Web Site: www.pacsi.org
   Days/Hours: Open daily, year-round. Monday–Friday, 10–5pm. Satur-
      day, Sunday, holidays, 10–6pm.
   Admission: Ranges from $7–$22.50; varies with exhibits, combined
      packages, etc.
   Wheelchair/Stroller Access: Yes

Children can always spot the Pacific Science Center, with its eye-catching white arches over large reflecting pools. Here there are dozens of hands-on activities for all ages. Toddlers will find a special room just for them, complete with bubble and water play, drums, and climbing/crawling toys. For the older children, there are some incredible exhibits that—once having visited—they talk about for days after: Dinosaurs – Journey Through Time; the Tropical Butterfly House; Desert Village; Puget Sound Model and Saltwater Tide Pool; Kids Works; Animal Exhibits; Body Works and more. Many locals visit several times a year to catch the rotating exhibits. Exhibit admission includes all exhibits plus the planetarium show. The Willard G. Smith Planetarium, open daily, is a live astronomy demonstration in a fairly intimate setting. Youngsters must be 4 years and older; seating in the theater is limited to 40 and you'd best be on time! No late seating. For reservations: 206-443-2920.

Special note to teachers and group leaders: The Center has traveling exhibits available by reservation. No shrinking violets here—the exhibits range from 2,000 to 10,000 square feet, and an instructor comes with them. Call 206-269-2145 for reservations and information.

On the inflatable rides at Seattle Center's annual Whirligig Festival

Photo courtesy Seattle Center

SEATTLE CHILDREN'S THEATRE   206-442-3322 (tickets)
   Location: Charlotte Martin Theatre on the west side of Seattle Center
   Web Site: www.sct.org
   Days/Hours: Call ahead for performance schedules.
   Admission: $18/adults; $12/children. These are for single tickets; prices
      are subject to change.
   Wheelchair/Stroller Access: Yes

Considered one of the country's finest children's theatres, SCT attracts award-winning productions to its two stages at the Charlotte Martin Theater. Most plays are designed for youngsters 6–12 years, but several appeal to those as young as 4. Look for one Shakespeare or another classic production each season. Some theatergoers love to sit on the carpeted area in the front of the comfy seats, getting as close as they can to the stage. Season ticket holders receive advance-show guides that help parents prepare their children with tips on what to watch for (or expect) in the production. The schedule will include performances that are signed for the hearing impaired. Off stage, classes in mask-making, comedy, movement and dance for children ages 4-1/2 to 19 years are available each quarter.

SEATTLE SONICS   206-283-DUNK (season tickets)
   Location: 190 Queen Anne Ave. N
   Web Site: www.nba.com
   Days/Hours: Preseason games begin in early October; regular season
      starts in November and runs through mid-May. Game times vary.
   Admission: Varies according to seating; call ticket office for current
      information.
   Wheelchair/Stroller Access: Yes

At home in the Key Arena, the Seattle Sonics provide slam-dunking action for all ages. During breaks in the game action, children love trying to catch the prizes dropped by the radio-controlled mini-blimp. At half times, fans compete in hoop shoot contests to win prizes.

SEATTLE THUNDERBIRDS   206-448-7825 (PUCK) (to order tickets)
   Location: Play is at Key Arena; Office: 1813 130th Ave NE, Bellevue WA
      98005
   Web Site: www.seattlethunderbirds.com
   Days/Hours: Office is open year-round; Monday–Friday, 9–5pm. Season
      is September to March.
   Admission: Kids' rates are $10 upstairs; some $8 tickets available 24
      hours in advance.
   Wheelchair/Stroller Access: Yes

For a team that plays on ice, this semi-pro hockey team can get really hot. Some fans like sitting right behind the players box to hear the coach bark orders. The season runs September through March. There are Kids' Birthday Party Packages; $96/8 tickets (two adults, six kids) for the best seats in the house. The birthday kid gets his/her name on the video board plus several other perks. Watch for cross-state rivalries with Portland and Everett. Note: The Thunderbirds were the 2003 U.S. Division champions. Not too shabby!!

SPACE NEEDLE   206-443-2100
   Location: At the Seattle Center
   Web Site: www.spaceneedle.com
   Days/Hours: Open daily; 9–11pm, Sunday–Thursday; 9–midnight, Friday and Saturday.
   Admission: $13/adults; $11/seniors 65 plus; $6/4–13; Free/3 and under.
   Wheelchair/Stroller Access: Yes

The Space Needle is a magnet to both visitors and "natives," especially those locals treating out-of-town guests. The glass elevators whisk you in seconds to the Observation Deck or restaurant for a 360-degree view of the city, Sound, mountains and outlying islands (always weather permitting). Gift shops at street level sell local and regional souvenirs. See the Sky City Restaurant listing for dining information.

THE CHILDREN'S MUSEUM   206-441-1768
   Location: Lower level, Seattle Center House
   Web Site: www.thechildrensmuseum.org
   Days/Hours: Monday–Friday, 10–5pm; Saturday–Sunday, 10–6pm.
   Admission: $7.50/adults and children; $6.50/seniors over 65; free/those under 1
   Wheelchair/Stroller Access: Yes

The centerpiece of the museum is a mountain forest so large it grows from the lower level of Seattle Center House into the main floor dining area. It's amazing the global ground they cover here. Children may explore nature in one corner-and a few yards away take an entertaining lesson in culture from Africa, China, or some other part of the world in the Global Village exhibit. Rotating exhibits frequently reflect different nations and their food, dance, architecture, art and music. The exhibits are hands-on, participatory learning, and meant to challenge the imagination, too. Permanent displays include Cog City, where children can track the route of ping-pong-sized balls as they roll along varying paths through tubes and pipes, and a child-size neighborhood with a fire truck, grocery store, restaurant and more. Even infants and toddlers become explorers in the Discovery Bay, a padded toy area for climbing and romping.

Special areas for workshops and classes include the Humanities Studio and the Artists Studio; group visits to the studios cost $5/person for groups of 15 or more.

Places to Eat

SEATTLE CENTER HOUSE   206-684-8582 (general info.); 206-684-7200
   Days/Hours: Labor Day–Memorial Day; open daily, 11–6pm. Remainder
      of year: Sunday–Thursday, 11–8pm; Friday–Saturday, 11–9pm
   Wheelchair/Stroller Access: Yes

Get your taste buds ready–it runs the gamut here! From hot dogs to fish and chips to pizza or numerous ethnic foods, the food court on the main floor of the Seattle Center House offers many dining choices. Come to buy or nibble or just wander and watch activities in the performing arts area on the main level. Surrounding shops carry both traditional and funky souvenirs. Almost daily entertainment includes local bands, energetic youth dance groups, square dancers and other cultural festivals throughout the year. Whirligig takes place here (in March and April) and Winterfest, a winter holiday celebration. People watching is a high priority as well.

SKYCITY RESTAURANT AT THE SPACE NEEDLE   206-905-2100
   Location: At the Center
   Web Site: www.spaceneedle.com
   Days/Hours: Daily, 8–10:30pm
   Wheelchair/Stroller Access: Yes, except restrooms. There's a restroom
      for the disabled on the 100-foot-deck; take elevator.

Your eyes aren't playing tricks on you. The restaurant on top of the 605-foot-tall space Needle is revolving constantly to give you a 360-degree view while you remain seated. Prices are definitely upscale, but locals and out-of-town visitors consider it a "special" occasion and worth the visit. Consider ordering the Space Needle punch for children; it comes in a plastic Space Needle cup kids can take home as a souvenir. Otherwise, the children's menu features burgers, fish and pizza.

Outside the Center

CHAMPION'S   206-284-1980

Location: 124 Denny Way
Web Site: www.championpartysupply.com
Days/Hours: Monday–Friday, 8:30–7pm; Saturday, 9–6pm; Sunday,
   11–5pm
Wheelchair/Stroller Access: Yes

On Denny Way, a few blocks above Elliott Bay and two blocks west of the Pacific Science Center, this party palace offers the wildest costumes, wigs and accessories around. Selection is amazing, from Halloween goblins and ghouls to some of your favorite celebrities. The "get-ups" can be rented or purchased, but it's wise to get in early for Halloween. They can supply anything–even palm trees. You bring the theme, they'll do the rest. Balloons for all occasions are also their specialty; party supplies available also include piñatas, stickers, party favors and more.

HELPFUL PHONE NUMBERS

Seattle Public Library and Visitors Bureau: 206-461-5840
Seattle Parks and Recreation Department information and recreation
   scheduling: 206-684-4075
Seattle Parks and Recreation Department Youth Sports Information:
   206-684-7091
King County Library System: 425-462-9600 (the "answer line");
   206-684-4494 (TDD)

Outside Seattle

What could be more fun than riding a giant toad?

Photo credit: Elliott W. Brogren

Seattle's residential areas originated in the 1880s, when trolleys made suburban life accessible. Today the metro bus system accomplishes the same purpose. Over 20 small communities surround Seattle's downtown core. Attractive walking trails, picnic grounds, greenbelts and parks, plus interesting shopping destinations are some of their best features.

NORTH KING COUNTY: Between Seattle and the Snohomish county line, three mostly residential communities predominate: Shoreline, Lake Forest Park and

Kenmore. At one time, these areas were so far removed from Seattle proper that most property was used only as summer or weekend homes for Seattle residents. It was easy for boaters to sail to Lake Washington's north end or along the Puget Sound shoreline and dock near the vacation homes. After World War II, the population here soared when veterans and their families settled in these communities. Today they are supported by major shopping centers as well.

EAST KING COUNTY: Of all the areas in Washington State, the Eastside– Bellevue, Mercer Island, Issaquah, Kirkland, Redmond and Woodinville—has probably changed the most dramatically. Growing from strawberry fields and summer homes reachable from Seattle only by ferry to a major business and technology corridor, this area is home to internationally known companies such as Microsoft and Nintendo, as well as cultural and recreation activities of high caliber. And while Eastside residents hate to admit it, Bellevue Square is no longer a shopping destination just for locals; tourists and visitors from around the country seek it out. Two freeway systems (with major bridges), I-90 and 405, can be charged with providing the access to accelerate the growth the area has experienced. Note: The hiking/biking trail from Marymoor Park around to the Burke-Gilman Trail is a must for both locals and visitors. You can launch a canoe or kayak at the Lake Sammamish State Park and go through miles of inland waterways, all the way to Puget Sound. While Lake Washington can take large ships, both Lake Washington and Lake Sammamish offer ideal small sailboat-kayak-canoe activity.

KIRKLAND: This is a very eclectic water-side city with art galleries, restaurants, excellent recreational facilities and some irresistible outdoor sculptures.

MERCER ISLAND: Once only a summer vacation destination, the I-90 corridor brought a new look to this mostly residential community. Although people still tend to zoom right by, the island has a reputation for excellent schools and recreational programs.

REDMOND: This city is an interesting association of suburbia and high tech. Redmond is home to Microsoft and Nintendo, along with recreational destinations such as the Sammamish River (favored for inert tubing and gentle rafting), a portion of the Burke-Gilman Trail, and Marymoor Park, which hosts many major activities (including the Evergreen Classic, a major show-jumping event benefiting the Fred Hutchinson Cancer Center.)

WOODINVILLE: An alluring little town that's growing up before our eyes, it still manages to cling to its rural roots even as encroaching suburbia and other signs of progress change the landscape. Major "names" here include Chateau Ste. Michelle Winery and Molbak's Nursery.

BOTHELL: Like Woodinville, Bothell suffered from the economic downturn that occurred when river traffic between Lake Washington and Lake Sammamish disappeared, due to completion of the ship canal. The ship canal lowered Lake

Washington and left the Sammamish river too shallow for navigation. Bothell is less suburban in appearance, but nevertheless bustling and full of energy.

DUVALL and CARNATION: The Carnation Milk Farm brought fame to the town in 1909 and now as Nestle's Training Center is still a destination for school field trips. But the countryside here is mainly agricultural, with some dairy and ranching activity.

ISSAQUAH: Don't blink or you'll miss another growth spurt here. The site of a coal find over a century ago, the settler's dreams of glory never materialized. Daniel Gilman planned to build a railroad (the Seattle, Lake Shore and Eastern) to carry his coal to national markets, but it was never completed and the old depot still stands at the corner of Front and Sunset Streets.

SNOQUALMIE VALLEY: Farming and mining attracted the hardy people who settled here, but the spectacular Snoqualmie Falls is the main attraction today.

SOUTH KING COUNTY: This part of Puget Sound is one of the industrialized arms of the region. Where coal mining once drove much of the economy and the Boeing Company was the link to prosperity for many, retail business now drives much of the reason for being here. The towns of Renton, Kent, Tukwila and Federal Way reflect this. While there is extensive suburban development and many families call this home, the population growth has been so rapid that the cities are working very hard to provide the recreational and cultural programs that round out the quality of life. The towns of Enumclaw and Black Diamond, located on the way to Mount Rainier, are home to horse farms and those seeking a rural setting.

North King County

Places to Go

HIGHLAND ICE ARENA   **206-546-2431**
    Location: 18005 Aurora Ave. N, Shoreline
    Web Site: www.highlandice.com
    Days/Hours: Sunday, 10am–noon, 1:30–7pm; Monday, 10:30am–12:30pm, 3pm–5:15pm; Tuesday, 10:30am–12:30pm, 3pm–5:15pm; Wednesday, 10:30am–12:30pm, 3pm–5:15pm, 8pm–10pm; Thursday, 10:30am–12:30pm, 3pm–5:15pm; Friday, 10:30am–12:30pm; 3pm–5:15pm, 7:30pm–midnight; Saturday, 10am–noon, 1:30pm–5pm, 7:30pm–midnight.
    Admission: Prices vary from $3.50–$5.50. Families can skate for $11.00 on Sundays from 2pm–5pm. Skate rentals are $2.50 each for all sessions. Call for information on free sessions and holiday schedules.

Checks not accepted.
Wheelchair/Stroller Access: Yes

What a cooool place for families. The Sunday skating session (see above) is a favorite and makes it easy for everyone to enjoy this very energetic activity—really takes the bounce out of the kids! For less experienced tots, consider classes for those 6 or younger. Some late evening sessions might be reserved for parties.

KENMORE AIR HARBOR   425-486-1257
Location: 6321 NE 175th St. Kenmore
Web Site: www.kenmoreair.com
Days/Hours: Monday–Friday, 9am–5pm
Admission: For flights, varies according to your flight plan.
Tours: By request, at no charge. Hours are flexible; tours last about
    thirty minutes. Self-guided tours welcome any time.
Wheelchair/Stroller Access: Yes

Kenmore Air is now the largest seaplane-based airline in the world, with two terminals, one on Lake Union, the other on the north shore of Lake Washington. The latter is a pretty exciting place to be when the float planes return from daily trips up north. In summer they transport fisherpersons on expeditions, returning midafternoon with the plane's pontoons filled with fish. The planes (and pilots) cover a 300-mile corridor from Seattle to the north end of Vancouver Island. From early September through winter and spring, they fly mainly to Victoria and the San Juans. Lots of visitors just hang around waiting to see a float plane come gliding in; if you have youngsters, bring plenty to feed the ducks. An interesting part of the place is their conversion program, in which they change regular aircraft to float planes (they build their own planes here). If you take a self-guided tour, don't hesitate to ask questions of the personnel. For special birthday ideas (great for teenagers and pre-teens) or out-of-town visitors, ask about their scenic flights. It will become a cherished memory.

SHORELINE HISTORICAL MUSEUM   206-542-7111
Location: 749 N 175th St., Shoreline
Web Site: www.shorelinehistoricalmuseum.org
Days/Hours: Tuesday–Saturday, 10am–4pm
Admission: Free; donations accepted and appreciated
Tours: Yes, by appointment
Wheelchair/Stroller Access: Yes

Local children discover the roots of their North King County community here. You can browse on a self-guided tour at this three-floor museum or reserve a forty-five-minute guided tour. Displays rotate regularly and curators make a point of including hands-on activities for children when possible.

RICHMOND BEACH SALTWATER PARK   **206-296-4232**
  Location: At Richmond Beach Rd. and 20th Ave. NW. From Aurora Ave.
  N and NE 185th St., turn west on NE 185th St until it becomes Rich-
  mond Beach Rd. At 20th Ave. NW, turn south for three blocks to park
  entrance.
  Days/Hours: Daily, dawn to dusk
  Wheelchair/Stroller Access: Yes

Local kids sometimes call this Puget Sound beach a "train park" because the noisy Burlington Northern cars rumble underneath a pedestrian overpass linking the parking lot to the beach. Friendly engineers frequently wave at children peering down through the fenced walkway. It can be both rocky and sandy here, fun for beachcombing and picnics. A playground near the parking lot is designed for both toddlers and older children, but lacks shade on warm days. On selected Saturdays, King County Parks Department naturalists lead families on tide-pool walks. In the summer there are midweek concerts for children and evening sunset concerts for families. Call King County Parks for a current schedule.

Places to Eat

GREAT HARVEST BREAD COMPANY   **(four Seattle locations)**
  West Seattle, 206-935-6882;
  Ballard, 206-706-3434;
  Lake Forest Park Towne Centre, 206-365-4778;
  Sand Point Village, 206-524-4873
  Location: West Seattle: 4709 California Ave. SW; Ballard: 2218 NW
    Market St; Lake Forest Park Towne Centre: 17171 Bothell Way NE; and
    Sand Point Village: 5408 Sand Point Way NE.
  Web Site: www.greatharvestsea.com
  Days/Hours: Lake Forest; Monday–Friday, 6am–8pm; Saturday–Sunday,
    6am–6pm. Sand Point Village: Monday–Friday, 6am–7pm; Saturday–
    Sunday, 6am–6pm. West Seattle: Monday–Thursday, 6am–6:30pm;
    Saturday–Sunday, 6am–6pm. Ballard: Monday–Saturday, 6am–7pm;
    Sunday, 10am–5.
  Tours: Yes; Tuesday–Friday in the morning. Call for appointment, at
    least one week ahead.
  Wheelchair/Stroller Access: Yes

Healthy, delicious oatmeal cookies are among the favorites at this friendly bakery, but the list of breads to choose from is impressive. From old-fashioned white to low-carb whole wheat to tomato asiago sourdough-you got it, there's something to suit everyone's taste. Great Harvest is widely known for their hot fresh ample sampling of the day's specialty breads on the front counter, with plenty of butter to go with it. Bakers knead the dough and pop loaves into the ovens right behind the counter so kids can see everything that happens. A window inside the Lake Forest Park Towne Centre gives you a peak at the machine that grinds the grains into flour. This is a popular stop for bicyclists just off the Burke-Gilman Trail at Sheridan Beach and at the Princeton St. Bridge.

Note: DON'T miss their brownies. And they make a whole-wheat challah on Fridays.

HOME DEPOT
>   Bothell, 425-806-9300;
>   Bellevue, 425-451-7351;
>   Federal Way, 253-661-9200;
>   Tacoma, 253-565-0334;
>   Seattle (on Aurora), 206- 546-1900;
>   Everett, 425-267-0337.
>   **Days/Hours:** The Saturday workshop schedule varies at each store; please call the store you're interested in for specific information. If we have not listed a Home Depot near you, call them to see if they offer this workshop.
>   **Wheelchair/Stroller Access:** Yes

For kids, the attraction to this mega-sized hardware store is the weekend Kids Workshop. Parents are encouraged (but not required) to attend. Kids will learn about tools and build a variety of small projects such as tool boxes, birdhouses, squirrel feeders and foot stools. All "Saturday's children" get a free child-size carpenter apron to take home.

Bellevue

Places to Go

BELLEVUE BOTANICAL GARDEN   425-451-3755
                                (Bellevue Botanical Garden Society)
>   **Location:** 12001 Main St., in Wilburton Hill Park
>   **Web Site:** www.bellevuebotanical.org
>   **Days/Hours:** Daily, dawn-dusk. Visitors Center: daily 9am–4pm
>   **Admission:** Free; donations encouraged
>   **Tours:** Guided tours, April – October. Free; they begin at the Visitor Center at 2 pm on Saturdays and Sundays.
>   **Wheelchair/Stroller Access:** Yes, but certain areas can be difficult to maneuver

No pets allowed here, but visitors abound. This is a 36-acre complex of display and demonstration gardens. The most attention-getting is the massive perennial border featuring some spectacular year-round color and foliage, seen over the past several years on the covers of numerous national gardening magazines. You'll stroll through the Yao Japanese Garden, a wetlands area, the Alpine Rock Garden, plus groundcovers, herbs and more. Each year this garden has something new to explore; the summer display of dahlias and fuchsias is worth planning for. There's a half-mile loop trail for walkers; families often continue down the hill past the soccer field to a small play area with climbing equipment for youngsters. If you're really hardy, you can continue down the path, walk through the neighborhood (right on 128th Ave. SE, left on Fifth NE) and into Kelsey Creek Park to extend your hike. On a seasonal note, don't miss the Holiday Lights display at Bellevue Botanical; it gets more impressive each year and it's free, although donations are much appreciated. Hot beverages are offered in the Visitors Center.

BELLEVUE MUNICIPAL PAR THREE GOLF COURSE   425-452-4873

Location: 1580 NE 15th St., just off 156th St. NE; tucked away just behind Crossroads Shopping Center (address is for the clubhouse)

Days/Hours: Call ahead; hours vary seasonally and according to daylight.

Admission: Nine holes: $7/adults; $6/youth and seniors. Eighteen holes: $12/adults; $10/youth and seniors

Wheelchair/Stroller Access: Possible, but difficult in places

This three-par, nine-hole course is a mini-version of the full-size courses and a great place for families to practice together. Lots of trees and grass traps keep it authentic. Although skill level is a critical factor, you can get around in approximately one hour. A good beginning place for the Tiger Woods wanna-bes and youngsters with motivation. It's always fun to watch an eager Dad coaching a three- or four-year old child swinging away.

BELLEVUE NATURE PARK   425-452-6881

Location: 1905 118th SE. Take I-405 to the Richards Rd. exit; drive west to SE 118th St. about a mile south of SE 118th.

Wheelchair/Stroller Access: Yes

Lake Washington receded when the Montlake Cut lowered the lake's level, leaving a huge peat bog that has become this park. Wear sturdy boots or old tennis shoes and stay on the wide wood-chip paths; the peat can be soft as butter. Hikers are asked to sign in and out of the park. In the center near the channel, the peat bog is six feet deep, a good reason to stay on the trails. In the swampy area look for water birch, the branches from which early pioneers made their brooms.

BELLEVUE PHILHARMONIC   425-455-4171
  Location: Subscription concerts at Meydenbauer Center (in the theater)
  Web Site: www.bellevuephil.org
  Days/Hours: Performances are Saturday evenings or Sunday matinees
  Admission: Vary; call for info or check Web site
  Wheelchair/Stroller Access: Yes

The Bellevue Philharmonic is now playing regularly in the theater at Meydenbauer Center in the heart of Bellevue. Except for the Young Artists Debut (usually in spring), there is little to engage the younger set, but older children would enjoy the regular concerts.

BELLEVUE SKATE (BOARD) PARK   425-455-2722
  Location: 14224 NE Bel-Red Rd.
  Web Site: www.cityofbellevue.org/parks
  Days/Hours: Winter hours: Closed Mondays; open from day after Labor
    Day to last day of school: Tuesday,Thursday, Friday, 3pm–9pm (one
    session). Wednesday: Session 1, 1pm–5pm; Session 2, 5:30pm–9pm.
    Saturday and Sunday; 12 and under only, noon–1:30pm; Session 1,
    1:30pm–5pm; Session 2, 5:30–9pm. Summer hours: day after school
    is out to Labor Day: Monday–Friday: Skate Camp, 9am–12:30pm; Session 1, 1–5pm; Session 2, 5:30–9pm.
  Admission: Skate Park ID card/$5; skate session/$3 (Bellevue residents).
    For non-Bellevue residents costs are slightly higher.

Those athletic wonders who love to maneuver their skateboards around obstacles, over ramps and between cones will consider this center a challenge. This indoor skate park has a street course with ledges, handrails, banks and a mini-ramp. The park was designed and built by skateboarders and because skateboarding on most King County streets is illegal, dozens of young people come here to practice and refine their skills. Helmets, knee and elbow pads must be worn at all times; if you don't have your own they can be rented here for about $1. If you're looking for lessons, they do give them here ($20/hr). Note: Scooters and BMX bikes are not allowed here. The park frequently hosts skateboard competitions and professional skateboard demonstrations; call for information.

DOWNTOWN PARK   425-452-6881
  Location: 10201 NE 4th St.. in downtown Bellevue, at the south end of
    Bellevue Square, between NE 4th St. and NE 2nd St.
  Web Site: www. ci.bellevue.wa.us
  Days/Hours: Daily, dawn to dusk
  Wheelchair/Stroller Access: Yes

On a warm summer day, the fountain at this park provides just enough spray to keep kids cool. At the southwest corner, a play area with swings, slides and a climbing fort designed for toddlers and preschoolers is very popular. Moms and strollers are frequent walkers on the half-mile promenade around the twelve-foot-wide canal; it's a social setting, especially popular in spring and summer when the gardens are in bloom.

BELLEVUE REGIONAL LIBRARY BRANCH   **425-450-1765**
    Location: 1111 110th Ave. NE, Bellevue
    Children's Program Line: 425-450-1775
    Days/Hours: Monday–Thursday, 10am–9pm; Friday, 10am–6pm; Saturday, 10am–5pm; Sunday, 1–9pm.
    Wheelchair/Stroller Access: Yes

As the busiest branch in the King County system, Bellevue Regional Library circulates more than 1 million items a year. Their Children's Department is like a "stand-alone" library—with its own children's reference collection and information desk, an area dedicated to children's books and reading area (with kid-size tables and chairs, of course) and hand puppets to play with. During the school year they offer story times for all ages (12 months and up) seven times a week, and twice a week during summer months. A stroll through the library reveals people of all ages tucked away in comfy chairs reading or perusing books and magazines. Also during the school year, there is a story time for infants 6–17 months old on Mondays at 11:15 am. Call to register.

GEER PLANETARIUM   **425-564-2323**
    Location: Bellevue Community College
    Web Site: scidiv.bcc.ctc.edu/Astronomy/GeerPlanetarium.html
    Days/Hours: Vary with tours
        Admission: Call for info; there is a charge for each presentation.
    Wheelchair/Stroller Access: Yes

Stars millions of miles away seem very close at the Geer Planetarium. Twice each year audiences are invited to study the night sky. Kids will understand better the earth's small role in our giant galaxy after hearing experts describe some of the constellations, planets and black holes of outer space. They use a modified Spita A4A Star Projector that displays all the visible stars on a 30-foot dome and also projects the sun, moon, planets and other celestial objects in their correct positions. Call ahead to find out when shows are scheduled. Seating capacity is 60 persons. The Geer Planetarium is the silver dome at the north end of the main cluster of buildings; it is on the second floor of the Science wing, B-244.

KELSEY CREEK PARK   425-452-6885 (information);
425-452-7688 (tours and parties)

Location: 13204 SE Eighth Pl. Exit 405 at SE 8th St.; head east, get in the middle lane and cross the Lake Hills Connector; stay on SE 7th St.. to 128th Ave SE; turn left and go to SE 4th St., turn right and proceed to the main parking lot.

Web Site: www.cityofbellevue.org

Days/Hours: Park: 7am–dusk. Barnyard area: open year-round; animals available for viewing from 9:30am–3:30pm.

Wheelchair/Stroller Access: Park paths: concrete, gravel or bark. Barnyard: asphalt, gravel and cement. Hiking paths: gravel and bark.

Kelsey Creek is unlike any park in King County. You can visit year-round to see farm animals in their natural environment and enjoy their antics. Interactive signs around the complex are great learning tools. It's a sprawling park with loads of running room, easy hiking trails and a delightful play area – a premier family-friendly place. There are a number of special events throughout the year that children will enjoy. Check their Web site or call for specific information. Note: They ask that you do NOT feed the animals and that you keep your dog on a leash.

**MERCER SLOUGH ENVIRONMENTAL
EDUCATION CENTER**   206-443-2925 or 206-443-2887 (TDD)
(party reservations); 425-450-0207

Location: 1625 118th Ave. SE

Web Site: ci.bellevue.wa.us

Days/Hours: Daily for strolls; weekdays for scheduled school field trips; weekends for birthday parties.

Wheelchair/Stroller Access: Limited

These are protected wetlands, great for family walking excursions. Programs here are run by the Pacific Science Center, and birthday parties–the Wild B'earthday Celebration-are a specialty. Naturalists lead up to 15 guests for ninety minutes of outdoor activities and games, exploring creatures in the mud, water and trees. If weather is inclement, the fun moves indoors. Older children may handle microscopes to study the creatures that live in the ponds. After the hike, the party guests are invited into a special room (for an hour) for cake and gifts. The Pacific Science Center provides the party invitations and much more. Boots are advised as the walk can be muddy.

ROBINSWOOD COMMUNITY PARK   425-452-7850 (for house rental)

Location: 2340 148th Ave. SE; Take I-90 east and exit at Bellevue Community College/148th Ave. SW. Drive north on 148th Ave. SE; turn right (east) on SE 22nd St.; parking lot is on your right.

Web Site: ci.bellevue.wa.us

Days/Hours: Daily, year-round
Wheelchair/Stroller Access: Yes

Originally a log cabin homestead in 1882, Robinswood is now a multi-use park with 13 acres of bridle trails and a public horseshoe ring south of the park's meadow. North of the meadow, there's a wonderful play area for young ones, with seesaws, climbing towers and swings for different sizes. The wide asphalt paths are perfect for strollers, tricycles and training wheels. You'll see lots of parents hauling bikes out of wagons and SUVs. There are benches and picnic tables for attentive parents, and the pond nearby is filled with water lilies and duck families. The older children usually head for the ball fields with bleachers, two lighted soccer fields and tennis courts. A cabana, swimming pool and main house, and tennis center (indoor and outdoor courts) are available for rental by reservation.

ROSALIE WHYEL MUSEUM OF DOLL ART　　　　　　　**425-4455-1116**
　　Location: 1116 108th Ave. NE
　　Web Site: www.dollart.com
　　Days/Hours: Monday–Saturday, 10am–5pm; Sunday, 1pm–5pm
　　　Admission: $7/adults; $6/seniors 65 or older; $5/ages 5–17; Free/4 and under
　　Wheelchair/Stroller Access: Yes

This extraordinary museum is totally dedicated to dolls—dolls of all sizes, from many countries, from many cultures. More than 1,200 dolls, teddy bears, toys and other favorites are on display with history and anecdotes to make them come alive. The dolls represent a collection dating from the year 1680 to present. The cases are irresistible but don't forget the drawers below; they're filled with other fascinating items. A special gallery features rotating exhibits during the year. If arrangements can be made, this is a special place to have a birthday party. Take a moment to visit the store (there is a second one offsite).

SHERWOOD FOREST SPECIALTY PARK
　　Location: 16411 NE 24th St.; Sherwood Forest Elementary School
　　Days/Hours: After school and weekends, dawn to dusk
　　Wheelchair/Stroller Access: Yes

Designed for physically-challenged children, this innovative playground is really a favorite for all children. Look for sand and water tables, textured paths, a sensory maze, and embankment slides that are accessible to visitors with nearly all abilities.

THISTLE THEATER　　　　　　　**206-524-3388 (box office)**
　　Location: 9450 NE 14th St.; Moore Theater at Sacred Heart School
　　Days/Hours: Schedule varies; call for information.

Admission: Varies; call for information.
Wheelchair/Stroller Access: Yes

Thistle Theater is a touring theater group; many of their performances take place in Bellevue and Burien. Appealing to children as young as 3, it's a delightful combination of a Japanese form of puppetry and acting. The musical tales range from children's classics to contemporary adventures. Watch for free performances at local schools and libraries.

Places to Eat

LIL JON'S RESTAURANT   425-746-4653
Location: 3080 138th Ave. SE at Eastgate
Days/Hours: Monday–Saturday, 5am–10pm; Sunday, 5am–9pm
Wheelchair/Stroller Access: Yes

Owned and operated by the Sjolanda family since 1967, Lil Jon's is a "staple" in east Bellevue. Best known for their fresh-baked cinnamon rolls laced with cinnamon and butter, topped with creamy frosting, they have an extensive breakfast and luncheon menu as well. For kids: the "good start" breakfast, hot cakes, French toast or a Kid's Breakfast with one egg, two pieces of bacon or sausage, and toast. For lunch, they offer chicken strips, fish and chips, half a grilled cheese sandwich with fries or plain cheeseburger. Eastgate has grown up around this restaurant. It's been a favorite coffee stop for policemen, fisherpersons, skiers, hikers and "locals." One of the ladies who serves you has been there for 28 years.

BURGERMASTER   425-827-9566
Location: 10606 NE Northup Way
Days/Hours: Sunday–Thursday, 10am–1am; Friday–Saturday, 10am–2am
Wheelchair/Stroller Access: Yes

Burgermaster Drive-In takes you back to the good old days. Sometimes it's fun to eat in your car—and they make it work. Service is fast and good; menu specials for kids include the Kiddie Combo (small burger, fries and soft drink) or just a Kiddieburger for $1.79. Kids can have a small fish and chip (one piece or two) or a veggie burger, but don't miss the milkshakes. They have the usual flavors plus hot fudge, banana, orange and pineapple (you'll have to ask, those are not on the menu), thick and yummy. Everything is made to order, no hold-overs here. And if it's not right, they'll fix it. You can also walk in and order take-out at the counter.

NOBLE COURT   425-641-6011
  Location: 1644 140th St. NE
  Days/Hours: Monday–Thursday, 11am–4pm (dim sum), 3pm–9:30 (dinner); Friday–Saturday, 10:30am–2pm (dim sum), 2pm–9:30pm (dinner); Sunday, 10am–3pm (dim sum), 5:30p0m–9:30pm (dinner).
  Wheelchair/Stroller Access: Yes

For dim sum on the Eastside, Noble Court offers a varied menu and it's definitely on par with the downtown restaurants (although prices may be slightly higher). Dishes start around $2 and go up. Ample free parking. It's pretty popular and can get crowded at lunchtime.

THE PANCAKE CORRAL   425-454-8888
  Location: 1606 Bellevue Way SE
  Days/Hours: Monday–Friday, 5:45am–2:30pm; Saturday–Sunday, 6am–3pm
  Wheelchair/Stroller Access: Yes

No question about it, Bill Chace's Pancake Corral is a Bellevue fixture and so are some of the regulars who make it a weekly (and some daily) habit. Its breakfast menu has changed little over the years; the pancakes are dependably good and filling, and the syrup comes heated. Not fancy (forget the lattes) but stable. It's standing room only most weekends; allow for a twenty to thirty minute wait. Parking is limited during busy times. They do like kids here. Bill may be gone but the memories and friendly service linger on.

YEA'S WOK   425-644-5546
  Location: 6969 Coal Creek Pkwy, Newcastle
  Days/Hours: Tuesday, Thursday, Sunday, 11am–9pm; Friday–Saturday, 11am–10:30pm. Closed Mondays. Reservations for six or more only.
  Wheelchair/Stroller Access: Yes, but narrow spaces between tables are challenging.

It's always fun to find a terrific restaurant tucked away in what seems to be a remote location. Newcastle's not remote any more, and Yea's Wok has probably contributed to that. Much of the crowd waiting at the door is there for take-out. The front of the restaurant looks small, but there's a good-sized second room that accommodates large family parties. Food is consistently good and service is friendly; portions are ample. High chairs and boosters available.

ZOOPA   425-453-7887
  Location: Bellevue Square; NE 8th St. and Bellevue Way. Other Zoopa locations:
  Southcenter Mall, 206-776-2600, Northgate Mall, 206-440-8136.
  Days/Hours: Open Square hours
  Wheelchair/Stroller Access: Yes

Hard to say who likes this restaurant more–kids or parents. It was designed with both in mind. Special trays with sections so foods don't touch are available for children who want to choose from the children's snack bar featuring raisins, fish-shaped crackers, favorite fruits and more. Or they may sample from the adult cafeteria-style counters with generous choices of salads, baked potatoes, pasta and soups. All-you-can-drink pop, ice cream sundaes—it just keeps going. Paper place mats and crayons make the visit more fun. Servers do the clean-up for you.

Shops to Browse

CROSSROADS SHOPPING CENTER   425-644-1111
    Location:15600 NE 8th St.
    Web Site: www.crossroadsbellevue.com
    Days/Hours: Monday–Saturday, 10am–9pm; Sunday, 11am–6pm.
    Wheelchair/Stroller Access: Yes

After struggling for years as an obscure Eastside location, Crossroads has redefined itself as a unique, interesting and entertaining destination. For families, there are some very particular reasons to come here. For little ones under 7, the carousel (25 cents a go-round) is magnetic; it's a short but delightful ride. For older children, the food court, king-size chess board and Marketstage are equally compelling. Called the Eastside Public Market, the food court offers an amazing variety of choices from sixteen international restaurants, including Indian, Korean, Mediterranean, Chinese and Japanese. The chess board is an ongoing game; it's usually a male contingent of players and onlookers, but kids into the game become easily engrossed and sometimes challenge the "old guys." On the stage, live music from jazz to folk on Friday and Saturday evenings is free; Thursdays is open mike. Children's events happen on Sundays. It's an amazing mix of people and a great family experience. Note: The restaurants of the Market are open for breakfast daily at 7am.

PETS 'N THINGS   425-746-9782
    Location: 14310 NE 20th St.
    Days/Hours: Monday–Friday, 10am–7pm; Saturday, 10am–6pm; Sunday, 1pm–5pm
    Wheelchair/Stroller Access: Yes, but the aisles can be tight

This is not your typical "cuddly creatures" pet shop. Owner Bob Mackin is a python breeder and he usually has a family of snakes brooding at the back of the shop. You may also see a pocket mouse, a red-foot tortoise, African spiny mice, iguanas, exotic birds, lizards of all sizes, tarantulas and scorpions.

Mercer Island

Places to Go

CHILDREN'S PARK
Location: Island Crest Way and 54th Ave. SE. From I-90, take the Island Crest Way exit south to just beyond Island Park School (about 54th Ave. SE).
Days/Hours: Dawn to dusk
Web Site: www.miparks.net
Wheelchair/Stroller Access: Yes

Conceived and designed by the Mercer Island Preschool Association, the park's unique climbing equipment was specifically designed for young children, but everyone enjoys it. Two tennis courts adjacent and small trails through shady woods make the park especially appealing and cool during the summer. A fence around the park keeps little ones from roaming; the older ones are busy playing on the dinosaur, in the forts, and crawling around the oversized drain tiles. There are a few picnic tables; space is limited.

CLARKE BEACH PARK
Location: 7700 Block of E Mercer Way (on the southeast part of Mercer Island)
Web Site: www.miparks.net
Wheelchair/Stroller Access: Yes, on a paved walking path

This is a small but very pleasant park offering delightful privacy. Donated to the city by the Clarke family, there are picnic areas and two swimming areas, one shallow enough for toddlers, and some marvelous views.

FIRST HILL LID
Location: W Mercer Way and I-90
Web Site: www.miparks.net

Creative park planners designed this site to hide from I-90 and they did it well. It features soccer, baseball and other play fields, two playgrounds, a basketball court, tennis court, restrooms and a picnic shelter. It's also a great place to wander with a latte (from nearby Tully's or Starbucks) and enjoy views of Seattle, the Eastside and Mount Rainier (Seattle's Lid Park is at 23rd Ave S and Yakima St.). Walkers and bikers frequent the area, too; you'll see many families biking together.

LUTHER BURBANK PARK   206-296-2966
  Location: 2040 84th Ave. SE (north end of the island)
  Web Site: www.miparks.net
  Wheelchair/Stroller Access: Yes

Originally a private estate, Luther Burbank Park is now one of the Eastside's favorites. It's a boating destination during warm weather, great for picnics or just hanging out. There are 77 acres of lake front, over a mile of hiking/biking paths, 3 tennis courts, fishing pier, a 2,000-person grass amphitheater well-used for summer concerts, and outstanding playgrounds with balance beams, climbing nets and other equipment for kids. For dog lovers, there's even an area for unleashed dogs to run. Skateboard enthusiasts cruise a downhill trail to the water's edge. Nearby moorage has room for eight craft. Picnic tables with small barbecues overlook the swimming beach; to use this area, you must make reservations with the King County Parks Department for weekends and holidays.

Shop to Browse

ISLAND BOOKS   206-232-6920; 800-432-1640
  Location: 3014 78th St.. SE
  Web Site: www.mercerislandbooks.com
  Days/Hours: Monday, Tuesday, Wednesday, Friday and Saturday,
     9:30am–7pm; Thursday, 9:30am–8pm; closed Sundays
  Wheelchair/Stroller Access: Yes

One of the Island's most dependable resources, Island Books, founded over 30 years ago, was formerly owned by Lola Deane, the very same person who was the inspiration for this book (and for whom the Children's Park is named). Not just an ordinary bookstore, their children's area is a veritable wonderland of books for all interests. They will special order for you, and if you order a book, it's mailed (book rate) at no charge. Their real specialty is getting to know their customers (including the youngest readers) and their reading habits very well. Great browsing place.

Kirkland and Redmond

Places to Go

FARRELL-McWHIRTER PARK   425-556-2309; 556-2300
  Location: 19545 Redmond Rd., off Novelty Hill Rd. from Avondale Rd. in
     Redmond
  Web Site: www.ci.redmond.wa.us

Days/Hours: Daily, 6am–dusk; animals visible from 9am–5pm.
Program times vary.
Wheelchair/Stroller Access: In most places

This 70-acre farm-turned-park is like a snapshot from your imagination. The sprawling acreage encompasses a lookout on top of an old silo, a forest with wheelchair-accessible Charlotte's Trail, and a collection of farm animals that includes pigs, chickens, goats and an albino cow named Ivory. Explore Mackey Creek Watershed Trail or picnic under one of the mammoth trees. Ask about pony riding classes and summer day camps here.

JUANITA BAY PARK   **425-828-1217; 425-828-2237 (tour info)**
Location: 2201 Market St., Kirkland
Web Site: www.elwas.org/juanitabay
Days/Hours: Dawn to dusk
Tours: Free tours on the first Sunday of the month
Wheelchair/Stroller Access: Yes

There's lots of space for pushing strollers in this 113-acre park with trails, boardwalks and observation areas. This is Kirkland's largest park and a unique urban habitat. Interpretive signs educate visitors about the animals that live and thrive in this wetland area. Be on the lookout for eagles, beavers and a variety of water birds. Nature tours are led by volunteer rangers; groups leave from the Juanita Bay parking lot at 2201 Market St.

KINGSGATE ICE ARENA   **425-823-1242**
Location: 14325 124th Ave. NE, Kirkland
Days/Hours: Open skating, April–August on; call ahead for hours.
Admission: Call for information.
Wheelchair/Stroller Access: Limited

What a great place to be in the summertime! Open skate times and admission prices vary, so it's important to call ahead. From August to April, they offer figure skating lessons and hockey competition.

MARYMOOR PARK   **206-205-3661**
Location: 6064 W Lake Sammamish Parkway NE, Redmond
Web Site: www.metrokc.gov/parks
Days/Hours: Daily, 8am–dusk
Admission: Yes
Wheelchair/Stroller Access: Limited

If you're looking for space, you've come to the right place. Marymoor features 500 acres of picnic grounds, baseball and soccer fields, swing sets, strolling paths and play places. When the weather's right, model airplane fanciers will be flying their radio-controlled aircraft. There is a new toddlers' playground near the Clise Mansion and windmill. Families with dogs can enjoy the 40-acre off-leash area.

Marymoor is also the push-off point for people drifting down the Sammamish Slough in rafts or inner tubes. Four tennis courts, a concession stand and the jogging track are here, also. In another section of the park, a large covered picnic area is frequently reserved for family reunions and birthday parties. One of the park's most amazing features is the Velodrome, one of a handful in the country; special bicycling activities take place here often.

Daring visitors may want to try scaling the manmade climbing rock south of the Velodrome. Thirty-five feet high and forty feet wide at the base, this is one of the largest free-standing climbing structures in the country. A series of intersecting walls with fixed handholds gives climbers different routes to the top. There's also a route for physically-challenged climbers.

NORTH KIRKLAND PARK AND COMMUNITY CENTER   **425-828-1105**
  Location: 12421 103rd Ave. NE, Kirkland
  Days/Hours: Dawn to dusk
  Wheelchair/Stroller Access: Yes

It's known as the "choo-choo train park" because its central climbing toy is a multi-car train with engine and caboose. Ladders, slides, windows and other features on the preschooler-sized train provide hours of imaginative play. Grassy hills a few feet away are a comfortable place on which sleeping babies and parents can relax. Shade trees planted some years ago are beginning to provide relief from the summer sun. The Community Center offers a variety of children's activities, by reservation. Currently there is an indoor playground area, open on Tuesday, Wednesday and Thursday, that's excellent for rainy day activity.

PAINT THE TOWN   **425-861-8388 (Redmond); 206-527-8554 (Seattle)**
  Location: 7529 164th Ave. NE, Redmond Town Center; 4527 University
    Village Court NE, Seattle
  Web Site: www.ceramics-painting.com
  Days/Hours: Monday–Saturday, 9:30am–9:30pm; Sunday, 11am–6pm
  Wheelchair/Stroller Access: Yes

The magic here is becoming a do-it-yourself artist with all of the materials just waiting for you. There are over 400 unpainted ceramic shapes, priced from $5–$40. From menorahs and Santa faces to tiny tea sets, plates and picture frames, you select the piece, then design and paint it. There are 30 colors on hand, from Salsa and Moody Blue to Leapin' Lizard and Rosey Posey. Kids can create personalized pieces for any occasion; perfect gifts for teachers, grandparents or a friend's birthday. The $6/per hour fee includes the paint and brushes, plus the glazing and firing (they do that for you); your piece is ready for pick-up in five to seven days. Great place for a birthday party; there's a party room in the back that accommodates up to twenty. They supply the activity; you supply the food. And it doesn't have to be kids! This could be a unique moms- night-out party, too. For parties and other groups, please reserve ahead. Paint the Town is also in Seattle at University Village (see number above).

REDMOND SATURDAY MARKET   425-556-0636
Location: 7730 Leary Way, northwest corner of Redmond Town Center
Web Site: www.redmondsaturdaymarket.homestead.com
Days/Hours: May-October, 9am–3pm, Saturdays

From a small collection of local vendors, this market has grown to include numerous booths and some interesting artisans. In 2004 they are in their 29th year, the first and oldest open air market in the state. Everything here is Washington-grown. They also feature music twice a month from noon–2pm. A trip to the Market can make your Saturday very productive. Fresh fruit and vegetables are always available; crafts will vary from week to week. Fun for the kids to learn some shopping skills here. Note: Kids who have something creative to sell can do so here on two selected market days. There's a small charge to set up a table and you must preregister. Pick up an application at the Market information table.

SAMMAMISH RIVER PARK
Location: NE 116th Ave. at the Sammamish River, Redmond
Wheelchair/Stroller Access: Yes

With 60 acres bordering the river, this park is a sports-oriented site that includes picnic facilities.

SAMMAMISH RIVER TRAIL
Wheelchair/Stroller Access: Yes

The flat surface of this ten-foot wide asphalt trail is a great place for young bicyclists to shed training wheels and give two-wheeling a try. It's a major favorite for bicyclists, joggers, skaters and pedestrians. If the trail, which begins in Redmond, seems longer, it's because it now connects with the Burke-Gilman Trail. No motor vehicles or horses allowed, but horseback riders do frequent the riverbanks. Popular access points are near Redmond City Hall and off Leary Way in Redmond. Be forewarned–it is very popular.

SKATE KING   425-641-2046

Web Site: www.BellevueSkateKing.com
Location: 2301 – 140th Ave. NE, Kirkland
Days/Hours: Open daily, year-round
Admission: $5/per person (admission and skate rental); $9/per person
(admission and roller blades)
Wheelchair/Stroller Access: In spectator area

Wheeling and dealing on roller skates is a totally different sport today. With in-line skating the hottest blades in town, there are new skills to be learned. Roller skating is an indoor/outdoor activity; at Skate King you don't need to worry about the weather. And it's still appealing to all ages, from toddlers to those 70 and up. They rent both quads (the four-wheel style) and roller blades here and offer a multitude of programs for everyone (singles, parents and toddlers, families, etc.). Birthday parties and special events happen here often. This is a great family activity—works off a lot of extra energy. Call or check their Web site for specific events. They offer lessons here; Skate Journeys offers in-line skating lessons on Saturdays (see Skate Journeys).

SKATE JOURNEYS   206-276-9328

Location: Most classes held at Skate King
Web Site: www.skatejourneys.com
Days/Hours: Varies; call for schedules.
Admission: $12/per person; ask about their Family Plan.
Wheelchair/Stroller Access: Yes, in the spectator area.

From Beginners I through Intermediate to Artistic, you can run the gamut if you have the energy! In-line skating is a whole new talent, but very exciting and energizing. If you've skated (either quads or ice) before, you'll find your balance easily and the lessons will move you along amazingly quickly. The instructors are both patient and supportive; the classes appeal to all ages. You can stay with indoor skating, or venture into Trails and Hills. It's a wonderful family activity and guaranteed to burn up the excess energy. Call Director Trish Alexander (number above) or check the Web site for complete information.

Places to Eat

BRITISH PANTRY   425-883-7511

Location: 8125 161st Ave. NE, Redmond
Days/Hours: Sunday–Tuesday, 10am–5:00pm; Wednesday–Saturday,
10am–9pm
Wheelchair/Stroller Access: Yes

What a charming introduction to the elegant sociability of a tea party at this very English restaurant. There are two rooms, separate but shared; one is an authentic English bakery with tasty scones, shelves of English teas, candies and other goodies. The other is a welcoming little tea room set with tea cozies and other appropriate accessories. Stop here for an afternoon respite or just to pick up some excellent baked goods. The wait staff will divide an adult portion for children with small appetites. Afternoon Tea is served daily from 2:30–4:30pm. You'll enjoy a pot of tea, accompanied by tea sandwiches, scones, jam and cream and a small pastry. Cost is $8.99 each. The owners tell us many of their customers are grandparents out with their grandchildren for the day.

GREAT HARVEST BREAD CO.   425-883-6909 (Redmond);
425-643-8420 (Bellevue)
Location: 17192 Redmond Way, Redmond; 3610-C Factoria Blvd. SE, Bellevue (Loehmann Plaza)
Days/Hours: Monday–Friday, 6:30–7pm; Saturday, 6:30am–6:30pm
Tours: At Redmond store only
Wheelchair/Stroller Access: Yes

Great Harvest is a franchised company, and the Eastside bakeries are under different ownership than the Seattle stores. But you'll find the same wonderful whole wheat bakery products and good bread. And the same delicious bread sampling. They bake many different kinds of bread, plus cookies, muffins and scones.

Store to Browse

CONFETTI JUNCTION   425-861-0567
Location: 17181 Redmond Way and Hwy. 520. Take Hwy 520 past Marymoor Park; exit at Redmond Way, turn left at the light.
Days/Hours: Monday–Friday, 9:00am–8pm; Saturday, 9am–6pm; Sunday, 10am–6pm
Wheelchair/Stroller Access: Yes

If you can't find it here, it probably doesn't exist. This is the "mega" party supply store. Take the kids along to help. They might come up with a novel idea, and you can certainly use an extra pair of eyes here. Confetti Junction can inspire imaginations with items ranging from candy eyeglasses to Dennis Rodman bubble gum to piñatas to–well, try football, soccer or Sylvester and Tweety cake icing decorations, or cowboy hat and dog bone cookie cutters. They rent Helium Express kits for blowing up your own balloons or will make the bouquets for you (up to $5.98/dozen). Costumes and favors exist here for every party theme imaginable.

Bothell and Woodinville

Places to Go

BOTHELL LANDING PARK
Location: At Bothell Way and NE 80th St.. in Bothell
Wheelchair/Stroller Access: Yes

Three important historical buildings–a Swedish immigrant's cabin, the home of the town's doctor, and the Hannan House (now a historical museum)—have all been moved to Bothell Landing Park to commemorate the pioneer families who settled the area. You can sit on the sloped and terraced hillsides next to the river to listen to summer weekend evening concerts. Kids can play nearby on the climbing toys and swings.

CHATEAU STE. MICHELLE   425-488-4633 (tour information)
Location: 14111 NE 145th St., Woodinville. Take I-405 to exit 223 (Monroe-Wenatchee) and follow Hwy 522 to the Woodinville-Redmond Rd. exit. In Woodinville, turn west at Rte 202; cross the railroad tracks. Turn south on Rte 202/Woodinville-Redmond Rd. In about two miles the road curves toward the east and the winery is on the south side.
Web Site: www.ste-michelle.com/
Days/Hours: Daily, 10am–4:30pm
Admission: Free
Tours: Tours are forty-five minutes long; tours are available during the summer every half hour, and winter tours every hour during the week, every half-hour on weekends
Wheelchair/Stroller Access: Yes

One of Washington's best-known wineries, Chateau Ste. Michelle is modeled after a French country chateau and is a welcome stop for families bicycling the Burke-Gilman/Sammamish River trails. Tours are interesting, geared more for adults than children. But youngsters in the tour group will enjoy grape juice samples at the finish (while adults sample wine). Of high interest are the special events and concerts that take place on the grounds; watch the local papers for announcements. There will be seating, but most families prefer to spread blankets and enjoy a grassy vantage point. There's usually ample parking.

SPIRIT OF WASHINGTON DINNER TRAIN   425-227-7245; 800-876-RAIL
Location: Departs from 625 S Fourth St. in Renton
Web Site: www.spiritofwashingtondinnertrain.com
Days/Hours: January–May; Tuesday–Friday, 6:30pm; Saturday, noon, 6:30pm; Sunday, 11am, 5:30pm. June–September; Monday–Friday, 6:30pm; Saturday, noon, 6:30pm; Sunday, 11am, 5:30pm.

Admission: Ranges from $49–$79
Wheelchair/Stroller Access: Yes

Trains have a mystique all their own. This three and a quarter-hour hour trip from Renton through Bellevue to Woodinville and back has become quite popular with both adults and children. Kids 12 and younger dine free from November to April; other months the fare is $20 in regular cars, full price in the dome car. Adult prices range from $47 to $69; reservations are required for all. Along with some delightful scenery and good food, a forty-five minute stop at the Columbia Winery adds to the ambiance of the experience.

GOLD CREEK TROUT FARM   425-483-1415
Location: 15844 148th St. NE, Woodinville. Take I-405 to exit 23 to Hwy 522/Monroe-Wenatchee. Follow Hwy 522 into Woodinville; turn west at 175th St. and right at 140th St.. Drive about a mile before turning left on 148th; go two more blocks.
Admission: Free; you pay only for the fish you catch.
Wheelchair/Stroller Access: Yes

Call before you go, as Gold Creek was closed for refurbishing until summer of 2004. You're charged according to the size of your catch; they do the cleaning and bagging for you. Bring a cooler with ice to take your catch home. This is a good birthday party option for younger kids.

Place to Eat

TEXAS SMOKEHOUSE BBQ   425-486-1957
Location: 14455 Woodinville-Redmond Rd NE (at Hollywood Corners). From I-405, take the 124th St. NE exit; head east across the valley; turn left at the Woodinville-Redmond light and continue toward Woodinville. Hollywood Corners is at the intersection of 145th Ave NE.
Days/Hours: Monday–Thursday, 11am–8pm; Friday and Saturday, 11am–9pm; Sunday, noon–7pm
Wheelchair/Stroller Access: Yes

This is great for dine-in or take-out. Kids' portions are half of adult portions of anything on the menu, and it's an ample serving, no matter what you order. Favorites here are baby-back ribs, chicken and brisket. They stop serving a half hour before closing for dine-in guests; for take-out, they take orders until closing. Their All You Can Eat menu is appealing: On Monday it's beef ribs; on Wednesday it's "burnt ends"of the brisket—a big favorite; and on Thursdays it's chicken. Texas Smokehouse is habit-forming for lots of families; high chairs available. Instead of napkins, you'll find rolls of paper towels at the tables. Great idea.

Shops to Browse

COUNTRY VILLAGE   425-483-2250
   Location: 23732 Bothell-Everett Hwy, Bothell. Take I-405 to exit 26; head
   south one mile.
   Web Site: www.countryvillagebothell.com
   Days/Hours: Monday–Saturday, 10am–6pm; Sunday, 11am–5pm
   Wheelchair/Stroller Access: In most places, but some of the boardwalk
   has stairs.

Located just off the highway, tourists can browse for knickknacks here, but kid-
friendly activities include dress-up teas at Peach Tree Bakery, birthday parties
at Classic Kids or The Iron Horse Railroad. You can feed the ducks and chickens
in the newly-remodeled center courtyard or ride the parent-powered merry-go-
round behind the Country Café. One of the best bets here is the Country Café
(425-483-6162), with generous breakfasts and desserts. Biscuits are a specialty.
You might enjoy the Farmer's Market here on Fridays from 10am–3pm, beginning in May. On Saturdays there are on-going demonstrations at the Wild Fire
glass-blowing studio.

MOLBAK'S GREENHOUSE AND NURSERY   425-483-5000, ext 400
                                                          (direction line);
                                               425-483-5000, ext 349 (tours)
   Location: 13625 NE 175th St., Woodinville
   Web Site: www.molbaks.com
   Days/Hours: Sunday–Friday, 9am–6pm; Saturday, 9am–6pm
   Tours: Groups of 10 or more only (plus chaperones); minimum age is 6.
   Tours usually one hour; Monday–Friday only.
   Wheelchair/Stroller Access: Yes

Molbak's is a good destination for children and families any time, but October
and November are perhaps the most magical. In October, watch for Molbak's
Floral Fairyland; the fun begins at the main entrance as you step into a story-
book world. Fairy tales come alive in the greenhouse as plays are comically
performed by professional actors. Ads in local newspapers will alert you, or
call Molbak's for a schedule or check their Web site. In November the Poinset-
tia Festival is enchanting, with thousands of colorful poinsettias blooming in
many colors. You can nibble on complimentary Danish pastry, but don't miss
the conservatory with its tropical birds. Cameras are welcome.

WOODINVILLE SATURDAY MARKET   425-481-8300
                                              (visitor information center)
   Location: 13203 NE 175th St. (City Hall parking lot)

Days/Hours: April–October; Saturdays, 9am–4pm
Wheelchair/Stroller Access: Yes

If you want to get away from the supermarket scramble, here's a nice collection of local produce, flowers and arts and crafts. This market has been growing, and you'll often see different vendors on different weeks.

Duvall, Carnation and Fall City

Places to Go

BALLOON DEPOT   425-881-9699
    Location: Launch sites will vary according to existing wind directions, although most trips will originate at Harvey Air Field in Snohomish.
    Web Site: www.balloondepot.com
    Days/Hours: Morning and evening flights daily, weather permitting. Reservations strongly recommended; allow a few days' notice. Sometimes they can accommodate day-of-flight reservations. Time will vary seasonally.
    Admission: From $155–$175.
    Wheelchair/Stroller Access: No

Children need to be at least four feet tall (and preferably without fear of heights) to venture into the loft of a hot air balloon. Usually four to nine passengers comprise a group, kids included. The one-hour rides will cost from $155–$175 per person; there are no discounts for children. Snohomish and Arlington (sometimes) are the departure points, and wind is a major consideration (see above). This is a very exciting excursion–the views (and thrills) are different than any other experience. Great birthday gift for a teenager.

CAMLANN MEDIEVAL FARE   425-788-8624
Location: 10320 Kelly Rd. NE, Carnation
Days/Hours: August–Labor Day; Saturday–Sunday, 11:30am–6pm. Call ahead.
    Admission: $5–$8 Gate admission could include the evening banquet but seating is limited.
    Wheelchair/Stroller Access: Yes

This fourteenth-century Olde English rural fair brings history to life for a time. Even children too young to understand the history will be entertained by the wandering minstrels, frolicking harlequins, historical craft demonstrations by peasant-clad performers, and puppet and magic shows. It's a whimsical environment and the food is authentic, too. It's a new experience for some (but old habit for others) to eat stew out of a bowl with no spoon; be sure to sample the zesty grape juice called ypocras.

FALL CITY FARMS 425-222-4553
   Location: 3636 Neal Rd., Fall City
   Web Site: www.localharvest.org/farms
   Days/Hours: Farm is open from August 1–October 31. Hours are: August
      1–September 30;Thursday–Monday, 10am–6pm, Sundays, 11am–6pm,
      closed Tuesday and Wednesday. October 1–October 31: open daily,
      10am–6pm; Sundays 11am–6pm (they close at dusk later in October).
      The U-fish is open weekends, April–June and September, or call for an
      appointment. U-cut Christmas trees, weekends in December.
   Tours: Yes; spring, summer and autumn; preschool – adult. Tours may
      be customized to group's interest.
   Admission: Farm admission/free. Tours: $5 minimum/per person. No
      charge for parents and teachers accompanying school groups. Octo-
      ber tour includes a pumpkin.
   Wheelchair/Stroller Access: Yes

Education and agriculture blend on this working farm and there is lots of "good, dirty fun," learning what working on a farm is all about. Animals are not in a petting zoo, but within reach in their barns and pastures. There are sunflower gardens galore here. You can stroll into the gardens that supply the on-farm market or get a bucket and get to work picking your own fruits, vegetables and flowers for dinner.

REMLINGER FARMS 425-333-4135
   Location: One mile south of Carnation on Hwy 203
   Web Site: www/remlingerfarms.com
   Days/Hours: May–October; daily, 9am–7pm. Closed remainder of year,
      except for holiday activities.
   Tours: Call or go online to reserve a tour.
   Wheelchair/Stroller Access: Yes

What's really fun here is riding the train that loops through the farm to pick a pumpkin in the fall or select a Christmas tree in winter. It's a real bonus for the hordes of kids who love to come to Remlinger. Ponies masquerade as reindeer in December for visitors who want a ride. In the fall a wild maze built from hay challenges visitors of all ages. During the holiday season there'll be weekend entertainment inside one of the barns; the audience sits on hay bales. Outside, kids are encouraged to feed the barnyard animals (with special edibles provided). And, of course, the general store, filled with fresh products, jams and other specialties is part of the ambiance here. If you want a special tour, pick your month and go for it; in May there's a Spring Planting and Bee Tour, in June it's a Pony and Baby Animal Tour and the Strawberry U-Pick. Go online to Calendar and decide for yourself which is the most appealing. If you stop in the cafeteria, you'll find hearty soups, sandwiches and bakery products.

Issaquah

Places to Go

BOEHM'S CANDIES   425-392-6652
   Location: 255 NE Gilman Blvd., Issaquah
   Web Site: www.boehmscandies.com
   Days/Hours: Monday–Saturday, 10am–6pm; Sunday, 11am–6pm.
   Tours: Children's Groups: Monday–Tuesday, Thursday and Friday, 1
      and 1:30 pm. Others: Monday, Tuesday, Thursday, Friday; 10:30am,
      2:15pm. Saturday–Sunday, 1pm. Children's groups must have one
      adult and five children. Age limit: 6 and up. Adult tours are thirty
      to forty minutes, children's tours twenty to twenty-five minutes.
      Reservations required; allow at least a week–they are very popular.
      Call number above; ask for Rebecca or Vienna. Note: No factory work
      on weekends.
   Wheelchair/Stroller Access: Yes

Popular—you bet! It's really a treat to visit this quaint Alpine chateau. Boehm's Candies is one of Issaquah's oldest and most charming attractions, and the tours are fascinating (and the sampling delicious). Candy makers here concoct more than 150 kinds of European and American sweets. During the tour, you'll see the work area with huge copper tubs and 3-inch-thick marble slabs. If you happen to be there when they're hand-forming the chocolates, you'll be intrigued by the precision of the chocolatiers. When you sample this delicious candy (at the end of the tour), you'll become a fan. Included on the tour is founder Julius Boehm's authentic Swiss chalet—the first one built in the Pacific Northwest. The chalet is filled with his collection of European art and mementos of a very unique and active life. Although he's been gone for some years, the owners have kept the premises as they were when Julius lived there.

COUGAR MOUNTAIN ZOOLOGICAL PARK   425-391-5508
   Location:19525 SE 54th St., Issaquah
   Web Site: www.cougarmountainzoo.org
   Days/Hours: February–November; Wednesday–Sunday, 10am–5pm.
      Closed Thanksgiving. December, 4 –23; 10am–7pm daily.
   Admission: $8.50/ages 13–61; $7/62 and older; $6/ages 2–12; Free/those
      under 2 and zoo members. Parking is free.
   Tours: Guided tours and birthday parties by request
   Wheelchair/Stroller Access: Limited

Small but very important, this 14-acre park is home to a number of endangered or threatened species. In an intimate setting, children get a chance to stop and "talk" with some brilliantly-colored exotic birds, or perhaps an alpaca, emu or cougar. In December, the Issaquah Reindeer Festival is quite authentic; reindeer live here, too. Select zoo exhibits will be open during the Festival. Birthday parties are available with special arrangements. Note: They do have some important guidelines for visitors; these include not feeding the animals, no pets allowed, no gum on zoo grounds, and please stay on pathways. Call before you go to visit; the zoo might be closed due to weather or other circumstances.

GEOLOGY ADVENTURES   425-413-1122
Wheelchair/Stroller Access: No

Whether it's crystals in the Cascades, amethyst in California or glowing rocks and palm trees in Issaquah, Geology Adventures takes you someplace out of the ordinary and off the beaten track. Bob Jackson is a geologist who loves to demystify science for children and adults, and offers opportunities for parents and kids to learn and explore together. Some trips are ideal for birthday parties; many are a great challenge for blasé teens. What age is the most curious? You'll have to ask Bob. He also provides a number of educational trips for schools, designing the field trip for the specific age group. Call for the brochure (be patient, he may be hard to reach when off on another exploration).

ISSAQUAH FARMERS MARKET   425-392-2229
Location: Community Center; 301 Rainier Blvd. S
Days/Hours: Saturdays, 9am–3pm
Wheelchair/Stroller Access: Yes

Another grand opportunity for a Saturday outing that accomplishes several purposes: shopping and fun. It's a good way to teach the kids how to select good produce and even plan some of the meals. What a concept for working parents!

ISSAQUAH SALMON DAYS FESTIVAL   425-270-2532
Location: Downtown Issaquah
Days/Hours: Always the first full weekend in October; 10am–6pm
Wheelchair/Stroller Access: Yes

Now one of the premier family events on the Eastside, Issaquah Salmon Days features hatchery tours, a Grande Parade, three stages of live entertainment, sporting events and the Field of Fun. That's where kids "reign"—there are pony rides, giant inflatables, a Nylon Zoo, a rock-climbing wall and more. The downtown streets become a mobile marketplace, with over 300 artists, food vendors and–importantly–local naturalists celebrating volunteer efforts to keep local waters clean so that our salmon can migrate upstream to spawn. All in all, a worthy event and a great family outing.

KING COUNTY LIBRARY SYSTEM
**425-462-9600
(answer line for all branches)**

Location: 960 Newport Way NW
Web Site: www.kcls.org (for all branches)

The King County Library System is one of the busiest in the country. There are 42 branches and all have access to the World Wide Web and all offer an extensive schedule of year-round reading programs and special activities, including a summer reading program immensely popular with youngsters. The programs are led by staff and/or experts from an amazing variety of disciplines. The KCLS Answer Line is a lifesaver for anyone looking for answers to homework or trivia questions. The three busiest branches are Bellevue, Redmond and Shoreline.

LAKE SAMMAMISH STATE PARK
**888-226-7688 (reservations);
360-902-8844 (information) or 425-455-7010**

Location: Off I-90; take exit 15 or 17; turn north to Lake Sammamish
Web Site: www.parks.wa.gov
Days/Hours: Winter: 8am–dusk; Summer: 6:30am–dusk. Open year-round for day use; no overnight camping here.
Wheelchair/Stroller Access: Yes

This was once a meeting place for local Native American tribes who held their potlatch at the south end of the lake; Sammamish comes from the Indian word "samena," which means hunter. This marvelous park offers an expansive beach and swimming area, and several play areas with climbing equipment made from rustic logs. A pagoda-covered eating area includes a central barbecue, running water and electricity. It's a popular spot for birthday parties, barbecues (there are 80 grills in the park), reunions and other large group events. Several areas can be reserved that accommodate groups of 100, 200 and 400; advance reservations are required (see number above). Boating is a favorite activity here; kayak rental is available during summer months and Klub Kayak is the place to go for rentals.

KLUB KAYAK
206-465-8372

Location: At Lake Sammamish State Park
Web Site: www.klubkayak.com
Days/Hours: Memorial Day–Labor Day, plus extended weekends
Wheelchair/Stroller Access: Yes

You must be 18 or older, or with an adult, to rent from Klub Kayak. They have pedalboats, kayaks and canoes; you can rent by the hour or by the day. Prices start at $16 an hour throughout the season. All adults and children (even toddlers) MUST know how to swim; you'll be given a safety check before going out on the water. If you want to "prep" ahead, take a Get In and Go class. These are lessons with rental, offered Saturday and Sunday. Life jackets are included in rentals; wet suits may be rented separately. Lake Sammamish is a great place to learn; once you know what you're doing, you can go anywhere!

VILLAGE THEATRE   425-392-2202 (Issaquah); 425-257-8600 (Everett)
   Location: 303 Front St. N; from I-90, take exit 17. In Everett, 2710 Wetmore Ave., Everett Performing Arts Center. From Seattle, go north on I-5; take exit 192 into Everett; drive about one mile north on Broadway, turn left on Everett Ave. Center is at intersection of Everett and Wetmore Avenues on the left.
   Web Site: www.villagetheatre.org
   Days/Hours: Box office: Tuesday through Saturday, 11am–7pm.
   Admission: Call for information.
   Wheelchair/Stroller Access: Yes

While older children will probably most enjoy the productions of this excellent local theater, there is a viewing room at the back of the Issaquah location where families with young ones can sit together. Here the toddlers can move around and feel less confined, yet parents can enjoy some good stage fare, mostly comical and musical productions. Scenery, costuming and production techniques are top-notch, especially for Broadway musicals. Schedules and prices vary; it's best to call ahead. Season tickets go quickly; there are singles to be had for individual performances. If you're new to this theater, ask ahead about parking.

Shops to Browse

GILMAN VILLAGE   425-264-0594 (main office)
   Location: Downtown Issaquah. Take I-90 to exit 17 (Front St.); turn south on Gilman Blvd.; turn right to cross the railroad tracks; turn left into Gilman Village. You can also take the Renton/Lake Sammamish exit (exit 16); turn right at the light, go to the next light (Gilman Blvd.); turn left; continue to Gilman Village (on your right).
   Web Site: www. gilmanvillage.com
   Days/Hours: Monday, Tuesday, Wednesday, Saturday, 10am–6pm; Thursday and Friday, 10am–7pm; Sunday, 11am–5pm.
   Wheelchair/Stroller Access: Yes; it's mainly a boardwalk, although a few stores are not accessible.

Gilman Village is a collection of old houses in the area, moved from their original sites and refurbished to form a cluster of 40 delightful specialty shops and restaurants. Especially in spring and summer, the bright, festive looks of flowers and outdoor accessories make it a most appealing and relaxing shopping venture. There's not a great deal for kids here, but the few shops that do attract them are charming. Call ahead for special events geared for kids and families.

While you're there, look for Mykens, a specialty boutique for dog and cat owners. Don't miss Lilypad Books; the shelves are filled with books just for kids and families (425-391-2758). And of course Sweet Addition is a draw; it's good for lunch or tea. In fact, their Wee Tea is tempting, a quiet celebration for a few moments, with treats. Wee Tea has a two-person minimum, reservations a must; at $10.50 a person, you'll be catered to with scones, pastries, finger sandwiches and confections, a beverage of choice (tea, juice, cocoa, soda and more). For $5 more, you can order a custom chocolate monogrammed platter. A long-time favorite here is The Boarding House, well-known for their homemade soups and breads. Just For Kids, 10 and under, is a half-sandwich (peanut butter or grilled cheese) with soup or salad, $4.50. Ask about their Sampler Plate Special.

SNOQUALMIE FALLS
Location: Town of Snoqualmie
Web Site: www. snoqualmiefalls.com
Wheelchair/Stroller Access: Yes

What a magnificent backdrop for your family and out-of-town visitor photographs. Some 26 miles east of Seattle, the falls plunge 268 feet into a 65-foot deep pool; that's almost 100 feet higher than Niagara Falls. Tourists and locals are elbow-to-elbow at this gorgeous waterfall. The roar of the spray, the gentle mists, and the fascination of the falling water attracts thousands. It's especially dramatic when the spring snow melts into the river, creating huge swells and currents. A little known fact: this is the site of the first major electric plant in the Northwest to use falling water as a source of power. Views of the Falls from nearby Salish Lodge make dining here a treat and usually require an early reservation.

SNOQUALMIE FALLS FOREST THEATER
425-222-7044
(Box Office only)

Location: Near Fall City at David Powell Rd. Take I-90 to exit 22; follow signs to Fall City for four miles; turn right on David Powell Rd. and go three miles to the gate.
Web Site: www.foresttheater.org
Days/Hours: Performances June–early September. Box office: Monday–Friday, 10am–5pm
Admission: Prices vary with performance; dinner also an option. Children 5 and under admitted free.
Wheelchair/Stroller Access: Limited due to a dirt path

For children, just getting to this outdoor amphitheater is half the fun. Performances are during summer months only. You'll hike down a dirt trail through a pristine forest to the stage; the audience is seated on the terraced hillside just above. The peaceful rhythm of Snoqualmie Falls and lush greenery on nearby mountains are the backdrop to the stage. The group performs at least one youth production each year; most shows are scheduled for Saturdays. Before or after the show, save time to stroll through the quiet woods. Schedules and ticket prices vary; do call ahead. Ask about their dinner options; it's a pleasant addition to the experience.

SNOQUALMIE VALLEY HISTORICAL MUSEUM 425-888-3200
Location: 320 Bendigo Blvd., North Bend; From I-90, take exit 31; proceed north approximately a half mile; the museum is on the right.
Web Site: www.snoqualmievalleymuseum.org
Days/Hours: April–October; Thursday–Sunday, 1pm–5pm
   Admission: Free; donations are appreciated
Wheelchair/Stroller Access: Yes

Children can travel back in time to 1917 and see what mill-town life was like in the Snoqualmie Valley. Sponsored by the Snoqualmie Valley Historical Society, the museum features both permanent and changing exhibits of Native American and pioneer life. You'll see models in authentic clothing from 1917-57 and a re-created kitchen and parlor. Out in the farm shed, some of the equipment and tools are over 100 years old. Special groups may make appointments to visit at nonscheduled times. As at other local museums, it's the volunteers that build and maintain these important reflections of our local history.

SNOQUALMIE VALLEY RAILROAD 425-888-3030
Location: 38625 SE King St. Corner of King St. and Railroad Ave. (Route 202)
Web Site: www.trainmuseum.org
Days/Hours: Summer weekends and holidays; 11am–4pm. Call for information.
Admission: Current train excursion is $5–$8 (call for update); Northwest Railway Museum is free.
Wheelchair/Stroller Access: No

Visitors climb aboard these vintage trains for a 10-mile journey through scenic Snoqualmie Valley. You can board at North Bend or Snoqualmie for a one-way or a seventy-minute round-trip. They've reopened the tracks to the top of Snoqualmie Falls; the sweeping view of the river valley below the Falls is quite something. Now on the National Register of Historic Places, the Snoqualmie Depot was built in 1890 by the Seattle, Lake Shore and Eastern Railway. December's Santa Train is very popular; tickets are often sold out by October, so call early. Ask about other special family events (Mothers Ride Free, Pops on Us, Day Out with Thomas). The Snoqualmie Railroad is part of the Northwest Railway Museum, which has a children's club called Cecil the Diesel Club (lots of perks when you join). While you're up there, look for the small locomotive on the Depot grounds for kids to play in; there's a self-guided walking tour that includes eight historic buildings around the town plus twenty-two railway artifacts.

KING COUNTY HIKES

ASAHEL CURTIS NATURE WALK   425-888-1421; 206-470-4060
Location: Snoqualmie Pass at I-90, exit 47

On the south side of I-90, just past Denny Creek, walk through a quarter-mile of old fir, cedar and hemlock. The Eastlake District of Federated Garden Clubs has identified more than 40 plants for novice botanists. The trail begins at the Asahel Curtis Picnic area. Four of the 28 picnic tables here are on the Snoqualmie River. There are fire pits for cooking; some kids enjoy drawing water from the hand pump.

DENNY CREEK CAMPGROUND   425-888-1421; 206-470-4060
Location: Snoqualmie Pass area

Located about 17 miles east of North Bend along I-90, this campground is a base for several short hikes. In spring, the rushing water in this creek poses a hazard to children. In summer, shallow spots offer safe wading and water play. The Franklin Falls Trail, a little more than a mile off the Denny Creek Trail, leads to a cliff face where water falls more than 70 feet to a pool. It's a nice place to feel the spray and watch for rainbows.

HIGH POINT TRAIL 425-888-1421; 206-470-4060
Location: West Tiger Mountain

Paint Seattle's downtown skyline, Bellevue's sprawling landscape and Issaquah's amazing growth on a picture postcard—these are the views you'll enjoy with a walk up Tiger Mountain. For children, it can be a new view of the world. To find the most traveled route up Tiger Mountain, leave I-90 at exit 20 (High Point Rd.); turn right at the stop sign. At the frontage road, turn left and park on the shoulder. This is one of the area's most popular trails, so don't expect privacy.

SNOQUALMIE TUNNEL   425-888-1421; 206-470-4060
Location: At I-90, exit 54 (Hyak)

This 2.3-mile-long abandoned railroad tunnel is the longest open to hikes in this country. The tunnel links the west and east sections of the John Wayne Iron Horse Trail, which begins at Rattlesnake Lake near North Bend. There are magnificent wild flowers growing at both ends of the tunnel in the spring, and dazzling colors in the fall. Because it's under the solid rock of Snoqualmie Pass, the tunnel is unlighted. Be sure to bring a flashlight, good walking shoes and a warm jacket. Some diehards attempt pushing strollers, but backpacks are the best way to get young ones through the tunnel. Check www.roadtripamerica.com for more information.

THE SUMMIT AT SNOQUALMIE

206-236-1600; 206-232-8182
(reservations for child-care)

Location: Just off I-90 at exit 52

One of the region's most popular downhill and cross-country skiing destinations, and only forty minutes from downtown Seattle, Snoqualmie Pass has consolidated its four areas—Alpental, Ski Acres, Snoqualmie and Hyak—into Summit East, Central and West. They are all part of The Summit at Snoqualmie. A single lift ticket is valid on all 25 chairlifts here. A new fixed-grip quad chairlift is a great feature of the area; 15 more quadlifts are planned to be built before 2007.

Parents with young children will appreciate the child-care services provided here (see number above). Snowboarding continues to grow in popularity. Ask about guided hikes for young teens. Advanced skiers may want to know about the guided tours to the back county. At nearby Snowflake Inner Tubing Center, you can flop onto an inflated tire tube and swoosh down the show. At the bottom, the rope tow hoists tubers back to the top for another ride.

SNOWFLAKE SUMMIT TUBING CENTER

206-236-7277; ex 3377

Location: Off I-90 at exit 52
Web Site: www.summit-at-snoqualmie.com/winter
Days/Hours: Friday, 9am–9pm; Saturday–Sunday, 9am–6pm.
Admission: Sessions are usually two hours: cost is $12–$15/adults,
13 and older, $10–$13/children. Free/children 5 and under; $5/inner
tube rentals
Wheelchair/Stroller Access: No

Now called Summit Central (formerly Ski Acres), this 400-foot snow hill has eight chutes, is lighted for late evening runs, and even has a rope tow on the hill's east side to pull tubers back to the top. Sleds and anything with metal runners are not allowed; only their equipment can be used. It's a good idea to make sure the tube is sufficiently inflated before starting out. There is a pressure pump site, but cold weather sometimes inhibits operation. This is one of the few inner tubing sites for kids to be found at Washington ski areas. Lift ticket and inner tubing prices may change yearly; it's best to call ahead.

RESOURCES:
King County Parks: 206-296-4232; www.metrokc.gov.parks
Shoreline Parks Department: 206-546-5041
Washington State Parks: 888-CAMPOUT (reservations);
425-455-7017 (information) info@parks.wa.gov online
Issaquah Chamber of Commerce: 425-392-7024
Issaquah Parks and Recreation: 425-837-3300
Bellevue Parks and Recreation: 425-452-6881
King County Library System: 425-452-9600 (Answer Line for all branches)

North Puget Sound and The San Juan Islands

A family outing at the popular North Bend/Snoqualmie Railroad

Courtesy, Northwest Railway Museum

North Puget Sound, the Kitsap Peninsula and the San Juan Islands offer some of Washington's most marvelous getaways, especially for one-day trips. Often, especially in summer, it makes more sense to drive through Tacoma, rather than fight the water traffic, but the trip is worth it. The Kitsap Peninsula is across the Sound from Seattle. To get there, go 30 miles south on I-5 to Tacoma, then 18 miles northwest on Hwy 16 to Port Orchard and Bremerton. There's lots of shoreline, but much is owned privately. Visiting Bainbridge, Whidbey and Camano Islands is a delightful day trip for kids. And the Skagit Valley is a haven for bikers, gardeners and weekenders.

North Puget Sound has some unique attractions. Anacortes, once a sleepy town, has come alive. More than just a gateway to the San Juans, it has a personality all its own and a certain whimsy, too. Watch all over town for the fabulous murals that artist Bill Mitchell has created. On almost every building there is a reminder of people and events from Anacortes's early history. Pick up a copy of The Clamdigger, a local paper that includes all kinds of helpful hints, information and some good coupons! You can definitely find a copy at the Visitors Center at 819 Commercial St. La Conner is a popular day's destination, especially around tulip time, and leaving Bellingham, coming down Chuckanut Drive is another heart-stopping experience at times.

Bremerton

Places to Go

BREMERTON NAVAL MUSEUM   360-479-7447
    Location: 402 Pacific Ave., Bremerton
    Web Site: www. museumsusa.org
    Days/Hours: Monday–Saturday, 10am–4pm; Sunday, 1pm–4pm
    Admission: Free
    Tours: Self-guided
    Wheelchair/Stroller Access:: Yes

This is the place for all things nautical and the people who are fascinated with them. The USS Washington and USS Puget Sound are docked here as well. You'll find ship models, naval weapons, and military historical artifacts to satisfy the most avid of naval buffs, and you'll probably be amazed at how much naval operations have changed over the past century. The collections include photos, books, cannons, uniforms, flags and more, some dating back to 1377.

KITSAP HARBOR TOURS   360-377-8924;
360-876-1260 (rates/reservations)
    Location: Departs from the boardwalk on the Bremerton waterfront
    Web Site:www.visitkitsap.com
    Days/Hours: Ship tours are May–October; every hour from 11am–4pm
    Admission: Call number above
    Wheelchair/Stroller Access: Yes

There is some breath-taking scenery on these Bremerton-area cruises. On a clear evening, Mount Rainier, the Olympic Mountains and Seattle's beautiful skyline are visible and astounding. Tillicum village is included in their itinerary (see Chapter One).

One of the cruises will take you around the harbor on a nostalgic look at some World War II ships. Aircraft carriers USS Nimitz and USS Midway and battleship USS New Jersey are on this narrated tour. The destroyer USS Turner Joy is docked here year-round.

Silverdale

Places to Go

ANNA SMITH'S CHILDREN'S PARK
Location: At the intersection of Tracyton Blvd. and Fairgrounds Rd., between Bremerton and Silverdale
Days/Hours: Daily, 9am–9pm
Wheelchair/Stroller Access: Yes

For families who like to feed ducks, this is an ideal place to stop for a while. A quiet park with a charming duck pond at the center, there are fragrant and colorful flower beds to stroll through. This beautifully landscaped area is linked to the saltwater below by a steep trail.

NAVAL UNDERSEA MUSEUM   360-396-4148
Location: In Keyport between Poulsbo and Silverdale. From Hwy 3, take Hwy 308; go east for three miles; follow the signs.
Web Site: www.kpt.nuwc.navy.mil/
Days/Hours: June–September; open daily, 10am–4pm. October–May; open six days, closed Tuesdays; 10am–4pm. Also closed Thanksgiving, Christmas, New Year's Day and Easter.
Admission: Free.
Tours: Self-guided; groups may call ahead to schedule.
Wheelchair/Stroller Access: Yes

This extraordinary museum documents the U.S. Navy's undersea heritage. Not only is the tour free, it's highly educational and entertaining. There are displays of diving gear and rescue vessels to explore, plus hands-on exhibits designed to teach about the diverse underwater life in our environment. Mini-subs and deep submergence vehicles are on exhibit for viewing. There are many other fascinating exhibits dealing with related subjects, including the physical properties below the water's surface, the use of ranging technology to track objects, and weaponry used by the Navy throughout its history dating back to the Revolutionary War. Parking is free; cameras are welcome.

Bainbridge Island

Places to Go

STRAWBERRY HILL
Location: Next to the Historical Museum

A park and playground for all ages. Includes a mini-gym, restrooms, tennis courts, baseball and football fields, and a skateboard court. There's a nice play area for the kids, with climbing equipment and a few picnic tables with outdoor barbecues. All in all, a nice place for a family.

BAINBRIDGE ISLAND HISTORICAL MUSEUM   206-842-2773
Location: 215 Ericksen Ave. NE; call ahead, they're planning a move
Hours: Tuesday, Thursday, Saturday and Sunday; 1–4 pm
Admission: No information at this writing.

The Museum is located in a one-room school, formerly the Island School built in 1908. It became a band room for a short time and was later turned over to the Historical Society, which has done a good job preserving Bainbridge Island history. Some of this history harks back to some ignominious times in our national history. Two videos are available for viewing: one is After Silence, the story of the Japanese internment, and is narrated by a man who experienced the internment as a child. The second is a documentary showing the "downing" of the 320 foot Ft. Ward antenna tower. The top part of that tower is on display at the Museum. Some very old school desks and chairs are there for children to enjoy, complete with buckets of blocks, crayons and pictures. The slate blackboard on the wall is from the original school; touch it and see howcool it is

BAINBRIDGE GARDENS   206-842-5888
Location: 9415 Miller Rd. NE. Coming off the ferry, take a left onto Winslow Way E and follow the road into town, turning right on Madison St. Stay on Madison until you reach the turnaround (can't miss it); go all the way around and turn right onto High School Rd. Follow High School Rd. to its end; turn right and continue through a four-way stop and go several more blocks. The Gardens will be on your left.
Web Site: www.bainbridgegardens.com
Days/Hours: Spring and summer: Monday–Saturday, 9am–5:30pm; Sunday, 10am–5:30pm. Closed Easter, Thanksgiving, Labor Day and December 25–January 1.

One would think a nursery would have no special attractions for children other than the beautiful flowers, but at Bainbridge Gardens there are some delightful surprises for kids. In the gift shop, called the Zen Building, a children's corner has kid-sized rakes, brooms and hoes, composting kits, animal soaps and much more. Outside a small playground has a climbing tower with a slide. School groups come here to plant bulbs and walk the Nature Trail. In the fall, they can watch Mother Nature put her plants to "sleep." Tucked away in a refrigerator in the main building are bags of ladybugs; kids are encouraged to take them home to treat garden aphids. Gardening parents will find it hard to leave, and fortunately the kids can enjoy it, too.

Note: Their annual Pumpkin Walk is great fun, with harvest light displays, a hay maze and the trail of pumpkins. Admission is free but donations for the Bainbridge Island Boys and Girls club are appreciated.

FAY BAINBRIDGE STATE PARK   206-842-3931
Location: 15446 Sunrise Dr NE. From the ferry, take Hwy 304 north to the traffic light at Day Rd.; turn right. The road dead-ends at Sunrise Dr.; turn left and follow the signs.
Web Site: www.parks.wa.gov
Days/Hours: Daily, 8am–dusk. Open year-round for day use; campgrounds close in September, reopen in April.
Admission: Call for current entry fee for campsites; first come first served here.
Wheelchair/Stroller Access: Yes

This is a beautiful 17-acre park with a waterfront view of downtown Seattle and a challenging driftwood beach. You can hike the beach for several miles at low tide. If swimming is your goal, be advised that these Puget Sound waters can be very cold!

SUQUAMISH MUSEUM   360-598-3311, ext. 422; 206-464-5456
Location: 15838 Sandy Hook Rd.; off Hwy 305 between Poulsbo and Winslow
Web Site: www.suquamish.nsn.us/museum
Days/Hours: October–April; Friday–Sunday; 11am–4pm; closed Monday–Thursday. May–September; open daily, 10am–5pm.
Admission: $4/adult; $3/seniors 55 and older; $2/ages 12 and under
Wheelchair/Stroller Access: Yes

The lifestyle and lives of the Suquamish people, past and present, are the focus of the museum, noted for its authenticity. The Suquamish have worked very hard at preserving their heritage and their history. Part of the museum is a longhouse replica. Inside, a fifteen-minute video, Come Forth Laughing, features tribal elders and their stories of growing up on the 8,000-acre Port Madison Reservation. The intricate basketry of the Suquamish is on display, as is a hand-carved canoe. If you go to the cemetery at St. Peter's Church nearby, you will find the headstone marking the grave of Chief Sealth (Seattle)—appropriately designed with painted canoes.

EAGLE HARBOR BOOK STORE 206-842-5332
> Location: 157 Winslow Way EWeb Site: www.eagleharborbooks.com
> Days/Hours: Monday,Tuesday, Wednesday, Friday, 9am–7pm; Thursday,
>   9am–9pm; Saturday, 9am–6pm; Sunday, 10am–6pm.
> Wheelchair/Stroller Access: Yes

Here's a bookstore to relax in. Comfy chairs to sink into and a very quiet atmosphere make reading easy. In the kids' area, which is large and offers both books and toys, there's a play table for the young ones. Out in the adult area, don't miss their REMAINDERS, bargain books at good prices

BLOEDEL RESERVE 206-842-7631
> Location: 7571 NE Dolphin Dr.
> Web Site: www.bloedelreserve.org
> Days/Hours: Open year-round; Wednesday–Sunday, except federal
>   holidays; 10am–4pm
> Admission: $6/per person; $4/seniors 65 and older and children 5–12.
>   Free/under 5. By reservation only; allow at least a week in good
>   weather.
> Tours: Guides available for groups of six or more by prior arrangement (no additional charge).
> Wheelchair/Stroller Access: Some areas not as accessible as others. The
>   Reserve has wheelchairs for your use (free and available by reservation) with wider than normal tires.

Described by a garden writer as an "artful woodland tapestry," Bloedel is worth a day's visit at the least (they suggest you allow two hours). By reservation only because they only "invite" a limited number of people per day, the Reserve is always a gift of privacy and reflection. There are two miles of trails on this 150-acre preserve; you'll stroll through "garden rooms," broad meadows, narrow ravines, woods and glens, and have the opportunity to explore the Bloedel home, with its magnificent Sound view and elegant furnishings. Be sure to see the Japanese Garden, the Moss Garden, the Reflection Pool and the Glen. There is something every season—you'll never be disappointed. Children can enjoy this panorama thoroughly; there is much to explore on their level.

Note: No food service or picnicking here; no pets allowed, in or out of the car.

Places to Eat

BLACKBIRD BAKERY   206-780-1322
> Location: 210 Winslow Way EHours: Monday–Friday, 6am–6pm; Satur-
>   day, 6:30am–6pm; Sunday, 7am–6pm
If you've just come off an early ferry or are waiting to leave in the weehours of the morning, stop at the Blackbird Bakery for some deliciouspastries and large,

tempting cinnamon rolls. For the kids, Charlie Browncookies and Super Chunks (totally chocolate) are appealing

BAINBRIDGE BAKERS   206-842-1822
   Location: Winslow Way EHours: Monday–Saturday, 6am–6pm; Sunday,
   6am–5pm
   Wheelchair/Stroller Access: Yes

Slightly more upscale and somewhat adult, still they serve hot chocolate,cookies with sprinkles and gingerbread men. On the sandwich list, tuna melt,plain tuna and grilled cheese are available in half portions.

STREAMLINER DINER 206-842-8595
   Location: 397 Winslow Way, Winslow
   Days/Hours: Monday–Saturday, 7am –12:30pm; Sunday, 7:30am–
   2:30pm
   Wheelchair/Stroller Access: Yes

Sometime during your stay or visit to Bainbridge Island, make sure you stop here. It's a longtime favorite with both visitors and locals and with good reason. Their country-style breakfasts and generous sandwiches create mouth-water-ing memories. Once there, one usually plans to go back.

Poulsbo

Places to Go

MARINE SCIENCE CENTER   360-779-5549
   Location: 18743 Front St. NE (across from New Day Fishery)
   Web Site: www.poulsbomsc.org
   Days/Hours: Open daily, 11am–5pm, except Christmas Eve, Christmas
   Day, News Year's Day and Thanksgiving
   Admission: $4/adults; $3/seniors 65 and older and students 13–17, and
   active duty military; $2/children 2–12; Free/under 2
   Wheelchair/Stroller Access: Yes

Here young marine biologists can examine plankton under microscopes, then watch their experiments on a nearby video monitor. Most of the exhibits here are touch tanks, allowing youngsters to get a hands-on feel for the underwater creatures. The jellyfish and octopus are especially popular!

SLUY'S BAKERY   360-697 2253 (BAKE)
   Location: 18924 Front St NE
   Web Site: www.poulsbo.net/sluysbakery

Days/Hours: Sunday–Thursday, 5am–6:30pm; Friday and Saturday, 5am–6pm
Wheelchair/Stroller Access: Yes

Starting as a local favorite, Sluy's fame has spread and Poulsbo bread has become a regional staple, available in many stores throughout the state. A tasty, multi-grain, generously sliced bread with a nutty flavor, it's popular for toast and sandwiches. But pastries are another specialty here, especially the Danish and the scones. It's a great stopping point for coffee and a sweet treat. If weather permits, take your reward over to Waterfront Park and enjoy.

Edmonds

EDMONDS UNDERWATER PARK
The Park is located just north of the ferry dock at the foot of Main St. In downtown Edmonds, it is also adjacent to the Brackett's Landing park facility.

Officially designated as one of the first underwater parks on the West Coast, the park is very popular and attracts scuba divers from all over the country. The area includes 27 acres of tide and bottomlands and was established as a marine preserve and sanctuary in 1970. The park's original feature, the "De Lion Dry Dock," is over 300 feet long and was sunk in 1935. It provides a haven for schools of fish and other extraordinary plant and invertebrate life. There are eight major structures underwater and many trails that provide diverse opportunities for exploration.

Place to Eat

MALTBY CAFÉ   425-483-3123
Location: 8809 Maltby Rd. in Snohomish. Take 405 north, exit on Hwy 522 East (Woodinville). Stay on the main road to the Maltby intersection (Bothell-Monroe Rd.). Turn left at the light; take the next right, then the next left.
Days/Hours: Daily, 7am–3pm
Wheelchair/Stroller Access: Yes

This is a place you go to eat. Breakfast is served all day weekends and until 11am on weekdays, lunch from 11am–3pm. They offer huge cinnamon rolls and delicious buttermilk biscuits; everything is fresh and there's Starbucks coffee to top it off. There is usually a wait (maybe twenty minutes) but it goes quickly. The kids' menu has crayons, too, with the smaller portions and prices. Lunch includes grilled cheese, turkey or junior pb&j sandwiches. Adults' portions are generous, but you can share at no extra charge (they don't do half portions). High chairs and boosters, but no changing table. Of interest: nearby Flower World.

North Snohomish County

Snohomish

Places to Go

HARVEY'S AIRFIELD   360-568-6894
   Location: 9900 Airport Way, Snohomish
   Web Site: www.harveyairfield.com
   Days/Hours: Field is open daily year-round
   Wheelchair/Stroller Access: Yes

There are a number of attractions here. The restaurant overlooks the airfield, has a kids' menu, and does birthday parties. The playground outside, plus outdoor dining, is great in good weather. While you dine, you can watch planes taking off and landing and skydivers wafting their way down. But for those bitten by the flying bug, there's magic here. Harvey's houses up to 300 planes, all privately owned, many of them of special interest. Snohomish Flying Service offers scenic airplane flights for one to three people ($85/half hour, $160/hour), helicopter flights for one to three people ($150/half hour, $290/hour), and Discovery Flights for two ($49 and $59, depending on the plane). For youths 12–17, the Summer Youth Camp is a good introduction to the world of flying; it's a week-long experience that includes two hours of flying (cost varies). Call about Harvey's Corn Roast Fly-In, usually in mid-September. An all-day affair, all the corn you can eat, with balloon rides, aerobatics contests, aircraft displays and much more.

PIONEER VILLAGE AND MUSEUM   360-568-5235 to arrange
                                                          group tours
   Location: Second and Pine Streets in Snohomish; parking is behind the
      Pilchuck Shopping Center
   Days/Hours: Mid-May–August: daily, noon–4pm
   Admission: $1/adults; 50 cents/seniors and students
   Wheelchair/Stroller Access: Possible, but be prepared for some rough
      grass.

The air is rich with the history of Snohomish of a hundred years ago at the Pioneer Village, a collection of cabins and other buildings from earlier days. Now restored and authentically furnished by the Historical Society, it's easy to imagine what life was life. The Kikendall Log Cabin, originally on the Pilchuck River, dates back to 1875. You'll find Cook's General Store, the blacksmith's shop, and even an outhouse out back.

Places to Eat

CABBAGE PATCH RESTAURANT AND INN   360-568-9081
Location: 111 Ave A, Snohomish
Web Site: www.cabbagepatch.com

Note: The Cabbage Patch had an unfortunate fire in spring of 2004 but plans to rebuild are already underway. Call for current information.

SNOHOMISH VALLEY ICE CREAM   360-568-1133
Location: 902 First St., Snohomish
Days/Hours: Summer: Monday–Saturday, 10am–9pm; Sunday, 11am–8pm. Winter; Monday–Saturday, 10am–5pm; Sunday, 11am–5pm
Wheelchair/Stroller Access: Yes

Milkshakes are special here. Real ingredients, made the old way in a metal cup on a long-arm blender—are we dating ourselves? They make their own waffle cones and do half sandwiches with pb&j on request. Plus sodas, floats and sundaes. Candy and popcorn, too.

Store to Browse

WEED'S VARIETY   360-568-5161
Location: First St. in Snohomish
Days/Hours: Monday–Saturday, 10am–5:30pm; Sunday, 11am–5pm.
Open year-round except for major holidays
Wheelchair/Stroller Access: Yes

If you're strolling First St., here's a well-remembered version of the variety store. Worth just ducking in for a look around.

Lynnwood

Places to Go

ROLL-A-WAY SKATE CENTER   425-778-4446
Location: 6210 200th St. SW
Days/Hours: Public Sessions: Wednesday–Friday, 4pm–6pm; Friday–Saturday, 7pm–11pm; Saturday–Sunday, 1pm–3:30pm, 3pm–5:30pm; Sunday, 7pm–9pm
Wheelchair/Stroller Access: In the viewing area

The price of admission is $2.50 during the day, $5 on weekend evenings, and skate rental is included

LYNNWOOD ICE CENTER   **425-640-9999**
  Location: 19803 68th Ave. W, Lynnwood
  Web Site: www.lynnwoodicecenter.com
  Days/Hours: Public Skating: daily, 11am–1pm; also, Tuesday–Thurs-
    day, 7pm–8:50pm; Saturday, 3:30pm–5:50pm, 9pm–1am; Sunday,
    3pm–5pm.
  Admission: $6.50/regular; $5.50/seniors and 12 and under; toddlers
    skate free. Cheap Skate: Wednesday evening for one hour/$4.50
  Wheelchair/Stroller Access: Yes, for viewing

Skating has always been a great family-togetherness experiment, and for some it's an ongoing resource for entertainment, exercise and even a stress-reliever. Just trying to get around the rink the first few times can provide great opportunities for laughter. It's a great place for kids' birthday parties, too. Formerly Sno-King, Lynnwood Ice Center offers a choice of three packages that include skate rental and admission; you bring the cake and they do everything else. The party takes place in the public area (no separate party room), but with all the commotion, no one ever seems to mind. It's fun—if your ankles hold up.

Mukilteo

Places to Eat

IVAR'S   **425-742-6180 (Mukilteo restaurant)**
  Location: Three locations in Snohomish County: Ivar's Mukilteo Land-
    ing and Seafood Bar, 710 Front St.; Ivar's Seafood Bar, 1520 41st St.,
    Everett; Ivar's Seafood Bar, 9910 Edmonds Way, Edmonds.
  Days/Hours: Mukilteo Fish Bar, Monday–Thursday, 10:30am–10pm;
    Friday–Sunday, 10:30am–11pm.
  Wheelchair/Stroller Access: Yes

This Puget Sound landmark dates back to the 1950s and was made famous by Seattle celebrity Ivar Haglund. From the Fish Bar, you can take your chowder or fish and chips and walk out to the adjacent dock to enjoy. Sitting over the water, the main restaurant offers a stunning, ever-changing view of the adjacent ferry traffic and sport fishing activities, plus the Olympic Mountains. It is so close to nature that in 2003 a huge wave burst through the front windows facing the Sound and inundated the room. They reopened in 2004.

Marysville and Snohomish County

Places to Go

BIG D's BATTING CAGE AND MINI GOLF   **360-659-4086**
  Location: 1070 Columbia Ave. in Marysville (behind gold's Gym)
  Days/Hours: Monday–Friday, noon–8pm; Saturday, 10am–8pm; Sunday,
    11am–7pm
  Admission: No admission fee; charges for individual activities
  Wheelchair/Stroller Access: Yes

Little Leaguers and other baseball advocates can sharpen their skills here quite nicely. With a ball coming at them every 10 to 20 seconds, they have to concentrate! You can select the speed of the pitch; the charge is 22 baseballs for $1. Reserve a cage in advance at $14 for 30 minutes or $25 for an hour. The minigolf is $2.50 for 12 and younger, $3 for 12 and up. Special note: They will close during thunder and lightning storms.

HORSE COUNTRY—PONIES TOO! 360-691-7509; 425-335-4773
  Location: 8507 Hwy 92 in Granite Falls. Take I-5 to exit 194; turn left onto
    Hwy 204, left again to Hwy 9, right onto Hwy 92. Horse Country is six
    miles up on the right. Look for a green fence and long driveway.
  Web Site: www.horsecountyfarm.com
  Days/Hours: Winter: Wednesday–Saturday, 9am–7pm; Sunday, noon–
    7pm. Closed holidays.
  Admission: Guided rides: $17.50/one hour; $25/ninety minutes; $5/fif-
    teen minutes (ponies). Call ahead—prices subject to change.
  Wheelchair/Stroller Access: No

Horse County covers 111 acres on the Pilchuck River. The guided trips go up into the Cascades; families often vacation together this way. There is no age limit to ride the ponies, and staff will help if needed. In case of rain, there's a spacious indoor riding arena. Western and English riding lessons are offered, plus there's a summer day camp for kids ages 7–16.

CENTENNIAL TRAIL
  Location: Snohomish to Lake Stevens. To start in Snohomish, drive
    Bickford Ave. into Snohomish; turn east on 10th Ave.; go north on
    Maple Ave., that becomes the Snohomish-Machias Rd. Look for a
    parking lot just past Three Lakes Rd. or park near Lake Stevens at
    the Bonneville field ballpark at the end of 16th Ave. NE.
  Days/Hours: The trail is always open, but unlighted at night; best to
    use between dawn and dusk.
  Wheelchair/Stroller Access:: Yes

It's amazing how many different modes of transportation can be seen on this modest, six-and-a-half mile paved trail. Bicycles, tricycles, walkers, strollers, roller skaters and bladers, skateboards and even horses share this Snohomish County trail. It's safe and flat, allowing a small measure of security to youngsters learning to ride. The trail winds through farmland, past horses and cows grazing in fields, and around waterways. The eventual destination is Arlington.

Everett

Places to Go

BIRINGER FARMS   425-259-0255

Location: 37th Ave. NE off Hwy 529. Heading north on I-5, take exit 195; turn left; continue two miles to Hwy 529; cross the Snohomish River Bridge; take the second right to 37th Ave. NW. Follow a bumpy dirt road into the farm.

Web Site: www.biringerfarm.com

Days/Hours: Seasonal; call for info.

Admission: For the pumpkin tours: usually $3–$4.50. Corn Maze: kids under 40 inches/free; other/$5.75–$9.00. Prices subject to change.

Wheelchair/Stroller Access: Yes

Biringer's attracts families for a number of reasons, not the least of which is their U-Pick berry fields. Strawberries and raspberries are irresistible in the summer months. Halloween is a wonderful time out here, with the "boo barn," the hay maze and pumpkins galore to choose from. In August and September, the Corn Maze is amazing. Check their Web site for other family-friendly events.

BOEING PLANT   206-544-1264;
                                        800-464-1476 (tour times and directions)

Location: 84th St SW. Take I-5 to exit 89; go west for two miles.

Web Site: www.boeing.com

Days/Hours: Monday–Friday, 9am and 1pm. Tickets available at 8:30 am.

Admission: $5/person charge for groups of 10 or more

Tours: Held at 9am, 10am, 11am, 1pm, 2pm and 3pm, Monday through Friday. Reservations may be made 24 hours or more in advance. Groups of 10 or more MUST make a reservation.

Tickets: Nonreserved tickets sold on site for same-day use beginning at 8:30am; available on a first-come, first-served basis.

Admission: Reserved tickets: $10/per person. Nonreserved tickets: $3/62 and over, 15 and under; $5/adults. Group tours: Commercial, $10/person; Nonprofit, $5/person.

Important Phone Numbers: General information/reservations: 800-464-1476 or 206-544-1264; Ticket availability for day-of-tour only: 425-342-8500 (8:30am–2pm, Monday– Friday)

Other: Children must be 4 feet, 2 inches tall to go on tour; children and/or students under 15 (meeting height requirement) must be accompanied by an adult. No babies; no personal items (purses, backpacks, cameras, cellphones, etc.).

Wheelchair/Stroller Access: Tour is wheelchair-accessible, but there are no wheelchairs available for visitors' use.

The Everett plant is considered the largest manufacturing plant in the world. The tour lasts a little over one hour; be there early to get tickets (if you haven't reserved them). Vacation months are by far the most popular. The tour includes a one-third mile walk, 21 steep stairs and an elevator ride. No restrooms are available on the tour, but there will be some before and after. Boeing has been Everett's main employer for some time, and while changes may be in the works, the company is a critical part of the community. Thousands of people come to tour this plant annually; it is the largest factory in the world, by volume.

EVERETT AQUASOX   425-258-3673

Location: Everett Memorial Stadium, 39th St. and Broadway St.
Web Site: www.aquasox.com
Days/Hours: Generally June–August (home schedule)
Admission: Prices vary
Wheelchair/Stroller Access: Yes

As the Class A farm team for the Seattle Mariners, the Aquasox continue to grow in stature and popularity. The lure of an outdoor game in a small ballpark, replete with hot dogs, hot chocolate and some pretty funky between-inning games and contests, is almost addicting. Bring a mitt—you never know when a ball may come your way. The concession stands have just the right snacks and treats. They work here to keep the park environment comfortable for families. It's great fun and you might recognize a budding star at the beginning of his career.

EVERETT FARMER'S MARKET

Location: Just off West Marine View Dr., north of Navy Home Port and Marine Village
Web Site: www.snohomish.org/activity
Days/Hours: June–September; Sundays, 11am–4pm.
Wheelchair/Stroller Access: Yes

This open-air market is a nice stopping point on a Sunday afternoon. Good selection of cut flowers, fruits, vegetables, herbs, honey and some crafts. Walk through once before selecting; prices will vary. All Washington-grown produce.

FOREST PARK   425-257-8300
Location: 802 Mukilteo Blvd.
Web Site: www.everettwa.parks
Days/Hours: Dawn to dusk
Wheelchair/Stroller Access: Strollers enter from the north parking lot;
wheelchairs from the south parking lot.

This is a lush green, 111-acre park with tempting paths. In summer, the playground is wonderful place for kids, while the rest of the family lounges on the grass. Lots of attractions here: ball fields, tennis courts, indoor swimming pool, outdoor wading pool and sprinkler pools. Big toddler favorite: the Animal Farm. The Concerts in the Park series is hugely popular for families in summer months.

JETTY ISLAND FERRY   425-257-8304
Location: Free ferry departs from the 10th St. boat launch and Marina
Park (ten blocks north of the Naval Base)
Days/Hours: July 5–August 31; Wednesday–Saturday, 10am–5:30pm;
Sunday, 11am–5:30am
Admission: Free
Wheelchair/Stroller Access: Ferry yes, island no

A free ferry is a wondrous adventure, especially to Jetty Island in the summertime. The five-minute ride goes VERY quickly and warm shallow water and a sandy beach are the reward. Jetty Island offers nature walks up to two miles, crafts projects and, survival adventure games, most appropriate for 5- to 10-year-olds. Guided nature walks are at 12:15pm and 3:15 pm. The ferry sails every half-hour and fills up very quickly. If you choose to arrive on your own craft, you may have to pull up on the beach, as the nearby dock has limited space. Special note: There is NO running water on Jetty Island. Restroom facilities are floating portable toilet stalls. Pets are not allowed. Also, during peak summer hours, the wait can be up to two hours. Parking adjacent to the boat launch.

Place to Eat

PAVE SPECIALTY BAKERY   425-252-0250
Location: 2613 Colby Ave.
Days/Hours: Monday–Friday, 7am–6pm; Saturday, 8am–4pm. Deli
Hours: Monday–Saturday, 10am–3pm.
Wheelchair/Stroller Access: Yes, but limited

It's a small place seating around 30 to 40 people; much of their business is take-out because the bakery goods are so good! Sandwiches and other portions are generous; they do half-sandwiches for smaller appetites. Box lunches are perfect for a picnic at Forest Park. Cookies are a good munching size; desserts are almost irresistible.

Store to Browse

DISPLAY AND COSTUME SUPPLY 425-353-3364
Location: 5209 Evergreen Way
Web Site: www.displaycostume.com
Days/Hours: Monday–Friday, 9am–8pm; Saturday, 9:30am–6pm; Sunday, 11am–5pm
Wheelchair/Stroller Access: Yes

An absolute haven for the party-giver, party lover and party-goers. Costumes for all occasions, decorations, paper supplies and balloons, specialty items—everything but the invitations—and they may have those by now! Helium tank rentals available, too.

Stanwood/Camano Island

Stanwood

From I-5, take Exit 212 and head west on Hwy 532 for about five miles. Stanwood is a historic laid-back little community serving surrounding agriculture and small industry and is a gateway to Camano Island. The city has several parks and playfield. The population has, for many years, been predominantly Scandinavian and German. The '"trademark" here is the popular snow goose; locks of them settle in the fields for weeks in early winter on their way to Siberia, where they summer.

Places to Go and Eat

THE PAVILION AT STANWOOD CAMANO VILLAGE
Location: 6996 265th St NW
Web Site: www.stanwoodcinemas.com
Days/Hours: Open daily, year-round

On your way to Stanwood from I-5, you'll want to stop at the Stanwood-Camano Village to see the Pavilion. When you first enter the building, come in from the west side and as you walk in, you'll see a 360-degree cyclorama of life as it was in old Stanwood circa 1910. To your right is a full-sized mural (40 feet high, 170 feet wide) depicting a Stanwood street scene complete with the early passenger train, storefronts and the people you would find there. The mural was painted by nationally known (local) artist, Jack Gunter, who says there are 100 flying pigs somewhere in that mural (look in the clouds above the town). You can stop at any of the three restaurants for a meal or a light bite. There's also a Game Room with 26 stations (great for the older kids) and a five-screen cinema with first run films. The entire Pavilion and all three restaurants are wheelchair and stroller accessible, although the flooring is a "cobblestone street." Many locals plan dinner first, then a movie, since the theater is just across the "street" from the restaurants.

CAFÉ CRAVINGS   360-939-2057
Days/Hours: Monday and Tuesday, 8am–4pm; Wednesday, Thursday, Friday, 8:30–9pm; Saturday, 10am–9pm; Sunday, 10am–4pm

They serve deluxe and panni sandwiches, salads, beverages, including espresso, and 16 flavors of hand-dipped ice cream. Sundaes and milkshakes are a specialty; no charge for splitting portions. Everything is made fresh here while you wait; pastry goods are baked there as well. Outside there's an eighteen-hole mini-putt golf course, open year-round (rates change, ask for information). For kids, there are coloring books, puzzles, boosters and high chairs. For kids 12 and under, all you can eat for $3.50. In winter months, sitting in front of the fireplace is a warming place to be. Checkers and chess games go on frequently. Computers are available for a small fee; customers are welcome to use their in-house Web site.

THE DRAGON PALACE   360-629-8106
Days/Hours: Monday–Friday; 11am–10:30pm; Saturday and Sunday, 11am–9:30pm
Dragon Palace has won recognition from many local papers for their cuisine. High chairs and boosters are available. It's very popular with families; the portions are generous and the food comes hot.

AMIGO'S MEXICAN RESTAURANT   360-629-5052
Days/Hours: Daily, 11am–11pm

Amigo's is a full-service restaurant with a full range of Mexican cuisine. There is a special senior and kids' menu with all choices, $3.75. For kids' entertainment, choose from coloring books and crayons and a box with toys. Amigo's portions are very generous; it's hugely popular with the family crowd.

HAGGEN FOOD AND PHARMACY   360-629-4400
Location: 26603 72nd Ave. NW
Web Site: www.haggen.com
Days/Hours: Open daily, twenty-four hours.

Haggen's is a good stop-over if you're planning a trip to the Camano Island State Park or a picnic of any kind. There are sandwiches ready for pick-up as well as lunch selections at the Deli counter. Sushi and hot dishes are available, too, and box lunches are possible, if you call ahead. There's a large seating area if you decide to eat right there (plus an in-house Starbucks). If you come late in the evening and can't find what you want, ask any of the store personnel; they'll make sure you get what you need.

D.O. PEARSON HOUSE AND MUSEUM   360-629-6110
   Location: 27112 172nd Ave. NW
   Web Site: www.whidbey.com/sahs
   Days/Hours: Wednesday and Sunday, 1–4pm; Friday, 10am–4pm
   Admission: Free; donations appreciated
   Tours: By special request only
   Wheelchair/Stroller Access: Pearson House, yes; museum, no

The circa 1890 Pearson House is furnished with authentic antiques donated and gifted from local families, providing a realistic reflection of the early Stanwood area. The adjacent museum has artifacts and photo displays describing Stanwood and the nearby Stillaguamish River Valley.

GARGOYLE BILLIARDS   360-939-0089
   Location: 8713 271st St. NW
   Days/Hours: Monday–Thursday, 2–10pm; Friday and Saturday, 2pm–
      midnight. Closed Sundays
   Wheelchair/Stroller Access: Yes

They've created a smoke-free entertainment center that welcomes families. With eight billiard tables, soft-tip dart boards, video games and Foosball, it's a gathering place for all ages. Located right near the police station in "Old Town," they have ample parking. Local musicians take advantage of Open Mike Night. Ping pong tournaments and DJ nights are equally popular.

Other Places to Eat

SCANDIA BAKERY AND CAFÉ   360-629-2411
   Location: 8704 271st St. NW
   Days/Hours: Tuesday–Saturday, 7am–5pm
   Wheelchair/Stroller Access: Yes

This Scandinavian style bakery (and there's no mistaking that!) and small restaurant is well-known in the area for its traditional lefse and bakery goods.

For children, there is pb&j and toasted cheese sandwiches, coloring books to work on; boosters and high chairs available.

JIMMY'S PIZZA & PASTA   360-629-6565
Location: 9819 Hwy 532
Days/Hours: Year-round (except four days over Christmas); Monday–
   Saturday, 11am–closing; Sunday, 4pm until closing
Wheelchair/Stroller Access: Yes

Hugely popular for both lunch and dinner, expect a wait on the weekends. Jimmy's food is consistently good and they do cater to kids. Much of their clientele is families and youth sports teams. They do orders to go, but only take reservations for groups of eight or more, Sunday–Thursday. Their mini-pizza for kids is $3.42 with two toppings; 50 cents for each extra topping. It comes with salad at lunch, no salad after 3pm. Boosters and high chairs are available. The big room gets noisy; it's quieter in the smaller area.

THE COOKIE MILL 360-629-2362
Location: 9808 Hwy 532
Days/Hours: Inside dining and drive-thru window: Monday–Saturday,
   6:30am–7pm; Sunday, 9am–6pm.
Wheelchair/Stroller Access: Not easy for wheelchairs; a few steps at the
   front door might be difficult to maneuver.

People love to stop here for a light breakfast or a quick lunch. Portions are ample and the baked goods (all made on the premises) are fresh. It's a cozy little place—seats about 30 to 40 people; friendly, country décor creates a warmth all its own. Another good stop for a picnic lunch.

Swushing down the slide at a Camano Island park

Photo: courtesy S. Cleveland

Camano Island

Camano Island is unique in its easy proximity to Seattle. Just an hour's drive, accessible by a small bridge (no ferry required!), tucked between Whidbey Island and the mainland, Camano offers all facets of marine and recreational activity, plus bird watching, camping, hiking, fishing and clamming (at the State Park). There are boat launches on all sides of the Island, and a natural harbor at the north end, Utsalady Bay, is a natural layover for sailboats going to and from the San Juan Islands. Skagit Bay is famous for its bountiful Dungeness crab harvests and secure anchorage. Camano Island is in the "Olympic Mountain rain shadow" and receives half the annual rainfall recorded for Seattle.

Places to Go

ALPACAS DE LA PATAGONIA   **360-387-9356**
  Location: 332 N East Camano Dr.
  Web Site: www.alpacapatagonia.com
  Tours: June–September, Fridays only. Tours last from forty-five minutes to one and a half hours; by appointment only. Allow 2–7 days.
  Wheelchair/Stroller Access: Not conducive.

Note: Tour guidelines include the following: no shouting, running or yelling. These movements frighten the animals; slow, gentle quiet movements are requested. Also: DO wear close-toed shoes, sturdy and meant for walking through muddy fields.

If it was possible to stroll through the herd while they're grazing, you'd hear them humming to each other. That's how they communicate. Alpacas are incredibly clean, gentle and quite lovable—and loved for their fiber (wool) as well as their good nature. Alpacas de la Patagonia is one of the top 10 farms in the United States; there are close to 600 animals on the 156-acre working farm. There's always something happening. Alpacas breed once a year but at different times; if there are some babies when you tour, you'll get to see them. Shearing takes place throughout the summer; if they are shearing on a tour day, visitors are welcome to watch. The tours are geared toward each group's interest; most school groups can do the walking tour, while seniors prefer the driving tour. If you're walking, you'll go into the fields and talk to the herd; they are very friendly and very curious, and most youngsters want to touch them. You'll see the barns, get to "feel" the raw fleece, and finish in the Show Room to admire their show ribbons. If you can't book a tour, drive south on E Camano Drive to see the herd grazing in the north meadow. Listen—you can hear them humming.

U-pickers harvesting oysters in Nahcotta.

Photo courtesy of Larry Warnberg

CAMALOCH GOLF COURSE   360-387-3084
Location: 326 E Camano Dr.
Days/Hours: Open year-round but availability is weather-dependent
Wheelchair/Stroller Access: No

During summer months Camaloch has a special twilight rate with an added special rate for juniors under 18 years of age (when playing with an adult).

OUT ON A LIMB ORCHIDS/CAMANO ISLAND LAVENDER FARM
360-387-2341
Location: 353 E North Camano Dr. From I-5, take exit 212, heading west on Hwy 532. Drive through Stanwood to Camano Island; proceed three and a half miles to a Y and stay right onto N Camano Dr. About eight-tenths of a mile, look for the Out on a Limb sign on the right hand side of the road; enter through the large gate.
Days/Hours: Open by appointment.
Tours: Wednesday–Thursday, 10am–4pm.
     Age minimum: 8 and up.
Admission: Free
Wheelchair/Stroller Access: Not advised

Out On a Limb is the largest orchid nursery in the Pacific Northwest. If you can't make a tour, watch for their Open Houses (four annually); call for dates and information. They have eight greenhouses filled with tens of thousands of exotic orchids of all varieties. You'll see everything, from babies to bloomers. It tends to be warm in here and the floors can be damp in places, so dress accordingly. Open-toed shoes not advised. People who don't know orchids come away completely amazed about the extraordinary selection, and how easy they are to grow. If you don't want to go home empty-handed, there are usually some plants available for sale.

CAMANO ISLAND STATE PARK

360-387-3031;
800-233-0321 (reservations)

Location: 2269 S Lowell Point Rd.
Web Site: www.parks.wa.gov
Days/Hours: April –September; 6:30am–dusk. October–March; 8am–dusk
Wheelchair/Stroller Access: Some parts are accessible; sometimes weather-dependent

This 134-acre park is very popular; part of the reason is that most of the waterfront on Camano is privately-owned. This is one of the few places on the Island—other than public boat launch areas—where clamming is accessible. There are 87 campsites (no RV hook-ups), restrooms, showers, a boat ramp and a trailer dump station. A group camp can accommodate 150 to 200 people. There are over five miles of hiking trails here, and 6,700 feet of beachfront facing Saratoga Passage. Licenses are required for fishing, clamming and crabbing. Picnic tables and a large covered picnic shelter are available as well. Call the park for details regarding the kayak/canoe camp and the amphitheater presentations. A grocery and restaurant are within four miles at the intersection of Elger Bay and Mountain View Roads.

Places to Eat

THE CAMANO

360-387-9972

Location: 170 Cross Island Rd.
Days/Hours: Monday, Tuesday, Wednesday,Thursday and Sunday; 7am–9pm. Friday and Saturday, 7am–10pm.
Wheelchair/Stroller Access: Yes
Driving Directions: Take Hwy 532 (exit 212) from I-5; travel through Stanwood onto Camano Island; stay on 532—it will change to E Camano Dr. The restaurant is located at the traffic light connecting E Camano Dr. to Cross Island Rd., just off to your right.

It's a lovely setting on Camano Island, looking out onto a lush green forest. Portions here are ample. The Kids' Menu includes eggs and waffles and French toast all day; for lunch there's also cheeseburgers, grilled cheese and chicken fingers. Prices are from $3.95–$5.50. This is a good stopping point.

ELGER BAY CAFÉ   360-387-2904
   Location: 1996 Elger Bay Rd.
   Days/Hours: April–September; 6am–8pm. October–March; 6am–3pm
   Wheelchair/Stroller Access: Yes

It's a cozy little café that attracts adults but does cater to children, as well. They will serve a large single pancake, and split meals for seniors and kids at no extra charge. Sundaes and milkshakes are made with hand-dipped ice cream. Coloring books and crayons are provided, along with boosters and high chairs.

Outside Stanwood

NOAH/NORTHWEST ORGANIZATION FOR ANIMAL HELP   360-629-7055
   Location: 31300 Brandstrom Rd., Stanwood. From I-5, take exit 215; go
      one mile east to Brandstrom; turn left; NOAH is one mile down the
      road.
   Web Site: wwww.thenoahcenter.org
   Days/Hours: Open daily; Monday–Friday, 11am–6pm; Saturday and
      Sunday, 11am–5pm
   Tours: Yes, anytime, but call ahead for an appointment.
   Wheelchair/Stroller Access: Yes

Located on over 17 wooded acres, NOAH is dedicated to rescuing pets from other animal shelters, and building a "Bond for Life" between pets and their families. They offer quality pet adoption, training, low-income spaying and neutering, education and volunteer programs. At any one time, the shelter houses 15–30 cats and 10–20 dogs, all ranging in age from one year to maturity. With acres of wooded wilderness trails, potential adopters can walk and bond with prospective dog companions. It's a different environment here and a great learning experience for children.

WILLOW & JIM'S COUNTRY CAFÉ   360-652-0372
   Location: 1421 Pioneer Hwy, Silvana
   Days/Hours: Open daily: Saturday–Thursday; 7am–3pm; Friday,
      7am–7pm.
   Wheelchair/Stroller Access: Yes

Previously Faye's, Willow and Jim have carried on the tradition of good country food in ample portions for their breakfast/lunch menu. Pancakes literally cover the entire 14-inch dinner plate; there's a good selection of breakfast side orders for small fry. Kids' lunch will include hot dogs, corn dogs, chicken strips and lots of deli and hot sandwiches. On the beverage menu, chocolate milk is a favorite; shakes, malts and sodas come in amazing flavors, including Green River, peanut butter and rocky road. Look for the flavor of the month. Boosters and highchairs are available. Cash or checks are preferred.

Skagit Valley

La Conner

The La Conner area is ideal for family biking. There are miles of perfectly flat bike lanes bordering roads passing through the tulip and daffodil farms. If you're hungry, stop in La Conner or (at Hwy 20) the Farmhouse Inn.

Places to Go

DECEPTION PASS VIKING CRUISES   **888-207-2333; 360-466-2639**
   Location: 109 N First St; in the Lime Dock building
   Web Site: www.vikingcruises.com
   Days/Hours: Cruises year-round
   Admission: Varies with cruise offered. See below
   Wheelchair/Stroller Access: No

They guarantee you'll spot whales, and they're probably right. From May through October, several Orca families play and feed in and around the San Juan Islands. Viking Cruises will take you there, and a number of other interesting places in the San Juans and Puget Sound as well. You can take a one-hour cruise along the Swinomish Channel in La Conner ($10/per person plus tax). You can take a three-hour Nature/Birdwatching cruise through Deception Pass ($30/adults, $15/youth 5–10 and seniors 62 and older). They love to cruise the area and know it well; call for available dates or more information. The boat is the Viking Star and is usually moored in front of the Channel Lodge in La Conner, on the Channel.

THE GACHES MANSION   **360-466-4288**
   Location: 703 Second St.
   Days/Hours: Open weekends in December; closed the first two weeks in January. Other: Wednesday–Saturday, 11am–4pm; Sunday, noon–4pm
   Admission: $4/adults; Free/children 12 and under when accompanied by an adult
   Wheelchair/Stroller Access: No

With its hundred-year history, this classic old mansion imparts a feeling of elegance to its visitors. Over the years, the mansion has been a home in high society, a hospital and a boardinghouse. A major fire destroyed the third floor, now restored by the La Conner Landmark Society. The upper floors are now also used for displays. Today it's considered primarily a quilt museum, one of only 10 in the country. On display is an international collection, including pieces from Asia.

MUSEUM OF NORTHWEST ART　　　　　　　　　　360-466-4078
Location: 121 First St.
Web Site: www.museumofnwart.org
Days/Hours: Monday–Sunday, 10am–5pm
Admission: $4/adults; $2/students over 12 or with college ID; Free/
　　those under 12 and members. Free admission first Tuesday of every
　　month.
Tours: Yes. Group tours: $1.50/elementary –high school students, must
　　be accompanied by one adult per five students (chaperones are free);
　　other groups/regular admission. Art Explorers Program: $95/in-
　　cludes one hour tour, one hour of art activity.
Wheelchair/Stroller Access: Yes

Founded in 1981, this petite museum has become an icon for northwest art—and
is dedicated to Northwest art of many kinds. There is a permanent exhibit by
regional artists, a glass gallery dedicated to Northwest artisans and changing
exhibits to pique curiosity. There are special programs for children, including
fish painting—with real fish! Take time to shop the museum store; there are
some kids' toys and games among the choices.

SKAGIT COUNTY HISTORICAL MUSEUM　　　　　　360-466-3365
Location: 501 S 4th St.
Days/Hours: Tuesday–Sunday, 11am–5pm. Closed major holidays
Admission: $4/adults; $3/seniors 65 and over, children 6–12; $8/fam-
　　ily (two adults plus children); Free/children 5 and under/Historical
　　Society members
Wheelchair/Stroller Access: Yes

One of the highlights of this delightful little town, the museum is a reflection of the rich history of the rural Skagit region. Perched on top of the hill,
the views from the observation deck are part of the charm. Some exhibits are
permanent, others change regularly, so there's always something interesting.
Most of the items in the collections have been donated (and were used, worn or
owned) by local families. From the observation deck, you'll see Skagit farmland,
Skagit Bay, the Cascades, and Mount Baker and Mount Rainier on good days.
During tulip season, you'll have a commanding and expansive view of these
colorful gems. Don't miss the museum store; if you come in to visit only the
store, no admission is charged.

LA CONNER MEMORIES　　　　　　　　　　　　360-466-9940
Location: 413A Morris St
Days/Hours: Monday, Friday, Saturday, 10am–4pm; Sunday, Tuesday,
　　Thursday, 9am–5pm. Closed Wednesdays.
Wheelchair/Stroller Access: Access through the back parking lot

Located on the main street going into town, just across from the Pioneer Grocery, this little shop can do some delightful things for you if you have something you want to memorialize. Pictures or names on mugs, t-shirts, baby bibs, baseball caps—you name it, they'll try it. If you're in town and want to develop pictures while you're there, try them.

BUNNIES BY THE BAY   888-229-5333
   Location: 617 E Morris
   Web Site: www.bunniesbythebay.com
   Days/Hours: Daily, 10am–6pm; November–March, 10am–5pm; Sunday, noon–5pm.
   Wheelchair/Stroller Access: No

This is a retail outlet for the original Bunnies in Anacortes, where the manufacturing is done. The La Conner store is charming and worth the visit, just to get acquainted with these often appealing "cuddlies."

O'LEARY BUILDING   360-466-2971 (Cascade Candy Company);
                                  360-466-1305 (From Grandma With Love)
   Location: 609 First St.
   Days/Hours: Generally open daily; winter hours will vary. Call to verify.
   Wheelchair/Stroller Access: Yes

A combination of candy and gifts and kids' clothing. On the candy menu, homemade fudge, truffles and chocolate suckers. At Grandma's, kids' toys, clothing and books to tempt you.

Places to Eat

CALICO CUPBOARD   360-466-4551 (La Conner);
                                      360-293-7315 (Anacortes);
                                      360-336-3107 (Mount Vernon)
   Locations: 720 S First St., La Conner; 901 Commercial, Anacortes; 121-B Freeway Dr., Mount Vernon
   Days/Hours: Daily, 8am–5pm
   Wheelchair/Stroller Access: Yes

No trip to La Conner is complete without breakfast or lunch at the Calico Cupboard. During summer months, expect a wait. Their home-baked breads and homemade soups are part of the draw; sandwiches are generous, fresh and hearty. Breakfasts are country-style; bring an appetite. Everything in the bakery is made fresh daily. Take something home for the freezer. If you're coming by boat, there's a public dock available; tie up and walk on up.

Whidbey Island

Whidbey and Camano Islands are rather unique destinations in Washington. Note: Overnight accommodations for families are sparse (if you're not camping).

Places to Go

CITY BEACH PARK   360-679-5551, ext 234
Location: At the end of 80th St. NW in Oak Harbor, off Hwy 20
Days/Hours: Daily, year-round; overnight camping allowed
Wheelchair/Stroller Access: Yes

The town's Dutch influence is quite evident here, with ornamental windmills and gardens alive with tulips in spring. For children, there are two playgrounds with swings and a slide, baseball field, wading pool and a swimming lagoon (with full-time lifeguard in the summer). The park is the stage for many community events; local families spend lots of time here.

DECEPTION PASS STATE PARK   360-675-2417;
                    888-CAMPOUT (campsite reservations)
Location: On Hwy 20, 10 miles north of Oak Harbor
Web Site: www.parks.wa.gov
Days/Hours: Summer, 6:30am–dusk; Winter, 8am–dusk. Open year-round for camping and day-use.
Tours: For the Historical Interpretive Center, tours conducted from mid-May –Labor Day. Contact the park for Center hours.
Wheelchair/Stroller Access: In some places

This has become one of the most popular parks and campgrounds in the state and for good reason. From 30 miles of hiking trails to an underwater park for divers, there's a wealth of activities. Statistics tell us that close to 4 million people a year enjoy the variety here. Don't be misled by the bridge; half the park is on Whidbey Island, the other on Fidalgo Island, but there are parking areas on both ends of the bridge to accommodate passenger vehicles. If you're hiking, the suggested route is the Discovery Trail, which begins at the Environment Learning Center on Whidbey and has side trails to Goose Rock. Other, more makeshift trails can be quite dangerous for children.

FORT CASEY STATE PARK   360-678-4519
Location: 400 Hill Valley Dr.; off Hwy 20, three miles south of Coupeville
Web Site: www.parks.wa.gov
Days/Hours: Year-round; 8am–dusk. Open year-round for camping/day

use. Winter: Day use on weekends and holidays only
Tours: Lighthouse tours, summer season; call 360-679-7391 for arrangements.
Wheelchair/Stroller Access: Yes

For Washingtonians, Fort Casey is part of a romantic, historical society. The fort was built in the 1890s, the lighthouse in the 1850s; they are said to be a corner of the "Triangle of Fire," a strategic defense against enemy ships attempting to sail through Admiralty Inlet in the late 1880s. With Fort Worden and Fort Flagler, Fort Casey was fortified against this and other military ploys. To the disappointment of some and relief of many, no ships ever appeared. Fort Casey did host training troops during World Wars I and II. Today the old cannons and bunkers provide a perfect opportunity for imaginative, energetic kids. But don't miss the park's water-view trails; two of these lead to Admiralty Head Lighthouse, which opened in 1861 and is now the park's interpretive center.

FORT EBEY STATE PARK
360-678-4636;
888-CAMPOUT (campsite reservations)
Location: 395 N Fort Ebey Dr.; off Libby Rd., south of Partridge Point, eight miles south of Oak Harbor
Web Site: www.parks.wa.gov
Days/Hours: Open year-round for overnight camping and day use
Wheelchair/Stroller Access: In some places

Originally intended as an antiaircraft/coastal defense fort, Fort Ebey saw no action and is now a 645-acre park with 48 campsites. There are some old bunkers, perfect for hide and seek. For hikers, the 28 miles of trails are beckoning; there are several paths down to Point Partridge, and near the park's north end is Lake Pondilla, noted for good bass fishing. There is an amazing variety of animal, bird and marine life here.

Place to Eat

MIKE'S PLACE
360-221-6575
Location: 219 First St., Langley
Days/Hours: Monday–Saturday, 8am–8pm; Sundays and holidays, 9am–2pm.
Wheelchair/Stroller Access: Yes

A very popular place is Mike's; they offer a bear-face shaped pancake for breakfast. The Kids' menu at lunch includes grilled cheese sandwiches. On Friday and Saturday, kids can do the all-you-can-eat thing with fish and chips; cost is 50 cents per year of age. The kids' dinner menu includes chicken and clam strips. Dessert is always a big surprise; the choice changes daily. If you're lucky, you'll choose the day they're offering blackberry cobbler or pie or chocolate cheesecake. Here's a stunner—their key lime pie recipe has been requested by Gourmet magazine. Don't bring willpower!

Mount Vernon

Places to Go

CHUCKANUT DRIVE
Location: Between Mount Vernon and Bellingham
Driving Directions: Heading south on I-5 from Vancouver, take exit 250, south of Bellingham's historical Fairhaven district and the northern entrance to Chuckanut Drive. Heading north: take exit 231 (60 miles from Seattle) marked Chuckanut Drive, Bow Edison, which leads to the southern entrance.

What used to be a four- or five-hour trip by horse and buggy to Bellingham over a rough gravel road is now a smooth, black-topped two-lane highway. Still narrow and definitely winding, Chuckanut Drive is one of the oldest scenic drives in the state. From top to bottom the drive can take only 15 minutes. The view of Guemes, Cypress, Lopez, Eliza and Sinclair Islands is quite breathtaking; add the Olympic and Coast Ranges and Puget Sound and it becomes an arresting and extraordinary sight. On the way down, Larabee State Park is the oldest park in the state and offers overnight camping and a railroad tunnel that has an enticing echo. Alert the kids to watch for a road sign that reads: "Please drive quietly. Meadowlarks singing."

LANG'S PONY AND HORSE RIDES   360-424-7630
Location: 21463 Little Mountain Rd., Mount Vernon. Heading north, take I-5 to exit 225; turn right on Anderson Rd.; go a quarter block, take an immediate left on Cedardale Rd. Heading north and running parallel to I-5, go right at Blackburn Rd.; travel about one mile. Road makes a 90-degree turn to the right and becomes Little Mountain Rd. Lang's is one and a half miles ahead on the left hand side; look for a large wooden sign. Drive up the driveway to the parking lot (near the horse barn). Heading south, take exit 225, turn on Anderson Rd.; cross over I-5, go a quarter block, turn left onto Cedardale and proceed as listed above.
Web Site: www.comeride.com
Days/Hours: Open year-round. Hours vary; call for information.
Wheelchair/Stroller Access: Yes

If you love horses, Lang's offers you a full menu of activity, including lessons, birthday parties, group trails rides and therapeutic riding. Trail rides are available for both individuals and families. Covered picnic facilities add to your day's outing. Some of their specialty services include Girl Scout Bead programs and one-day and overnight camps. Their traveling ponies will come for school carnivals, birthday parties and other special events. Rides are by reservation only; be sure to call ahead, and plan to arrive at least 15 minutes prior to your schedule riding time for check-in and preparation.

PADILLA BAY NATIONAL ESTUARINE SANCTUARY/BREAZEALE INTERPRETIVE CENTER

360-428-1558; 360-757-1549 (TDD)

Location: 10441 Bay View-Edison Rd., Mount Vernon. Take exit 230 off I-5; head toward Anacortes, follow the signs to Padilla Bay.
Web Site: www.padillabay.gov
Days/Hours: Interpretive Center; Wednesday–Sunday, 10am–5pm, except holidays
Wheelchair/Stroller Access: Yes, at the center

Padilla Bay is the only National Estuarine Research Reserve in Washington State. The large sea-grass meadows and mudflats support many invertebrates and migratory animals as well. In the Interpretive Center, kids can touch the bones, teeth, feathers and pelts representing the inhabitants of the estuary. The hands-on exhibits and presentations are put together with kids' curiosity in mind, showing children how the delicate balance in the bay is a natural wonder. There are tanks here full of marine life such as sea perch, sculpins, flounder and salmon. Much of the research done here is to monitor the plant and animal populations, protect water quality, and understand better the ecological processes. Outside, you can walk or bike the two-plus mile trail along the shoreline, or absorb the view from the observation deck.

ROOZENGAARDE GARDENS

360-424-8531; 800-732-3266

Location: 15867 Beaver Marsh Rd.
Web Site: www.tulips.com
Days/Hours: Open daily year-round except Christmas, New Year's and Thanksgiving. Monday–Saturday, 9am–5:30pm; Sunday, 11am–4pm. Winter hours will adjust slightly due to daylight saving.
Wheelchair/Stroller Access: Limited. The fields are not hospitable but the retail store and display gardens are accessible.

Roozengarde is the place to be when the tulips bloom, but don't overlook the daffodils. The Tulip Festival is a grand occasion, happening the last weekend of March through the second week of April (sometimes dependent on the weather). The fields of blooms are a magnificent sight and have become a huge tourist attraction. You can purchase daffodil, tulip, crocus, hyacinth and iris bulbs here, or just enjoy the brilliant colors in the three-acre display gardens. People love to have their picture taken in front of the authentic windmill. Daffodils usually start blooming in March; the tulips erupt in late March and early April and continue until early May (unless the winds take over). Even the locals take a day to "do the tulips."

SKAGIT COUNTY CHILDREN'S MUSEUM   360-419-7474
Location: 419 First St., Mount Vernon
Web Site: www.skagitchildrensmuseum.org
Days/Hours: Tuesday–Saturday, 10am–5pm; Sunday, noon–5pm
Admission: $3.50/per person. Family membership/$55 per year

Always a big undertaking, the folks behind this new museum have put in much time and effort to bring this new experience to Mount Vernon families. There are eight main areas in the museum, with familiar themes, including: transportation with a truck stop diner, a farm theme at the toddler play station, an art studio, the always popular drama theme complete with costumes, props and a ticket booth, a quiet reading area and a natural habitat (with a tree house, mountaintop and sand). The Birthday Party room is separate and has chalkboard walls. It's a welcome addition to the family scene in the Skagit Valley.

Places to Eat and Stay

CALICO CUPBOARD (see La Conner)

BENSON FARMSTEAD   800-441-9814; 360-757-0578
Location: 10113 Avon-Allen Rd., Bow (Skagit Valley)
Web Site: www.bbhost.com\bensonbnb
Days/Hours: Open year-round.
Wheelchair/Stroller Access: No

The Farmstead, owned by Sharon and Jerry Benson, is a 17-room Scandinavian farmhouse with a family cottage across the yard. The cottage is equipped with a kitchenette, living room, TV and sleeping accommodations. Outside there are lovely gardens to stroll through and a playground with a playhouse. There's a hot tub for a relaxing soak. The full farm breakfast in the morning includes homemade breads. A good place for families.

BIG SCOOP   360-424-3558
Location: 327 E College Way, Mount Vernon
Days/Hours: Sunday–Thursday, 11am–10pm; Friday–Saturday, 11am–
11pm.
Wheelchair/Stroller Access: Yes

Although a franchise, Big Scoop's a downscale version of the old-fashioned ice cream parlor. Loads of choices here, especially in burgers and sundaes. They do birthday parties in a special area; there's no age minimum and they provide party hats, decorations and place mats as well as a free sundae for the birthday person. High chairs and boosters available.

Sedro Woolley

Places to Go

WOOLLY PRAIRIE BUFFALO COMPANY   800-524-7660; 360-856-0310
   Web Site: www.BuffaloRanchTours.com
   Days/Hours: Daily, April 1–September 1
   Tours: For groups and private parties; reservations are required.
      Groups of 10 or more preferred. The charge is: $7 each/groups of
      10–19; $6 each/groups of 20–39; $5 each/groups of 40 or more.
   Wheelchair/Stroller Access: Yes. You will ride on the "Prairie Schoo-
      ner." Strollers can be folded up.

If you've noticed, there's no address available. That's because drop-ins are not welcome, for a very good reason. There are some big bison here, and people wandering around without invitation could cause problems. This is a very unique experience, one you won't soon forget. Groups can ride among the herd on the Prairie Schooner; you can picnic on the grounds after the ride, shop at the Buffalo Trading Post or visit the hay barn. It's great for birthday parties. The size of the herd fluctuates, but they thrive on "neglect." Buffalo pretty much take care of themselves but they do expect to be fed, which includes grass hay and grass. The owner will feed the bull and some of the cows from the viewing platform; apples are a favorite. Kids can feed them hay (with preparation from the leader). You'll get to "know" Coach, the 2000 lb. male of the herd. The babies are born in spring, usually in May. Kids may not care, but parents will be interested in the value of buffalo meat. It's high in protein, low in fat and quite delicious when prepared well.

Place to Eat

THE FARMHOUSE INN   360-466-4411
   Location: At Hwy 20 and the La Conner-Whitney Rd., Mount Vernon
   Days/Hours: Daily, 7am–10pm
   Wheelchair/Stroller Access: Yes

A local favorite since 1980, farm-style meals are the ticket here with generous portions of everything. The specialty of the house is homemade pies—15 kinds. The kids' menu (for those under 12) has nine entrees to choose from, and includes a choice of soda. The collection of Tulip Festival posters on the wall is eye-catching (this is the heart of tulip country). Note: The inn is located on the highway to Anacortes; you may want to plan your stop accordingly. High chairs and boosters are available. Also, many families stop here to unload their bikes and pedal over to La Conner and back—it's pretty flat in these parts!

San Juan Islands

Anacortes

Places to Go

CAUSLAND MEMORIAL PARK
Location: 8th St and N Ave.
Days/Hours: Dawn to dusk
Wheelchair/Stroller Access: Yes

This park is on the National Register of Historic Places, but you'll enjoy it for its unique walls and gazebo, which are constructed of rock and decorated in mosaics of colored rock. Be sure to walk around the entire park—there are hidden facets waiting to be discovered.

GUEMES ISLAND FERRY
360-336-9400 (Skagit City Department of Public works);
360-293-6356 (ferry schedule)
Location: Just off 6th St.
Days/Hours: Monday–Thursday, 6:30am–6pm; Friday and Saturday,
6:30am–midnight. Sundays and holidays, 7am–10pm
Fee: For walk-ons: $1.25/adults; 50 cents/children under 6
Wheelchair/Stroller Access: Yes

This little ferry could almost be called "cute," but they probably wouldn't appreciate it. It's a mini-ferry with a flatbed that holds up to 22 cars and takes you from Anacortes to Guemes Island in a five-minute shuttle. You can walk on, ride over and ride back (all fares are round-trip), or walk off and spend some time on the beach next to the landing, where kayakers launch their boats for island explorations. You can enjoy the view and boat traffic, then ferry on back. Kids will get quite a kick out of the experience. Something different, that's for sure!

W.T. PRESTON   360-293-1915
Location: 703 R Ave. (James Rice Civic Park)
Days/Hours: Memorial Day–Labor Day: daily. September and April,
weekends only. October–March, closed. Tours by
appointment only in winter months.
Tours: Self-guided only

Wheelchair/Stroller Access: Not really

The W.T. Preston, a steam–wheeler snag boat, cruised Puget Sound and tributary rivers to clear the waterways of navigational hazards. Big (and handsome for a work boat, they like to say), she and many other snag boats performed an invaluable service for Puget Sound marine transportation. When retired in 1981, the Preston was the last large, active sternwheeler remaining in the Sound. Now stationed at the James Rice Civic Park in Anacortes, you can tour the boat all summer long. It's a self-guided tour with an excellent brochure and some interesting side notes. A trip to the top to view the pilot house through its window is worth the climb (the pilot house is locked).

MARINE SUPPLY AND HARDWARE   360-293-3014
    Location: 202 Commercial St.
    Web Site: www.marinesupplyandhardware.com
    Days/Hours: Monday–Saturday, 8:30am–5pm
    Wheelchair/Stroller Access: Yes

From glass floats to Greek fisherman hats to a Russian diving helmet, this is almost a museum. With an unbelievable variety of merchandise, this is a throwback to the old days when you could find anything at your local hardware store. The Demopoulos family has owned and run the store since 1913, making it the only—and oldest—continuously operating marine supply store in North America. Theirs and the surrounding buildings are on the National Register of Historic Places. The kids may not get as big a kick out of this place as their parents, but it's worth a look-in. There's enough history here for you to spin a dozen stories and enlighten your kids about their grandparents' lives in new ways.

Places to Eat

VILLAGE PIZZA   360-293-7847
    Location: 807 Commercial Ave.
    Days/Hours: Monday–Wednesday, 11am–9pm; Thursday–Saturday,
      11am–10pm; Sunday, noon–9pm
    Wheelchair/Stroller Access: Yes

They provide dine-in, take-out and delivery service. Most amazing—their pb&j pizza. Plus mini-pizzas for kids, with a choice of one topping (additional toppings cost extra). They offer child's portions for pastas, and lots of beverages and desserts. Pretty quaint and fun.

Orcas Island

Places to Go

MORAN STATE PARK 360-376-2326; 888-campout (for reservations)
   Location: Take the ferry to Orcas Island; exit the ferry and turn left;
      drive five miles south on Eastsound Dr.
   Web Site: www.parks.wa.gov
   Days/Hours: Daily: Summer, 6:30am–10pm; Winter, 8am–dusk. Camp-
      ing and day use year-round
   Wheelchair/Stroller Access: In some places

Even with 165 campsites, reservations are highly recommended to secure a place. It's very popular. Moran is not on the Sound, it's on an island in the Strait of Juan De Fuca, with children's play equipment and 33 miles of hiking trails. Cascade Lake has freshwater swimming beaches and rowboat rentals; Mountain Lake has trout fishing and an almost four-mile walk around its perimeter. Also for hikers is a quarter-mile trip to the 100-foot Cascade Falls. For the hardier, bike or walk to the top of Mount Constitution, where the road climbs 2000 feet in 6 miles. At the summit, you can climb the winding staircase to the top of a four-story observation tower modeled after a twelfth-century watch tower. The view is incredible, rated as one of the most spectacular mountain and marine vistas in North America.

Places to Eat and Stay

ROSARIO RESORT AND SPA 360-376-2222; 800-562-8820
   Location: On Orcas Island; from the ferry terminal, drive 17 miles
      north and around East Sound to Rosario.
   Web Site: www.rosario.rockresorts.com
   Days/Hours: Open year-round for overnight accommodations
   Wheelchair/Stroller Access: Yes

One of the charms of the San Juans, Rosario is a majestic mansion set on a rocky bluff. Visitors are delighted with its old-style charm. This 85-year-old estate was once the home of shipbuilder Robert Moran; today it houses a restaurant and exercise and relaxation facilities. There are close to 200 rooms on the adjacent hillside where guests can relax on their balconies and enjoy the water view. Boats are moving in and out of the marina, seaplanes are approaching and leaving the water. Friendly deer often appear to munch on the grass. For kids, there are indoor and outdoor swimming pools, but no lifeguards.

San Juan Island

Places to Go

LIME KILN POINT STATE PARK   **360-378-2044**
   Location: 1567 Westside Rd., Friday Harbor
   Web Site: www.parks.wa.gov
   Days/Hours: Year-round, 8am–dusk
   Wheelchair/Stroller Access: No

In the 1880s the lime quarries attracted a big limestone manufacturing busi-ness to the Island. Today the quarries are mostly good for whale-watching. The Orca pods (or killer whales) frolic and dine on salmon and other marine life in these waters, generally in early spring and summer. Their antics are highly vis-ible as they plunge and surface in the Strait; quite captivating for children, who love to learn about the whale families and their relationships. There are rough trails to the bluff, with a few picnic tables. Sorry, there's no running water or flush toilets. Binoculars recommended!

WHALE CRUISES

There are a number of charter operations that will take you close to the whales without interfering with the pod. Charter trips vary in length and price; some set an age minimum of 6 years old. When checking out the companies, be sure to inquire about bathroom facilities. Here are some resources:

   San Juan Visitors Information Center:

   Orcas Island Eclipse charters: 800-376-4663

   San Juan Boat Tours: 800-232-6722 (Friday Harbor)

   Western Prince Cruises: 800-757-6722 (Friday Harbor)

   Deer Harbor Charters: 800-544-5758 (Deer Harbor)

WHALE MUSEUM
                 800-562-8832 (hotline for sightings and beachings);
                                            360-378-4710
   Location: 62 First St. N, Friday Harbor
   Web Site: www.whalemuseum.org
   Days/Hours: June–September; daily, 10am–5pm. October–February, call
      for schedule.
   Admission: $6/adults; $5/seniors 62 and older; $3/students with ID and
      those 5–18; Free/children under 5
   Wheelchair/Stroller Access: At video program and gift shop only

The humming sound inside the museum's blue interior might be the whales talking to you. The gigantic whale skeletons on display give you a very keen sense of the size of these mammals—and a healthy respect for what they can do. Explore the children's room; take time to see the video, a delightful story of how the whales feed and care for their young.

Bellingham

AMERICAN MUSEUM OF RADIO AND ELECTRICITY 360-738-3886
Location: 1312 Bay St.
Web Site: www.americanradiomuseum.org
Days/Hours: Wednesday–Saturday, 11am–4pm; and by appointment
Admission: Donation of $4
Tours: By request
Wheelchair/Stroller Access:Yes

What used to be the Bellingham Antique Radio Museum is now the next step in a dedicated "love affair" with radio and the story of electricity. Founder Jonathan Winter, with extraordinary support from friends such as John Jenkins, now has space to stretch out with more than 1,200 radio artifacts and 11 galleries showcasing scientific discoveries and cultural history. Plan to spend time here; you'll want to explore. The exhibits cover, among other things, The Dawn of the Electrical Age, The Beginnings of Radio and The Wireless Age. Already imposing in scale but still in developmental stages, the Museum will eventually feature nearly 25,000 exhibits. You don't need to be a radio buff to be amazed and entertained here. Of special interest to many will be the Marconi Wireless Room. This full-scale diorama reproduces, quite accurately, the actual radio room on the Titanic, complete with an original (and rare) Marconi wireless set. You will hear the sounds of the spark transmitter's SOS call at sea. Those that remember will be moved by this experience. To prepare for this visit, you might want to visit their Web site.

BELLINGHAM RAILWAY MUSEUM   360-739-9091
Location: 1312 Bay St.; From I-5, take the Lakeway Dr. exit; turn right (west) on Lakeway Dr.; proceed through the lights and bear right on Holly St.; turn right on Bay St.
Web Site: www.bellinghamrailwaymuseum.org
Days/Hours: Fridays and Saturdays, 11am–4pm
Tours: Open by appointment for tours; to book a tour, call the museum or email trainsnc@cs.com
Admission: By donation; $3/per person suggested or $5/per family. No one will be refused admission.
Wheelchair/Stroller Access: Yes

We've said it elsewhere—those that love railroads and railways REALLY love them. The volunteers who have put this museum together fit into that category. They have collected historic artifacts and exhibits from the railroads of Whatcom and Skagit counties and are working on new layouts. The exhibits will tell you the story of the street and electric railways that transported people all over the area (for example, Railroad Ave.). Model railroads are important here; there are several and one is an interactive Lionel layout where visitors can actually run the trains. A floor level model encourages kids to get down and play, featuring a well-known tank engine—is there a five-year-old who doesn't know who that is? Eventually they plan to have traveling exhibits as well, taking the stories to the public.

BELLINGHAM HATCHERY/DEPARTMENT OF FISH AND WILDLIFE   360-676-2138

Location: 1700 Silver Beach Rd. Take I-5 exit 253 (Lakeway); continue past Woburn and Yew Streets, past Bayview Cemetery; at Kenoyer intersection turn left onto Silver Beach Rd.

Days/Hours: Daily, 8am–4:30pm. Groups coming on weekends should call ahead to book tours.

Wheelchair/Stroller Access: Yes

Formerly known as the Whatcom Falls Park and Hatchery, there are interurban trails around the park, swimming holes, Whatcom Creek, tennis courts, baseball, and, of course, the fish. The hatchery raises fish for release into Whatcom, Skagit and San Juan waters. Nine outdoor ponds and seven raceways house about 100,000 trout annually. Guided tours are an option, but call at least two days ahead for reservations.

BELLINGHAM/WHATCOM COUNTY CONVENTION AND VISITORS BUREAU   800-487-2032; 360-671-3990

Location: 904 Potter St.

Days/Hours: Open daily year-round except for major holidays; 9am–5pm

Wheelchair/Stroller Access: Yes

We normally don't tout a visitors' center as a stopping point, although it's recommended for any trip you take. But this one is quite special. They have two maps: one in green, the second a large multi-colored affair with many of Bellingham's "hot spots." Be aware that the streets aren't easy to follow. Look for the Discount Coupon booklet (it's free) with 56 pages of money-saving coupons. Then head out and enjoy…it's a fabulous town.

FAIRHAVEN PARK   360-676-6985

Location: 107 Chuckanut Dr.

Days/Hours: Daily, 8am–dusk.

Wheelchair/Stroller Access: Yes

This is a sprawling park with lush greenery, especially dedicated to families with young children. A new Splash or Spray Pool for toddlers and preschoolers is under construction at this writing; they are hoping to open it in summer 2004. Call ahead for the hours. The playground has swings and equipment for older children. It's a short stroll to the fish ladders nearby.

MARINE LIFE CENTER   360-671-2431
   Location: Harbor Center Building at Squalicum Harbor; 1801 Roeder Ave.
   Days/Hours: Daily, 8am–sunset. Open year-round
   Admission: Free. But your donation will help to feed the fish.
   Wheelchair/Stroller Access: Yes
   Email: marinelifecenter@msn.com

Visiting the harbor is a treat but the Marine Life Center makes it more so. There is a Touch Pool with hardy, small marine life that accept the attention of young hands. You are welcome to gently touch hermit crabs, several kinds of seastars, anemones, sea cucumbers and snails. In the Observation Pool, there are larger versions of these animals, plus more delicate specimens including white and giant green anemones, leather stars, sunflower seastars, copper rockfish, Dungeness crabs, sea perch, kelp crabs, and perhaps a fish with an eel-like shape called a potatohead! All the critters are from the marine waters of Washington. New this year is a Giant Pacific Octopus; at two and a half years, she weighed 10 pounds and is expected to grow to between 35 and 50 pounds before she is released. Look for a new octopus to arrive at the Center soon after that. Note: Stepping out onto the docks, you'll see over 1500 boats moored in Squalicum Harbor. Wear sturdy shoes and don't forget to admire the view!

MINDPORT   360-647-5614
   Location: 210 W Holly St.
   Web Site: www.mindport.org
   Days/Hours: Wednesday–Friday, noon–6pm; Saturday, 10am–5pm; Sunday, noon–4pm. Closed Monday and Tuesday.Admission: $4/adults; $2/ages 15 and under
   Wheelchair/Stroller Access: Yes
   Groups: Groups up to 20 accepted; must schedule visit in advance. Children under 6 must have one adult per child; ages 6–12 requires one adult for every two children; 13 and up requires one adult for every five children. Adults MUST accompany their group.
   Driving Directions: From the Lakeway exit turn right and go to the Lakeway Dr. light; Lakeway turns into Holly St.; follow Holly to Mindport, approximately five blocks on the right side before Bay St. Metered parking during the week, free parking on weekends.

Mindport is a nice surprise. The brainchild of three enterprising people, Mindport challenges your perception of how the world really works. Using essential theorems from physics and related sciences, they have developed incredibly basic (but incredibly interesting and amazing) mini-exhibits that test your sense of reality. There are things to push and squeeze, and holes to peer through. Here are few: Marbellous Indeterminacy (a marble maze); The Creek, a simulated creek with moving water and tiny wooden boats to play with (you can get wet—there's a towel handy); the Eye Mirror; One Hundred Compresses, a marble pump. Don't miss the Air Machine with balls. You can choose a color path and follow the ball as it travels through an extended circuitry of pneumatic tubes (all air powered). Next door, the Art Gallery and Gift Shop may look more adult but there are some enchanting pieces of art that will intrigue children. They must be accompanied by an adult.

WESTERN WASHINGTON UNIVERSITY   360-650-3440; 360-650-3000
  Location: Visitors Center is on S College Dr. at the main entrance to
    campus.
  Web Site: www.wwu.edu
  Tours: Monday–Friday, 11 am and 2 pm (except for holidays and school
    breaks). No reservation necessary; just show up!
  Wheelchair/Stroller Access: Yes

A university student will be your guide for this one-hour tour. For older children, the academic buildings and residence hall may hold some interest, but the primary attractions here are the campus viewpoints of Bellingham Bay and the San Juan Islands. There are nearly two dozen pieces of contemporary outdoor sculptures to admire (only a few to climb on).

WHATCOM CHILDREN'S MUSEUM 360-733-8769
  Location: 227 Prospect St.
  Web Site: www.whatcommuseum.org
  Days/Hours: Tuesday, Wednesday and Sunday, noon–5pm; Thurs-
    day–Saturday, 10am–5pm. Closed Mondays. Tuesday and Wednesday
    mornings are reserved for school groups. Tours and birthday parties
    need reservations.Admission: $2.50/per person; babes in arms free.
  Wheelchair/Stroller Access: Yes

This delightful place is strictly for children, especially those ages 2–8. The docents make you feel very much at home. The model train is a permanent exhibit; larger exhibits are on display for long periods. Smaller exhibits change and revolve throughout the year. Through August 2004, the Centennial Time Machine (conceived and built by Whatcom Museum folks) is on display. It covers the 1700s, 1800s and The Future—quite a presentation for young ones. Watch for a new exhibit in the fall of 2004. A bonus is the nice clean restrooms with a changing table.

WHATCOM COUNTY MUSEUM OF HISTORY AND ART
Location: 121 Prospect St.
Web Site: www.whatcommuseum.org
Days/Hours: Tuesday–Sunday, noon–5pm. Closed major holidaysAdmission: None, but donations are appreciated
Wheelchair/Stroller Access: Yes

This is an outstanding museum, well-known for its excellent exhibits of Northwest Coastal Native American artifacts. Also intriguing are the timber industry dioramas, telling the local story in a more multi-dimensional manner. Originally in the town's city hall and courthouse, the attractive, ornate, hand-carved staircase on which you ascend from the first floor is an elegant and artistic reminder of an earlier Victorian era. The museum has expanded into the nearby ARCO building, housing works by local artists, and into the former firehouse adjacent, allowing for more attention to children's exhibits. In the Syre Educational Center the exhibits are permanent. Featured are Birds of Washington (an extraordinary collection), a Victorian Parlor circa 1890–1910, The First Nation—Inuit (including an interesting basket collection), a Settlement Cabin from the period 1890–1920 and Tools From Settlement Days. Don't miss the Victorian clock collection on the third floor.

VILLAGE BOOKS AND COLOPHON CAFÉ
360-671-2626 (bookstore)
360-647-0092 (café)

Location: 1210 11th St. in Old Fairhaven
Web Site: www.villagebooks.com
Days/Hours: Summer: Monday–Saturday, 9am–10pm; Sunday, 10am–10pm. Remainder of year: Monday–Saturday, 9am–10pm; Sunday, 10am–8pm.
Wheelchair/Stroller Access: Yes

Village Books has been here a long time and they do love kids! There's a cozy reading corner where kids can settle in with a new book or old favorite while the older folks browse. There are a number of special events: monthly and bimonthly Saturday programs, bookmark contests, and writing contests. Colophon Café has a "Mug a Mocha Moo," steamed milk with hot fudge and whipped cream, perfect on a cold or rainy day. Ice cream in waffle cones are a spring and summer favorite. The Kids' Menu has basic sandwiches (toasted cheese), both whole and half portions. Eat inside or take your meal out to the square behind the café and enjoy the sun.

Places To Eat

BERGSMA CAFÉ AND GALLERY 360-733-1101
Location: Just off I-5 at exit 253, across from the Visitors' Center
Web Site: www.bergsma@bergsma.com
Days/Hours: Gallery: Monday–Saturday, 10am–6pm; Sunday,11am–
5pm. Café open 11am–2pm daily
Wheelchair/Stroller Access: Yes

A stopping point for a light lunch or snack, the café offers lots of beverage choices, sandwiches (halves available) and soup. Pb&j is an option. The gallery has art predominantly by Jody Bergsma, but there is a Kid's Room with stuffed animals and toys.

BAYSIDE CAFÉ 360-715-0975
Location: Squalicum Harbor (next to Marine Life Center)
Days/Hours: Monday–Friday, 7am–3pm and 4pm–8:30 pm; Saturday
and Sunday, 8am–3pm and 4pm–9:30pm
Wheelchair/Stroller Access: Yes

Of course the outlook here is fantastic. Sitting waterside is a kaleidoscopic view of hundreds of boats, water and sky. The Kids' Menu for breakfast includes pancakes, French toast and eggs, for lunch and dinner, pb&j and grilled cheese sandwiches. The adult menu is large and varied.

North Whatcom County

Places to Go

BERTHUSEN PARK 360-354-2424
Location: 8837 Berthusen Rd. Take I-5 to exit 256; go north 12 miles to
Hwy 546; turn left and follow the signs.
Days/Hours: Daily, 8am–dusk. Both day use and overnight camping
available.
Wheelchair/Stroller Access: Limited

This 236-acre park is rich with opportunities for families to enjoy hiking, stream fishing, a playground, and an old homestead barn with vintage farm equipment. The park is named for the Berthusens, an immigrant Norwegian family with ten children, who left the acreage to the city. There are over four miles of hiking paths, 85 picnic tables and a few barbecue pits. Overnight campsites are available from March to October.

HOVANDER HOMESTEAD PARK 360-384-3444
Location: 5299 Nielson Rd., Ferndale. Take I-5 to exit 262 west; less than a mile ahead you'll take a hard left under the railroad trestle.
Days/Hours: 8am–dusk.
Admission: $3/for the park; $1/for the house
Wheelchair/Stroller Access: Yes, at the park; no, at the house

Adjacent to the Tennant Lake Natural interpretive Center, Hovander is a delightful place for kids to spend time. The equipment they play on is from the turn-of-the-century lifestyle lived by the Swedish immigrants who used to farm here. There are farm animals—goats, rabbits, pigs and peacocks—all cared for by 4-H Club members, and a viewing tower overlooking the Nooksack River. Inside the farmhouse, vintage woodwork and décor is another reminder of earlier times.

MOUNT BAKER WILDERNESS AREA
Location: On Hwy 542, 56 miles east of Bellingham
Days/Hours: Varies; some roads will be closed in winter due to snow.
Wheelchair/Stroller Access: In some areas

The west side of North Cascades National Park and Recreation Area (at the Mount Baker Wilderness Area) is very popular with skiing families. You can downhill and cross-country daily in winter, mid-November through December, and on weekends during the rest of the season. After the snow melts, it's a spectacular hiking area; you can even find blueberries in late summer and early fall.

The Heather Meadows Visitors Center is open daily, July through September, from 10am–5pm. Nearby are two half-mile hikes, The Fire and Ice Trail and Picture Lake Path, that are wheelchair and stroller friendly. For more information, call the Glacier Public Service Center, 360-599-2714; they're open daily, 9am–5pm during summer months, 9am–3pm on weekends in winter (this may change due to budget constraints).

PEACE ARCH STATE PARK   360-332-8221
Location: On I-5 at the U.S.-Canadian border
Web Site: www.parks.wa.gov
Days/Hours: Daily, 8am–dusk
Wheelchair/Stroller Access: Yes, at the garden

It's difficult to leave the car if you're trying to get through the border. Stopping here requires you to park off to the side. The 67-foot Peace Arch is a monument to over 200 years of peaceful relations (most of the time) between our two countries. The span is placed in the middle of the 40-acre park, resting one column in Canada, the other in the U.S. Seasonally, the flowers are quite beautiful and, if it's been a long ride, this is good place to let the kids get out and run. On the second Sunday in June, the annual Peace Arch celebration takes place, in which thousands of American children are invited to exchange flags and other friendship symbols with Canadian children. A touching ceremony, if you can be there.

PIONEER PARK   360-384-6461
Location: At the end of First St., Ferndale
Days/Hours: Tours given from mid-May to mid-September
Wheelchair/Stroller Access: Yes

This is a large play and recreation area, but the fascinating part is the collection of authentic pioneer homes, reconstructed from those originally in the locale. Most were built to withstand lonely, isolated environments. Along with the homesteads are a general store, a schoolhouse, a printer's shop and a church (which still accommodates weddings).

TENNANT LAKE NATURAL INTERPRETIVE CENTER   360-384-3064
Location: 5236 Nielsen Ave., Ferndale
Web Site: www.co.whatcom.wa.us/parks
Days/Hours: June–Labor Day, Thursday–Sunday, noon–4pm. After
     Labor Day, call for schedules.
Wheelchair/Stroller Access: Yes

The Fragrance Garden is a must. You'll develop a keener sense of smell and a deeper appreciation for the incredibly diverse scents to be found in nature. Expect bees! A favorite, the chocolate mist, of course. The plants are tended in raised beds within cement walls; running along the top of the cement wall, the full length of the garden, is a wooden rail. On the inside of that rail are Braille signs for those visually-impaired; visitors are encouraged to feel the plants. The gardens were begun in 1985; today the collection is quite mature and the variety amazing. Late spring and summer are best times to visit. For strolling or walking, take the half-mile boardwalk as it looks around the 200 acres of marsh. You might spot hawks, beavers or muskrats as you go. The Interpretive Center is the Neilsen farmhouse, preserved and adapted for present use.

Birch Bay

MINIATURE WORLD FAMILY FUN CENTER   360-371-7511
Location: 4620 Birch Bay Rd.
Web Site: www.miniatureworld.org
Days/Hours: Mid-June through Labor Day: daily, 10:30am–8:30pm.
     March, April, May, September and October: open Saturday, Sunday
     and holidays. Call for hours of operation.

Admission: Family train special, 4/$10. Kids 1 year and younger free with a paid adult; 4 years and younger must be accompanied by paid adult.

Wheelchair/Stroller Access: Limited

Driving Directions: From I-5, take exit 270 and head west three miles. Can't miss it on your right.

Miniature World has been here for 32 years, but it looks brand-new! A testimony to the folks that own and run this very kid-friendly place. There's a Go-Kart Racing Track with kid-size karts, single and double-seaters. If you buy three race passes, you get one free. The eighteen-hole miniature golf course (with par 72) is good for all ages, but the high spot of the day here is the train ride. It leaves on the hour and half-hour, travelling over an 80-foot trestle and through 10 acres of forest, with delightful scenery along the way. The engine that pulls the train is a giant replica of a well-known toy (any 4- or 5- year old boy will recognize that immediately), complete with bright blue and red paint and shiny wheels. One of the stops is the Petting Zoo, where you can feed the goats. There's a snack bar, large picnic areas and birthday party packages available.

Note: Check their Web site for the Christmas Wonderland Ride, with thousands of twinkling lights, hot chocolate and cookies.

BIRCH BAY WATER SLIDE   360-371-7901

Location: 4874 Birch Bay-Lynden Rd.

Web Site: www.birchbaywaterslides.com

Days/Hours: Open daily, Memorial Day–Labor Day; 11am–6:30pm. Closed September–MayAdmission: $13.95/ages 6 and older; $8.55/ ages 3, 4 and 5 years old; 2 and under/free.

Wheelchair/Stroller Access: Yes, around the park; there are stairs to the slides.

There are three slides for the 8-and-under crowd, and five regular slides for the daredevils. The Black Hole is the challenge. There is no age limit to use the slides but there is a height and weight requirement for the HydroCliff (a drop slide). This is a place to make a day of it; there's a snack bar and restaurant on the premises, but you are welcome to bring your own food and picnic there. PLEASE NOTE: No glass products and no alcohol. On a warm day, this is the place to be! A great co-op adventure—both parents and kids can enjoy this together.

HELPFUL PHONE NUMBERS:
Chambers of Commerce:

Arlington: 360-435-3708
Bainbridge Island: 206-842-3700
Birch Bay: 360-371-5004
Burlington: 360-755-0994
Central Whidbey/Coupeville: 360-678-5434
Edmonds: 206-670-1496
Everett: 425-257-3222
Ferndale: 360-384-3042
Greater Oak Harbor: 360-675-3535 or 360-675-3755
La Conner: 360-466-4778
Langley: 360-221-6765
Lummi Indian Nation: 360-384-2304
Lynden: 360-354-5995
Marysville: 360-659-7700
Mount Baker Foothills: 360-599-1205
Port Orchard: 360-876-3505
Poulsbo: 360-779-4848
Sedro Woolley: 360-855-1841
Silverdale: 360-692-6800
Snohomish: 360-568-2526
South Snohomish County: 425-774-0507

OTHER RESOURCES
Anacortes Visitor Information: 360-293-3832
Bellingham/Whatcom County Convention/Visitors Bureau: 800-487-2032; 360-671-3990
Blaine Visitors Center: 800-624-3555
Bremerton/Kitsap County Visitor Convention Bureau: 360-479-3588
North Cascades National Park Visitors Information Center: 360-856-5700
San Juan Islands Bed and Breakfast Inns: 360-378-3030
San Juan Islands Visitors Information Service: 360-378-9551; 888-472-7923
Snohomish County Visitors Center: 425-745-4133
Snohomish County Tourism Bureau: 425-348-5802
Washington State Ferry Information: 206-464-6400; 800-84-FERRY (800 is in-state only)

South King County

The new Library Connection at Southcenter in Seattle

Photo: courtesy King County Library System

Auburn, Renton, Kent, Tukwila and Federal Way

CANTERBURY FAIRE   253-859-3991
Location: Mill Creek Canyon Earthworks Park, 742 E Titus St., Kent
Days/Hours: Usually a mid-August weekend; call ahead for schedule
Admission: Usually $1
Wheelchair/Stroller Access: Yes

It's a slice of merry Olde England at this annual fair, and a good weekend family experience. Creative children can try their hands at creating a coat of arms or weaving with a floor loom; these and other hands-on activities usually happen between noon and 5pm. Or you may prefer just milling among costumed lords and ladies, brave knights and comical jesters, or having a spot of high tea served in the English Tea Garden. Shuttle buses carry passengers every half hour between the fair and Metro Park-and-Ride at Lincoln and Smith Streets. Call ahead to check on seasonal changes.

EMERALD DOWNS 253-288-7000
Location: East of Hwy 167/Valley Freeway near Auburn. Take the 15th St. NW or 37th St. NW exits
Web Site: www.emdowns.com
Days/Hours: Gates open at 11:30am on Sundays; post time is 1pm. Season runs early May–late September.
Admission: $3/general; free/children 10 and under
Wheelchair/Stroller Access: Yes

Even if you don't like the betting, there's frequently a Sunday afternoon slate of activities for children throughout the racing season. Pony rides, on-stage musicians, face painters, jugglers, mimes and inflatable jumping toys are set up for youngsters on a grassy lawn at the northwest edge of the track; most activities are free. Picnic tables are available if you've brought your own food, or you can purchase ice cream and other snacks inside. Between races, families may wander down to the paddock where stewards bring the horses near the rails so children can see these sleek, muscular animals. General parking is free, but it can be a long hike for some children; you may want to ride the free shuttle bus. Reserved parking is $3.

ENCHANTED VILLAGE/WILD WAVES WATER PARK
253-661-8000; 253-661-8001 (groups and birthday parties)
Location: 36201 Enchanted Parkway S in Federal Way. Take exit 142B
Web Site: www.sixflags.com
Days/Hours: Memorial–Labor Day; 11am–7pm. Weekends during spring and fall; 10am–6pm. Call or check Web site for specific dates.
Admission: $29.99/child over 4 feet tall; $24.99/child under 4 feet tall; $24.99/tickets purchased at any Safeway. Group rates available for 12 or more; call number listed above.
Wheelchair/Stroller Access: Yes at Enchanted Village, not at Wild Waves

With the wonders of a fantasyland and the exhilaration of a water park, these side-by-side attractions draw a variety of visitors. At Enchanted Village, activities are geared to younger children and there's a lot to do. The colorful carousel, small train and padded jumping area are favorites. Admission also includes on-stage entertainment featuring costumed animals.

Wild Waves is popular with preteens and teens. A river ride and slides attract little ones; older kids go for the Raging River Ride, Cannonball Ride and a giant wave pool. The highlight is the Wild Thing, zipping through a 60-foot loop to a 64-foot drop, calling itself the largest roller coaster in the northwestern U.S. In 2004 they introduced Washington's largest wooden roller coaster, called "Timber-Hawk, Ride of Prey," with an 84-foot drop and speeds of up to 50 miles per hour. In the evening hours from late November through December, Holiday Lights is a spectacular display of holiday characters throughout the park. Rides, trees and other structures twinkle and sparkle, creating a very festive atmosphere.

GENE COULON MEMORIAL PARK   425-430-6700
Location: In Renton at Lake Washington's south end. From I-405, take the Sunset Hwy exit to Lake Washington Blvd.; follow the signs.
Web Site: www.ci.renton.wa.us
Days/Hours: Daily, dawn to dusk. Call for current hours.
Wheelchair/Stroller Access: Yes

Formerly known as Lake Washington Park, this is a delightful public beach with ample parking, a good boat launch site and excellent picnic facilities, especially the covered pavilion with cooking areas. There are lots of ducks to feed, a complete first-aid station, bike racks, volleyball and tennis courts, horseshoe pits and concessions stands. The playground has small swings for small persons. A wooden bridge takes you to a small, grassy island on which you can picnic. There are eight boat launches, and you can rent canoes, sailboards and rowboats, picnic, listen to summer concerts, ride bikes, or take a stroll. The park prohibits kite flying because of nearby power lines. No animals or alcohol allowed. Lifeguard on duty only during summer months. For boat rental, call the Cascade Canoe and Kayak Club at 425-439-0111.

PACIFIC RIM BONSAI COLLECTION
253-924-5206 (info); 253-924-3153 (group tour reservations)
Location: 33553 Weyerhaeuser Way S, Federal Way (next to Rhododendron Species Botanical Garden on the Weyerhaeuser campus). From I-5, take exit 143 (Federal Way/320th St.) to the east side of the freeway onto Weyerhaeuser Way S. Follow signs to gardens.
Web Site: www.weyerhauser.com
Days/Hours: June–February, 11am–4pm (closed Thursday and Friday); March–May, 10am–4pm (closed Thursday)
Admission: Free
Tours: Guided tours each Sunday at noon; no charge or reservation. Request a tour at the Rhododendron Garden Shop. Self-guided tours anytime with a complimentary guidebook.

Wheelchair/Stroller Access: Yes

As you enter, be sure to pick up a brochure for the Bonsai Collection, considered an "outdoor museum of living art." Each specimen is identified with a history and description, which will enhance your understanding of this remarkable display. Children are usually quite amazed at the dwarf varieties, so perfect in their presentation. There are more than 50 trees here in this ancient art form; each is unusual for a different reason. The park was created in 1989 as Weyerhaeuser's tribute to the Washington State Centennial. To honor the company's trade relations, the plants on display come from Taiwan, Japan, Korea, China, Canada and the United States. If you are interested in bonsai on a personal level, there are some internationally known experts right here in Washington. Tour guides are very knowledgeable and share volumes of information.

PATTISON'S WEST SKATING
253-838-7442; 253-838-5788 (recorded information)
Location: 34222 Pacific Hwy S, Federal Way; one mile south of Sea-Tac Mall
Days/Hours: Seasonal; call the recorded information line for current schedule.
Admission: $3 with your own skates; $3/includes skate rental; $6/for in-line skates
Wheelchair/Stroller Access: Yes

It's a large skating arena with a capacity for a thousand. Best to call ahead for detailed information; depending on the time of year, there might be special sessions for youngsters. It's very popular for school parties, service groups and birthday parties. There's a snack bar on site.

RHODENDRON SPECIES BOTANICAL GARDEN   253-681-9377
Location: 2525 S 336th St., Federal Way (right next to the Pacific Rim Bonsai Garden)
Web Site: www.rhodygarden.org
Days/Hours: March–May, daily except Thursday, 10am–4pm; June–February, Saturday–Wednesday, 11am–4pm
Admission: $3.50/adults; $2.50/seniors and students; Free/children 12 and under and school groups
Wheelchair/Stroller Access: Yes

There's so much more than just rhododendrons here, although you'll find more than 500 species with 2,000 varieties displayed by the Rhododendron Species Botanical Garden. The nonprofit garden is on 22 acres and is maintained magnificently. Did you know that the rhododendron is Washington's state flower? Other areas of the garden include a fern collection and an alpine garden, plus the woodland and azalea varieties. Don't overlook the plant sale area (some beautiful specimens here) or the gift shop, with a wonderful selection of floral-related items.

RENTON CIVIC THEATRE 425-226-5529
Location: 507 S Third St.
Web Site: www.rentoncivictheatre.org
Days/Hours: Box office: Monday–Wednesday, 10am–5pm; Thursday–Saturday, noon–6pm
Admission: $18/adults; $14/students and seniors
Wheelchair/Stroller Access: Yes

With musicals and other family-oriented productions, this is a wonderful community theater for children. Many performances are ideal for children 7 years and older; past productions include The Secret Garden and Godspell. The season runs September – June; you can purchase season tickets, but it's also possible to find a good seat by arriving at the box office thirty minutes before show time.

RIVER BEND MINI PUTT   253-859-4000
Location: 2020 W Meeker St., Kent. From Hwy. 167, take Hwy 516/Willis St. exit. On Willis St., turn north on Washington Ave.; drive several blocks to Meeker St. From I-5, head south to the Kent-Des Moines exit, staying in the left lane. Turn left at the light; head down the hill to the light at Meeker St., turn left; the mini-putt is on your right.
Days/Hours: Mid-spring–Labor Day; daily, 7am–10pm. Remainder of year: daily, 8am–9pm.
Admission: $5/adults; $4/children 12 and younger
Wheelchair/Stroller Access: Yes

This lighted eighteen-hole mini-putt course is next to a larger driving range. Miniature golf is a great family activity, especially for those new at the game. There is a room for birthday parties here.

SPRINGBROOK TROUT FARM   253-852-0360
Location: 19225 Talbot Rd., Renton. Take I-405 to exit Hwy 167 heading south; take SW 43rd St. exit off Hwy 167 to Valley General Hospital one block east. Trout Farm is a mile south of the hospital.
Days/Hours: March–October; Monday–Saturday, 10am–dusk; Sunday, 10am–6pm.
Admission: Cost for fishing only; depends on the size of the fish
Wheelchair/Stroller Access: Yes, but ground can be soft in wet weather.

It's a delightful woodsy setting, appealing to kids of all ages. Even toddlers can watch Dad pull one in—or even help him. The cost depends on the size of the catch—it will range from 10 inches/$3.50 to up to 19 inches/$9.50 (prices subject to change). They do birthday parties (three packages available) and educational tours (groups of 10 or more) and provide picnic rentals for a minimum charge. Best of all, they clean and bag the fish; you take it home to the freezer or for dinner.

Shops to Browse

THE FISH GALLERY

(two locations) 425-226-3215 (Renton); 253-852-9240 (Kent)
Location: Renton Village, Renton; Easthill Plaza, Kent
Web Site: www.fishgallery.com
Days/Hours: Monday–Friday, 9am–9pm; Saturday, 9am–7pm; Sunday, 11am–6pm
Tours: Group tours by request; morning hours preferred; reserve at least one week in advance.
Wheelchair/Stroller Access: Yes

The tropical fish collection is extraordinary, but you'll also find some flamboyant parrots whose life span can be as long as 150 years. Pet choices here range from the traditional to the exotic; families are welcome to drop in and handle the animals or talk to the birds. The owners are happy to give group tours, but need plenty of warning.

Black Diamond and Enumclaw

Places to Go

BLACK DIAMOND HISTORICAL MUSEUM   **360-886-2142**
Location: 32627 Railroad Ave. and Baker St.
Web Site: www.ohwy.com/wa
Days/Hours: Thursday, 9am–3pm; Saturday–Sunday, noon–3pm.
Admission: Free; donations appreciated
Tours: By arrangement only
Wheelchair/Stroller Access: Yes

There was a time when the railroad was the best transportation in this area. The museum is an old train depot, restored and transformed, with interesting tidbits about the region's old coal-mining communities. Look for the 1920s caboose at the museum's depot entrance. Next door is the old Black Diamond Jail, built in 1910. Families may drop in to visit; special groups should make arrangements. The small museum can accommodate between 50 and 75 visitors.

BLACK DIAMOND BAKERY AND RESTAURANT
360-886-2741 (bakery); 360-886-2235 (restaurant)
Location: 32805 Railroad Ave., Black Diamond
Days/Hours: Bakery: Monday, 7am–4pm; Tuesday–Saturday, 7am–5pm.
Restaurant: Monday–Friday, 7am–4pm; Saturday–Sunday, 7am–5pm
Tours: Yes, for groups of less than 15. Call ahead for arrangements.
Wheelchair/Stroller Access: Yes

The bakery has grown up and includes a small coffee shop as well. The restaurant is a perfect opportunity to sit down and enjoy something with, or on, their famous bread. On a clear day, the picture window with a southern exposure frames Mount Rainier. A most extraordinary dining experience! Some good advice on the wall for bakery visitors: "don't count your calories, count your blessings!" That helps when you're tempted by their fresh-baked pies. The old brick ovens are still there and very much in use, turning out those delicious doughnuts for which skiers and hikers go out of their way.

CJ'S BAKERY   360-886-0855
Location: 30800-A 3rd Ave., Black Diamond
Days/Hours: Tuesday–Saturday, 4am–6pm.
Wheelchair/Stroller Access: Yes

Folks get up mighty early in these parts! If you're on your way to somewhere along Hwy.169 (usually Enumclaw or Crystal Mountain), CJ's is right off the road. There are scrumptious doughnuts and muffins (caramel bran looks good), but the high point for kids is the cookies – dinosaurs, dogs and butterflies. For birthday parties or special occasion, Jim will "bake" your picture right onto the cake. You can use any photo you wish (within reason). If you need more of a snack, try their jalapeno and cream cheese roll.

THE SALES PAVILION   360-825-3151
Location: 22712 SE 436th St., Enumclaw. Take I-5 to Auburn. Drive five
miles on Hwy. 18 to the Auburn/Enumclaw exit; turn east and drive
another twelve miles on Hwy 164.
Days/Hours: doors open at 8am; sales start at 10am, every Saturday
and Sunday. The first Sunday of every month is horse tack; on Saturdays it's poultry, sheep, calves, cows and goats.
Admission: Free
Wheelchair/Stroller Access: Yes

If you think your children talk fast, take them to hear the prattling of the auctioneers who sell pigs, sheep, goats, poultry and horses at the Sales Pavilion auctions. Much of the countryside near Enumclaw and Black Diamond is farmland, so this is a center of activity year-round. Auctions take place in a barn, and the atmosphere is ripe with animal sounds and smells. The audience is seated in rows of old theater seats, steeply banked, surrounding the stage. There's a snack bar nearby. In the lobby near the entrance to the auction, you'll often find vendors displaying Western-style goods. This is a great, no-cost weekend experience for families who appreciate new environments and enjoy people-watching. Become part of the audience, sit back and enjoy.

Helpful Resources

CHAMBERS OF COMMERCE:
  Federal Way: 253-838-2605
  Kent: 253-854-1770
  Renton: 425-226-4560
  King County Park District: 206-296-8687
  Northshore/Shoreline District: 206-296-2976
  South District: 206-296-4232
  Mercer Island Parks and Recreation Department: 206-236-3545
  Bellevue Parks and Recreation Department: 425-452-6881
  Snoqualmie Pass Visitor Information Center: 425-434-6111

OTHER RESOURCES

East King County Convention and Visitors Bureau: 425-455-1926

King County Library System: 425-462-9600 (the "answer" line); 425-450-1788 (TDD)

Snoqualmie Pass Visitor Information Center: 425-434-6111 (Thursday–Sunday only; Backcounty and Avalanche Center)

Lake Washington beaches with daily summer lifeguards: Lake Washington's Juanita Beach in north Kirkland; Mercer Island's Luther Burbank Park; Issaquah Plateau's Pine Lake Park; Lake Wilderness east of Kent and Five Mile Lake Park near Federal Way.

Go to: www.metro.kc.gov to access links to bus and ferry schedules.

Tacoma and Southwest Washington

Celebrating the power of play!

Photo: courtesy Children's Museum of Tacoma

In many ways, Tacoma is the gateway to southwestern Washington. As you travel southward, you have the option of interesting inland towns or the mosaic coastline and coastal beaches. Some of Washington's most important history came from the economies of the lumber industry, inherent in towns like Shelton, Longview, Raymond and Kelso. As the economics of these cities have changed, families find other interesting aspects of the area to explore.

TACOMA: Nicknamed the City of Destiny, Tacoma is the second largest city in

Washington. While the citizens are still working to define that destiny, Tacoma has developed an ambiance all its own. The Tacoma Dome hosts world-class sporting events, top-drawer entertainers, and some of Puget Sound's most popular annual festivals. The historic Pantages Theater was restored in 1932 and today showcases many different stage productions. Tacoma's Metropolitan Park District has developed one of the state's finest parks and recreational systems; Point Defiance Park is part of that system. And Tacoma's downtown core is fast becoming a cultural Mecca, with three of the state's most interesting museums sharing the tourist trade and attracting art lovers of all description.

OLYMPIA: Here lies the heart of the state's eminent political system. Olympia is the state capital, residing on a 35-acre campus that is jumping when in session (usually the first four months of the year) and much more subdued in the off-season. Elected officials represent a great mix of the rural and metropolitan, sophisticated and naive, and to the public's credit, diversity in ethnicity. There is much history in this city; some of the old homes here reflect some grand traditions of the past.

LEWIS and COWLITZ COUNTIES: Lewis County is named for famed explorer Meriwether Lewis, and of course the historical Lewis and Clark journey permeates many aspects of the area. Cowlitz County is home to the mountain that blew its top. In May of 1980 Mount St. Helens drew international attention when it erupted, sending 8.8 billion cubic yards of ash, ice, rock and dirt 75,000 feet into the atmosphere. The mushroom cloud was seen through most of the state; 57 people died and 300 homes were demolished. The fall-out affected areas as far away as eastern Washington; people are still talking about it and hundreds of families drive through the area each year, although the landscape has changed considerably through growth and reclamation. Thousands of acres of trees were demolished, but Weyerhaeuser, which operates the forestry center with the state Department of Transportation, has reforested much of the land. The Mount St. Helens National Volcanic Monument is accessible from two directions. From the west via I-5, exit 49 at Castle rock, drive five miles to the Visitors Center at Silver Lake. From the north, take Hwy 131 south from Randle, via Morton and Randle to Windy Ridge on the crater's east side.

CLARK COUNTY: Clark County can boast of numerous parks for recreational enjoyment. Along the shores of the Columbia River you'll find a working model of Fort Vancouver, one of the first settlements in the Oregon Territory. A number of popular hikes to Mount St. Helens are accessible through Clark County.

South Puget Sound

Tacoma and Greater Pierce County

Places to Go

PORT OF TACOMA OBSERVATION TOWER   253-383-5841
  Location: From I-5, take exit 136; head north of Port of Tacoma Rd.; go
    left on E 11th St. and drive a quarter mile to the Port Administration
    Bldg; Tower is at the west end of the parking lot.
  Web Site: www.portoftacoma.com
  Days/Hours: Open twenty-four hours
    Admission: Free
  Wheelchair/Stroller Access: Not to the Tower, but a kiosk on the first
    floor has an ongoing video with interesting information on Port
    activities.

It's a free view of the Olympic Mountains, especially gorgeous at sunset. You'll climb three flights of stairs to the top of the tower where cameras are definitely encouraged. You'll watch marine traffic of all kinds moving in and out of the port; there's a free telescope as well.

CHILDREN'S MUSEUM OF TACOMA   253-627-6031 (information)
  Location: 936 Broadway
  Web Site: www.ChildrensMuseumofTacoma.org
  Days/Hours: Tuesday–Saturday, 10am–5pm; Sunday, noon–5pm. First
    Friday of each month is free, 10am–7pm.
    Admission: $3/13 and older; Free/2 years and younger. Free the first
    Friday of the month,10am–7pm.
  Wheelchair/Stroller Access: Yes. There is a ramp between 9th and 11th
    Streets at Court St.
  Groups: Group visits: Tuesday and Wednesday, 11am–5pm; Thursday
    and Friday, 9am–5pm.

In keeping with children's museums around the state, this one is totally dedicated to children and families. Activities and offerings within the museum are free with museum admission. Most exhibits are hands-on, always giving children (and parents) a chance to do something creative. Becka's Studio is filled with art-related materials, giving youngsters a chance to explore art processes. The exhibit Under the Big Top—a Circus Adventure probably speaks for itself. There are current features that will change regularly (for example, Emotion Play with Dr. John Gottman was scheduled for January of 2004). Building on Play is a toddlers' area designed for those 3 and under. Motor skills, early childhood development, exploration in the arts, sciences and creative play are all enhanced through exhibits and activities that are meant to entice children into learning while playing, a most enjoyable situation for parents and offspring.

Note: There is free one-hour parking along Broadway and surrounding streets.

FREIGHTHOUSE SQUARE   253-305-0678
Location: 430 E 25th St.
Web Site: www.FreighthouseSquare.com
Days/Hours: Varies with merchants
Wheelchair/Stroller Access: Yes

It's called Freighthouse Square because it's the Milwaukee/St.Paul Railroad freighthouse rejuvenated. There are numerous small shops to browse through, not much of interest to kids except those with food. These include Subway, Mocha Stop (milkshakes and ice cream here), McGregor's Scottish Tea Room (older children preferred, but it's a nice, dignified experience for all ages) and Gourmet Pizza, among others. Close to the Tacoma Dome, it's a good stop-over coming or going.

FORT LEWIS MILTARY MUSEUM   253-967-7206
Location: At I-5, exit 120; Fort Lewis' main gate is just west of the free-
way. Note: If you do not have a military sticker on your car and a
Federal ID card, you will need to go to the Main Gate Visitors Center
pass. You must have a driver's license, vehicle registration and proof
of insurance at that time.
Web Site: www.lewis.army.mil.DPTMS/POMFI/museum.htm
Days/Hours: Wednesday–Sunday, noon–4pm; closed Federal holidays
Admission: Free; donations welcome
Tours: Mostly self-guided. Special tours can be arranged from Mon-
day–Sunday by calling 253-967-7207, 967-7208 or 967-7800.
Wheelchair/Stroller Access: Yes

The museum was built by the Salvation Army as a guest house and used from 1919 to 1972; it has been a museum since. Tanks, jeeps, rockets, missiles and armored cars are on display, plus galleries with nearly 2000 northwest military artifacts. Objects, uniforms and weapons from the 1770s to the present day are part of the presentation, including Stormin' Norman Schwarzkopf's Jeep.

RUSTON WAY
Location: From I-5 south to Tacoma, take a City Center exit and follow
signs to Ruston Way.

Ruston Way runs along Commencement Bay and overlooks the Port of Tacoma. There are patches of beachfront up and down the parkway, with benches and grass for water gazing, strolling, picnicking and even swimming. A two-mile pathway dedicated to bikers, walkers and skaters becomes a sidewalk intermittently. There's a fragrance here you find only near saltwater byways. Trains go rolling by periodically; bike and blade rentals available. Mount Rainier is in full view on a good day. This is a picturesque part of Tacoma.

DICKMAN MILL PARK
Location: Ruston Way
Web Site: www.metroparkstacoma.org
Wheelchair/Stroller Access: Yes

The nine-acre Dickman Mill Park is historically significant in Tacoma. The Dickman Lumber Mill operated continuously from the 1890s until 1974, the last in a long tradition of lumber mills on Tacoma's "Old Town" waterfront. After a fire in 1979, the mill's remnants slowly deteriorated. The park opened in 2001 and tells the mill's story through the old wood burners and signage with old photos. On public display next to the Lobster Shop is a Headsaw and Carriage. It's 61 tons, stands two stories tall and was salvaged from the Dickman Lumber Company.

LES DAVIS PIER
Location: 4303 Ruston Way
Web Site: www.metroparkstacoma.org
Wheelchair/Stroller Access: Yes

The Pier offers public fishing and ample parking, with a bait and tackle shop and a fish and chips stand and restrooms nearby. On the pier are benches and picnic tables. You'll see divers, too, as this is the site of an artificial reef.

MARINE PARK
Location: 4303 Ruston Way
Web Site: www.metroparkstacoma.org
Days/Hours: Open dawn to dusk
Wheelchair/Stroller Access: Yes

Very popular in the summertime with families and singles. There are grassy areas with benches and picnic tables, good access to saltwater swimming and fishing. Fabulous views of mountains and water traffic.

MUSEUM OF GLASS   253-284-4750; 866-4museum
Location: Thea Foss Waterway; 1801 E Dock St.
Web Site: www.museumofglass.org

Days/Hours: Fall–winter: Wednesday–Saturday, 10am–5pm; Sunday, noon–5pm; third Thursday of each month, 10am–8pm. Closed Mondays and Tuesdays; also New Year's Day, Thanksgiving and Christmas. Summer hours will be posted on the Web site.

Admission: $10/adults; $8/seniors 62 and older, students 13 and older with ID and military with valid ID; $4/children 6–12; Free/under 6 and museum members. Free/every third Thursday, 5–8pm. $30/ familes with two adults and up to four children under 18.

Tours: $8 per person/adults in groups of 10 or more; $3/per person for youth and school groups. To book a tour, call 253-284-4713 or 253-284-4709.

Wheelchair/Stroller Access: Yes. Wheelchairs and hearing assistance devices available for loan at the coat check in the Grand Hall.

Aside from the building itself creating national attention for its state-of-the-art design, the Museum of Glass celebrates the beauty and unique qualities of glass as a contemporary art form. The $58-million building is 75,000 square feet, with 13,000 square feet of exhibition space. Along with Tacoma's native son, Chihuly, you will see a vast array of ever-changing exhibits featuring artists from around the world working with glass and other media. Not to miss: the Hot Shop Amphitheatre, where blowing glass is sheer entertainment. There are two furnaces, four glory holes and other special equipment for the artisans who work, demonstrate and talk to you at the same time. It's both fascinating and amazing. You will, of course, want to walk across the Chihuly Bridge of Glass; you can only access this from outside, using either the Grand Staircase or the outdoor plaza ramps, which offer more art installations. The 500-foot bridge connects the Thea Foss Waterway and Museum of Glass to the Washington State History Museum and downtown Tacoma. The bridge features one of the largest outdoor installations of Chihuly's glass, with 1,500 pieces. Save time to enjoy the walk over and back. You might need an umbrella for inclement weather.

TACOMA NATURE CENTER   (at Snake Lake) 253-591-6439

Location: 1919 S Tyler St.

Web Site: www.metroparkstacoma.org

Days/Hours: Monday–Friday, 8am–5pm; Saturday, 10am–4pm.

Admission: Free, but there is a voluntary $3 day pass for families

Tours: Guided tours for groups for 12 to 60 people; call ahead

Wheelchair/Stroller Access: Yes

Snake Lake has long been one of Tacoma's special places and is an important part of the Metro Parks Department. In partnership with the Tahoma Audubon Society, this 54-acre wildlife preserve has 35 educational stops along wooded paths that extend almost two miles. Visitors are asked NOT to feed the waterfowl, which exist here in their natural setting. In the Interpretive Center there's a wetlands diorama, a small beaver lodge for small ones to crawl through, and many hands-on exhibits that are entertaining as well as informational. Get on their mailing list for some exciting classes and workshops.

POINT DEFIANCE PARK   253-305-1000
Location: N 54thSt. at Pearl St. Take I-5 to Exit 132; follow to Hwy 16; take the 6th Ave. exit and turn left. Turn right at Pearl St.; follow this into the park.
Web Site: www.metroparkstacoma.org
Days/Hours: Daily, dawn to dusk
Wheelchair/Stroller Access: Yes

Tacoma and its Metropolitan Park District are known for an outstanding park system, and this is the jewel in their crown. We've offered the various areas in separate blocks so you can plan your trip accordingly. You can easily spend an entire day in the park.

POINT DEFIANCE ZOO AND AQUARIUM   253-591-5227
Location: Near Park's eastern entrance
Web Site: www.pdza.org
Days/Hours: January 1–March 31, 9:30am–4pm; April 1–May 28, 9:30am–5pm; May 29–September 6, 9:30am–6pm; September 7–September 30, 9:30am–5pm; October 1–December 31, 9:30am–4pm. Closed July 16, Thanksgiving and Christmas.
Admission: $8.25/general; $7.50/62 and older; $6.50/ages 4–13; Free/3 and under (Rates will be slightly lower for Pierce County residents). Discounts available for groups of 12 or more, AAA members and military; reserve at least one week in advance.
Wheelchair/Stroller Access: Yes

If you like zoos, you'll love this one! This combined facility offers something for everyone in the family, from the outdoor elephant exhibit to the indoor shark tank. There are two aquariums in one here: North Pacific and Discovery Reef. North Pacific is home now to a delightful new seahorse exhibit as well as cold water fish and invertebrates, many found here in Puget Sound. Discovery Reef is definitely more tropical, with brilliantly colored fish, sharks and eels. Kids can see as much as they want, pressed against the floor-to-ceiling windows. At Rocky Shores, the bigger guys are busy—sea otters, walrus, beluga whales and harbor seals are at home here. A "new zoo" is emerging in 2004. On May 1, the new Wild Wonders Outdoor Theater opened, with films of exciting animal encounters and in July, the new Asian Forest Sanctuary exhibit with tigers, two species of primates, tapir and other endangered Asian animals. A zoo tradition for many years here is the Zoolights holiday display from the day after Thanksgiving through New Year's, when a half-million lights decorate the grounds, buildings, trees and walkways. You'll recognize northwest landmarks and zoo animals in the hand-crafted glitter and sparkle. Admission is $4 in advance (at the zoo before 4pm or online at www.pdza.org) or $4.50 at the gate. Note: If you're wondering why Pierce County residents enjoy a lower admission, it's because they support the Zoo through a special sales tax.

POINT DEFIANCE PARK/BOATHOUSE MARINA   253-591-2068
Location: Park's northeast corner near the Vashon Island ferry terminal
Web Site: www.metroparkstacoma.org
Days/Hours: Varies with available daylight and fishing seasons. Call for updated information.
Wheelchair/Stroller Access: Yes

Commencement Bay offers good fishing here. Rent a small boat with or without a motor, buy bait in the tackle shop, or check out the boats moored nearby at Old Town dock. The ferry to Vashon Island docks near here, also.

POINT DEFIANCE PARK/CAMP 6 LOGGING MUSEUM   253-752-0047
Location: Park's southwest corner
Web Site: www.camp-6-museum.org/c6.html
Days/Hours: Outdoor exhibits open year-round, dawn-dusk, as long as the Park is open. Park may close during severe winds or weather. Indoor exhibits: October 1–October 26, Wednesday–Sunday, 10am–4pm, closed Monday and Tuesday. Closed from October 27–April 3. For Logging Train Riders; April–May; Saturday, Sunday, holidays, noon–4pm. Memorial Day weekend thru September; Saturday, Sunday, holidays, noon–6:30pm
Wheelchair/Stroller Access: Yes

Keeping the old logging days alive, the museum is modeled after an authentic logging camp. Steam–powered locomotives and equipment from the 1880s to the 1940s are on display. The train is great fun; it operates spring and summer weekends and selected holiday afternoons. Mark your calendar for the Santa Claus train ride through the park (first weekends in December). Note: All train rides subject to equipment availability.

POINT DEFIANCE PARK/FORT NISQUALLY
Location: Park's southwest corner
Web Site: www.fortnisqually.org/
Days/Hours: January 1–March 31, Wednesday–Sunday, 11am–4pm.
April 1–May 22, Wednesday–Sunday, 11am–5pm. May 23–September
3, open daily, 11am–6pm. September 4–December 31, Wednesday–
Sunday, 11am–4pm.
Admission: Winter rates: November–February: $2/adults; $1.50/seniors
and students; $1/children. Regular rates: March–October; $3/adults;
$2/seniors and students; $1/children.
Tours: Call for reservations and fees
Wheelchair/Stroller Access: Yes, but grass and wood paths can make it
slow going.

Summer visits are the most fun here; interpreters are on hand, dressed in costumes, and full of information and anecdotes. The Hudson Bay Company fur
trading and farming post south of Tacoma was lively 160 years ago; it's been
reconstructed here at Fort Nisqually, with great attention to detail and authenticity. The outhouse is especially interesting! Take your imagination with
you—the blacksmith shop is aromatic. The Factor's House symbolizes a delightful lifestyle even then. Now that there is a stove in the Trading Store, lectures
are offered during winter months. The majority of customers at the original
fort were Native Americans, so bartering and trading were the norm. Ask about
their fall candlelight tours; they are a magical experience and sell out early.

POINT DEFIANCE PARK/NEVER NEVER LAND   253-591-5845
Location: Park's southwest corner
Web Site: www.metroparkstacoma.org
Days/Hours: Memorial Day–Labor Day, 11am–6pm
Admission: Free
Wheelchair/Stroller Access: Yes

What a great place for little ones! Mother's Goose's messenger, Humpty Dump-
ty, greets you from atop the arch as you enter this 10-acre haven. While the
nursery rhyme characters are gone, it's still a great place to picnic and let the
little ones work off some energy. To reserve a group picnic site, call 253-305-
1010.

TACOMA ART MUSEUM   253-272-4258
Location: 1701 Pacific Ave.
Web Site: www.TacomaArtMuseum.org
Days/Hours: Tuesday–Saturday, 10am–5pm; Thursday, 10am–8pm; Sun-
day, noon–5pm. Closed Mondays. For holiday hours, call the number
listed above

Admission: $6.50/adults; $5.50/seniors 65 and older, students and military; free/children under 6 and members. The Third Thursday Art Walk is also free.

Tours: Guided tours available; call number above, ask for Education Dept.

Wheelchair/Stroller Access: Yes

The adult displays predominate here, but on the second floor is a Creative Room, where youngsters can come in, choose a project and work on it there. There are worktables, materials and usually an adult on hand to help lead you through the process. The Museum's Kid and Family Programs are designed to get everyone involved and they focus on all ages. Young at Art is for ages 2–6 (with an adult), Art Stories are for 10 and younger, Mask Making is for ages 7–10, and the Family Art Affair is for 10 and under with an adult. Some require pre-registration; call for updates.

TACOMA RAINIERS   253-752-7707 800-281-3834

Location: 2502 S Tyler; Cheney Stadium

Web Site: www.tacomarainiers.com

Days/Hours: April–September

Admission: Ticket prices range from $4–$12; Family Fun Pack 4/$40. Lots of other packages available. Ticket office at Cheney Stadium is open Monday–Friday, 9am–5pm, year-round.

Wheelchair/Stroller Access: Yes

As the Triple A affiliate of the Seattle Mariners, the Tacoma Rainiers draw a vocal, enthusiastic crowd throughout their season at Cheney Stadium. It's a great place to get autographs of soon-to-be big leaguers or see some of the big guys come down from the majors to play for a while. Autograph time is best about one hour before the game, during batting practice. Groups (and Little League teams) can reserve blocks of seats by calling ahead. Fridays are a great day for kids; it's fireworks day!

WAPATO PARK AT WAPATO LAKE   253-305-1070

Location: S 68th St. at Sheridan Ave., south Tacoma

Web Site: www.tacomaparks.com

Days/Hours: Daylight hours

Wheelchair/Stroller Access: Yes

Wapato Lake is a great place for kids to fish because only those 13 or younger may dip their lines into the waters.

WASHINGTON STATE HISTORY MUSEUM

253-272-WSHS; 888-BE-THERE

Location: 1911 Pacific Ave. Take Exit 133 off I-5; take the E 26th St. exit; turn left on E 26th St. and head three blocks to Pacific Ave. Turn right, continue five blocks. The museum is on the right.

Web Site: www.wshs.org

Days/Hours: Tuesday–Saturday, 10am–5pm, except Thursday, 10am–5pm with free admission from 5–8pm; Sunday, noon–5pm. Closed Mondays.

Admission: $7/adults; $6.50/seniors 60 and over; $5/students 6–17; Free/5 and under.

Tours: Call 253-798-5876, Monday–Friday, 8am–noon to book a tour. There are numerous tour opportunities; be specific about what you want to see.

Wheelchair/Stroller Access: Yes

If their slogans "history with an attitude" and "first person present-tense exhibits" are accurate, you'll enjoy this museum even more because it's about where you live (if you're a Washingtonian, of course). If not, you'll learn heaps about this wonderful state and enjoy your visit even more. They present Washington State historically, culturally and even philosophically, using well their 106,000 square feet of space. For kids, the largest model railroad in the state is here. The museum covers events electronically, using visual, audio and interactive aides. Motion sensors in mannequins trigger characters to "talk" about state history, including some of the tragedies that were endured. There's also a replica of a covered wagon, perfect for climbing on and pretending an adventure. There are continuing exhibits, temporary exhibits and coming attractions; there's ALWAYS something interesting happening here, including lectures and demonstrations covering a multitude of things. The gift shop and café are nice amenities, and there are indoor and outdoor theaters, dioramas and videos. You can easily spend several hours there; it's worth it. Hint: No food or drinks, but flash cameras or large bags are allowed.

*Note: Triple Tuesdays are a great value. WSHM, Tacoma Art Museum and the Museum of Glass offer a joint ticket to all three facilities on Tuesdays; cost is $17/adults, $14/seniors (60 and older) and military w/ID; $12/students with ID and children 6–18.

W.W. SEYMOUR BOTANICAL CONSERVATORY

253-591-5330

Location: Wright Park, 316 S G St., Tacoma. From I-5, take Exit 133 to City Center; follow signs for 705 St. N; take the Stadium Way exit; turn right on Stadium Way, left on 4th St.; follow G St. into Wright Park.

Web Site: www.metroparkstacoma.org/parks/conservatory

Days/Hours: Open Tuesday–Sunday, except for Thanksgiving and
Christmas. Conservatory, 10am–4:30pm; Plant and gift shop,
10am–4pm.

Admission: Free; donations welcome

Tours: Yes; $1.50 per person; groups up to 25. Call ahead for informa-
tion and reservations (subject to change).

Wheelchair/Stroller Access: Yes, although aisles may be narrow in
places

This lovely Victorian-style building, built in 1908, has recently been renovated
and sparkles with new glass. It is listed on the state and national historic regis-
ters, and features a 12-sided central dome and over 3,500 panes of glass. With
the 550 species of exotic tropical plants in the permanent displays, an amazing lemon tree with fruit the size of grapefruit, and seasonal displays that
sometimes change monthly, there is always something new to see. The holiday
floral displays are especially enticing. Also, look for the goldfish and the waterfall. Kids can run off some energy in the park as well.

Places to Eat

ANTIQUE SANDWICH COMPANY   253-752-4069
Location: 5102 N Pearl St.
Days/Hours: Monday–Saturday, 7am–7:30pm; Sunday, 8am–7:30pm
Wheelchair/Stroller Access: Yes, main floor; ask regarding restroom
facilities for disabled.

Here's a favorite of ours; they've grown up with this book. There are 19 sandwiches (whole and half) to choose from (pb&j still a favorite) and homemade
pies are created right here. There is a good drink selection and a great play
place for the kids. Toy baskets are full of irresistibles. If you wonder what's
going on in town, glance at the posters that line the counter. Don't miss the
lovely old ceramic chandelier. Restrooms are up the loooong staircase. Fresh
fruit milkshakes are a specialty, but they've added espresso and lattes.

C.J. SHENANIGAN'S   253-752-8811
Location: 3017 Ruston Way
Days/Hours: Monday–Saturday from 11am; Friday and Saturday, clos-
ing is at 10pm, Thursday at 9pm. Sunday brunch, 9:30am–1:45pm,
dinner, 2pm–9pm
Wheelchair/Stroller Access: Yes

Ideally located, overlooking Commencement Bay, you can eat on the deck at
umbrella tables in summer. The seagulls paddle back and forth, biding their
time, waiting for the inevitable tidbit. For kids, a Little League menu has some
specials under $6.

THE LOBSTER SHOP   253-759-2165

Location: 4015 Ruston Way

Days/Hours: Monday–Friday, lunch is 11:30am–2:30pm, dinner from 4:30. Saturday, dinner only, 4:30pm. Sunday brunch 9:30am–1:30pm, dinner from 4:30.

Admission: For Sunday brunch, kids under 5 are free, ages 6–12 are $8.95.

Wheelchair/Stroller Access: Yes

Looks like a very adult dining spot but they do have menu items for kids, including cheese pizza, fish and chips, chicken strips, a grilled cheese sandwich and fettuccine alfredo. High chairs and boosters available.

Outside Tacoma

NORTHWEST TREK   253-847-1901; 360-832-6117; 800-433-TREK

Location: 11610 Trek Drive E, Eatonville. Take I-5 exit 127 to Hwy 512. Turn on South Hill Mall/Eatonville exit to Hwy 161.

Web Site: www.nwtrek.org

Days/Hours: Open daily at 9:30am, mid-February–October. Open Friday–Sunday, November–mid-February and selected holidays

Admission: $8.75/adults; $8.25/seniors 62 and older; $6/ages 5–7; $4/ages 3–4 (slightly lower for Pierce County residents)

Tours: Yes. There are discounted rates for groups of 15 or more; make reservations at least 15 days ahead.

Wheelchair/Stroller Access: Yes

Northwest Trek's 615 acres of natural wetlands, forests and grasslands are home to hundreds of animals, including grizzlies, black bears, big-horn mountain sheep, shaggy goats, Roosevelt elk, bison, beaver, wolverines and much more. They thrive in a very authentic environment; the Trek Tram carries visitors through the park to view them foraging for food, building homes and at play. Start with a fourteen-minute show at the Forest Theater, save time for the hands-on exhibits in the Cheney Discovery Center. Spring is a special time here, with babies everywhere. You can explore by Trek Tram (in winter they're heated and closed) through wooded paths and along nature trails. This can be an all-day destination; a picnic area, restaurant and covered outdoor eating space offer you choices. Call ahead to learn about their special events or camping in your own tent on Trek grounds. Go online to get a discount coupon. Ample parking here.

PIONEER FARM MUSEUM   360-832-6300

Location: 7716 Ohop Valley Rd., Eatonville
Web Site: www.pioneerfarmmuseum.org
Days/Hours: Farm Tours: March 20–June 19, Saturday and Sunday.
   Father's Day–Labor Day, daily. September 5 –November 21, Satur-
   day and Sunday. Farm tours start at 11:15am and run continuously
   until 4pm (last tour ends at 5:30pm) Native American Season Tours:
   Father's Day–Labor Day; Friday–Sunday; 1pm and 2:30pm
Admission: Farm Tours: $6.50/adults; $5.50/ages 3–18; $5.50/seniors. Na-
   tive American Tour: $6/adults; $5/ages 3–18 and seniors. Note: If you
   do both tours on the same day, you can save $1.00 per person.
Wheelchair/Stroller Access: For strollers only

This is the hands-on place to get a taste of the Pacific Northwest back in the
1880s. From milking cows and churning butter to hand-washing clothes, you'll
get an authentic view of how the early settlers lived. The ninety-minute tour
includes visits to a trading post, barn, blacksmith shop, a vintage log cabin and
more. Another opportunity here is the Native American Seasons Tour focusing
on the life of the Salish Indians (see above). This tour has access for strollers
but not wheelchairs.

MOUNT RAINIER NATIONAL PARK

Our state's trademark is—currently—a dormant volcano. It is also the highest
volcanic peak in the Cascade Mountains. Of course, there's no guarantee it will
remain dormant; predictions include a possible eruption several hundred years
from now. Hikers, climbers and tourists ignore all predictions and flock to
the mountain by the thousands. Many are looking for old-growth forest, to be
found at Ohanapecosh at the park's southeast corner. Here some of the Douglas
fir, western hemlock and red cedar are 500 to 1,000 years old. A walk through
the Grove of the Patriarchs will give you an appreciation of the grandeur here.
Read further to find out more about other activities in the area.

CRYSTAL MOUNTAIN RESORT   360-5-663-2265

Location: Just off Hwy 410 on Crystal Mountain Blvd. Take I-5 exit
   142A; follow Hwy 164 through Enumclaw to Hwy 410; drive 33 miles
   east to the Crystal Mountain turnoff (just before entering Mount
   Rainier National Park). Yakima Route (closed during the winter):
   follow Hwy 410 from Yakima west, over Chinook Pass; turn onto
   Crystal Mountain Blvd., just after leaving the national park.
Web Site: www.skicrystal.com
Days/Hours: Lifts closed September 7 till the snow starts (hopefully
   mid-November)
Summer rates: $10/adults; $60/summer pass; $7/seniors 65 and older;
   Free/children 8–17. Winter rates vary, call for information.

Washingtonians know Crystal as an exceptional winter destination for skiing and other snow activities, but Crystal is great in summer time as well, especially in June when the wild strawberries are out. The chairs run to the top of the mountain; you'll think you can practically reach out and touch Mount Rainier (you're only 12 miles away). It's an exquisite view and a perfect place to bring visitors. Summer activities include hiking, picnicking and horseback riding. Trail maps are available at the hotels. A tram for summer recreation will be opening in summer of 2006.

Crystal Mountain has been voted by Ski Magazine as one of the top 25 winter sports areas in North America. During winter, you can ski, snowboard, snowshoe and telemark. Overnight accommodations include Crystal Mountain Hotels (888-754-6400), Crystal Mountain Lodging (condos, 888-668-4368) and Alta Crystal Resort on Hwy 410 (800-277-6475). For skiing parents with young ones, a winter day care center will be available in 2005.

LONGMIRE MUSEUM   360-569-2211
    Location: Take Hwy 706 to Longmire
    Days/Hours: Daily, 9am–4:30pm
    Admission: Free
    Wheelchair/Stroller Access: Yes

There are no tours at Longmire; the emphasis is on the exhibits and displays on the biology, geology and history of the area. Longmire is one of the oldest museums in the National Park Service, established in 1928. The Trail of Shadows, a three-quarter mile loop, takes you by some of the mineral springs in the adjacent meadow; it's a 275-foot elevation. The loop includes interpretive signs and a pioneer cabin.

MOUNT RAINIER SCENIC RAILROAD   360-569-2588; 1-888-STEAM11
    Location: In Elbe. Take I-5 exit to Hwy 512; turn on the Mount Rainier
    exit to Pacific Ave./Hwy 7. Turn right and follow the arterial for 33
    miles.
    Web Site: www.mrsr.com
    Days/Hours: Open daily, July 1–Labor Day; weekends only, Memorial
    Day –June 30, Labor Day–mid-October. The train leaves Elbe Station
    at: 11am, 1:15pm and 3:30pm.
    Admission: $12.50/adults; $11.50/seniors; $8.50/ages 3–12; Free/under 3.
    Group discounts for 20 or more. Telephone reservations accepted for
    groups of 25 or more.
    Wheelchair/Stroller Access: Yes

Riding a train is one of those unexplainable, simply terrific experiences—and this one is no exception. For ninety minutes you'll rumble across bridges, through lush forest to Mineral Lake and back again. The ride passes too quickly. There's also a premier forty-mile, four-hour dinner train that includes a five-course prime rib dinner, hors d'ouevres and surprises, such as handmade chocolate truffles!; prepaid reservations required. Box lunches are available by reservation, also. Ask about their monthly special themed excursions.

NATIONAL PARK INN AT MOUNT RAINIER
Location: Longmire. From Tacoma take Hwy 167/161 through Eaton-ville to Hwy 7; follow the signs.
Web Site: www.guestservice.com/rainier
Days/Hours: Open daily, year-round
Admission: Rooms range from $87–$177
Wheelchair/Stroller Access: Yes

Originally built in 1912, this historic, rustic inn provided the only overnight winter accommodations on Mount Rainier at the time. The facility burnt down in the 1920s and fortunately was rebuilt in 1930. Along with overnight lodging, visitors can enjoy a full-service restaurant, gift shop and advantages of the Ski Touring Center.

SKI TOURING CENTER, LONGMIRE   360-569-2411
Location: Mount Rainier National Park
Web Site: www.nps.gov/parks
Days/Hours: Mid-December–April; daily (depending on snow conditions)
Wheelchair/Stroller Access: At shop only

Paradise is considered a premier destination for snow fun and this is a central stopping point. Snowshoes may be rented here, also cross-country equipment (for touring or telemarking). If you're planning to do some sledding or inner tubing, you'll have to bring your own equipment.

PARADISE INN   360-569-2413
Location: Mount Rainier National Park
Web Site: www.guestservices.com/rainier/
Days/Hours: Closes last Monday in October, reopens third Friday in May
Wheelchair/Stroller Access: Limited

If you're planning a trip to the "Mountain," you might want to stay overnight. The inn is a rustic lodge built in 1917, with massive stone fireplaces, exposed beam ceilings. And log furniture. Rooms for families with small children can accommodate up to five.

The Let's Pretend Circus at the Puyallup Fair.

Photo courtesy Puyallup Fair

Puyallup

THE DAFFODIL FESTIVAL   **253-627-6176**
  Web Site: www.daffodilfestival.net

In 2004, the tried and true Puyallup Daffodil Festival entered its 71st year. This is one of the state's revered and honored events, attracting people from all over the state. The Grand Floral Parade commands attention with over 130 daffodil-decorated floats, classic automobiles, marching bands and more. Not limited to Puyallup, they travel to Tacoma, Sumner and Orting as well. The Festival happens every April. Call the number above or go online for current information.

WESTERN WASHINGTON FAIR/THE PUYALLUP FAIR   253-841-5045
   Location: Puyallup Fairgrounds, 110 9th St. SW. From I-5 take exit 127
      (Hwy 512) east to Puyallup.
   Web Site: www.thefair.com
   Days/Hours: Daily for 17days; 8am–11pm. Always starts the first Friday
      after Labor Day.
   Admission: Varies; grandstand tickets are separate; kids under 5 are
      free
   Wheelchair/Stroller Access: Yes, strollers and wheelchairs available for
      rent

Exhibits open at 10am but the first thing to do is buy your bag of scones. Rides open at noon weekdays, earlier on weekends. If this is your first visit to The Fair, allow the whole day–it's a total experience. From the food to the exhibits to the grandstand shows, time will disappear. A discount ride bracelet for kids is offered Monday–Thursday. Parking can be difficult on crowded days. Wear good walking shoes and bring an appetite. Onion burgers are one of the favorites here. Weather is no hindrance.

The corn's delicious...with or without teeth!

Photo courtesy Puyallup Fair/Western Washington Fair

PUYALLUP SPRING FAIR   253-841-5045
   Location: Puyallup Fairgrounds; 110 9th Ave. SW. From I-5, take exit
      127 (Hwy 512) east to Puyallup.
   Web Site: www.thefair.com

Days/Hours: Four days in April (always Thursday–Sunday). Thursday, 3–10pm; Friday and Saturday, 10am–10pm; Sunday, 10am–7pm
Admission: Varies; kids under 5 free
Wheelchair/Stroller Access: Yes; available for rent

Lots of kid-oriented activities at this Fair, including the KidZone with special booths and hands-on activities. Kids can enjoy the display, Creative Kids Exhibit— fun to see how imaginative others can be. Pre-entry is required for this exhibit; check the Web site for details. There's also free face painting, pig races, strolling entertainment and the baby animal petting farm. A Puyallup School District science fair and midway rides for kids of all ages, plus the usual tempting foods and free parking makes this a great springtime experience.

THE MEEKER MANSION   253-848-1770
Location: 312 Spring St.
Web Site: www.meekermansion.org
Days/Hours: Mid-March–mid-December; Wednesday–Sunday, 1–4 pm
Admission: $4/adults; $3/seniors and students; $2/under 12; half-price
    on Thursdays
Wheelchair/Stroller Access: No

Ezra Meeker was a name to reckon with in early Puyallup. A pioneer and leading citizen, he earned acclaim for his earnest and devoted preservation of the Oregon Trail. He built the ornate Italianate Victorian mansion to please his wife (they had been living in a log cabin) and they lived there from 1890 to 1909, when she died. The mansion has had several "lives" since, including that of a hospital. The Ezra Meeker Historical Society has restored the Mansion, which is now considered a National Historic Site. Events throughout the year that appeal to families include a Cider Squeeze in October and a Mother's Day Victorian Tea. A tour of the house includes the Small Parlor, Morning Parlor and Drawing room, all authentic examples of an early elegant lifestyle.

Olympia

Places to Go

HANDS ON CHILDREN'S MUSEUM OF OLYMPIA   360-956-0818
Location: 106 11th St. SW
Web Site: www.hocm.org
Days/Hours: Monday–Friday,10am–5pm; Friday, 10am–9pm; Saturday,
    10am–5pm; Sunday, 10am–5pm. Members only, Sundays, 10am–
    noon.
Admission: $6.50/adults; $5.50/seniors and grandparents; $6.50/ages 2
    and up; $3.50/10–23 months; Free/birth–9 months

Considered the second largest children's museum in Washington, they've given careful consideration to their age groups; all activities are dedicated to what children in each age group can learn most easily. In the Backyard Wilderness exhibit, there's a Musical Garden Bench where little ones can pick up the mallets and play the slats. It's a Habitat experience here. Another exhibit, Body Sounds, is just what toddlers need. Push a button and get a cough, or a sneeze or a giggle. The play areas include Medic One, Emergency Room, and an Animal Hospital (with Spanish titles with every English heading). In the Build It area, kids can build different things; tools and building materials are readily available.

Young ones can crawl through Arnold's mouth, through his teeth and over his tongue and into different parts of the body, all scaled for young ones to play in, around and through. Birthday parties (do it yourself or let them do it for you!) and overnights are popular here; the facility lends itself well to these events.

OLYMPIC FLIGHT MUSEUM   360-705-3925
    Location: 7637-A Old Hwy 99, SE Olympia
    Web Site: www.olympiaflightmuseum.com
    Days/Hours: Open daily, 11am–5pm. Closed Mondays in winter
    Admission: $5/adults; $3/ages 7–12; Free/6 and under
    Tours: Yes; call for arrangements
    Wheelchair/Stroller Access: Yes

There's an interesting collection of aviation history here, from pre-WW II trainers up to a supersonic jet interceptor. The hangar holds about seven airplanes; these will vary each month, from a fleet of about 26. The oldest here is a 1939 biplane; there are several small jets and helicopters, too. Now on interactive display is a Bell UH-1 helicopter, or the "huey," a warbird from the Viet Nam tour. Its "hands-on" cockpit gives the youngsters a taste of reality. From the P-51 Mustang to the F-104 Starfighter, you can be assured that most kids will find this an appealing place to visit. Call about their annual Gathering of Warbirds, usually held in June. An air show is part of the excitement.

BIGELOW HOUSE MUSEUM   360-753-1215
    Location: 918 Glass Ave. NE
    Web Site: ohwy.com/wa/b/bigeloho.htm
    Days/Hours: Open weekends from 1–3pm; groups by appointment on
        Thursday and Friday afternoons
    Admission: $3/adults 18 and older; $1/children under 18
    Wheelchair/Stroller Access: Yes

Fortunately the Bigelow family saved things–for nearly 140 years. So visitors today can enjoy authentic antique furnishings, including books, paintings, photographs, tools and household items, all still in remarkable condition. The first floor of the house is the museum; family members still reside upstairs. To their credit, the original Daniel Bigelow and his wife Ann were ardent supporters of important movements such as education and suffrage for women. Susan B. Anthony is reputed to have visited them; the chair in which she sat is on display.

CAPITOL TOURS

360-664-2700 (visitor services and reservations); 360-586-8687 (Capitol Visitors services)
Location: Olympia State Capitol. Take I-5 to exit 105; follow signs west
Web Site: tours@leg.wa.gov

At this writing, several major facilities at the capitol were under construction and tours have been suspended. However, there are a number of interesting sites you can visit.

Capitol Campus: Tours are available daily, every hour on the hour from 10am–3pm. Tours are 45 minutes and free to the public.

Capitol Conservatory: Home to tropical plants and bedding plants for the Capitol Campus. There are more than 30 landscaped areas and some outstanding floral displays that change seasonally.

Old Capitol Building: Built in 1892 and the Capitol from 1901-1928. Self-guided tours, 8am–5pm weekdays. For group tours, call numbers listed above.

Temple of Justice: When in session, the Washington State Supreme Court meets here and the State Law Library is housed here.

Legislative Building: Closed for renovation; reopens in November of 2004

Executive Mansion: Tours suspended until December of 2004. Call the number or email listed above for reservations and information

State Capitol Visitor Center: Call 360-586-3460.

MILLERSYLVANIA MEMORIAL STATE PARK/DEEP LAKE

360-753-1519; 888-226-7688 (campsite reservations); 360-902-8600 (Environmental Learning Center)
Location: Ten miles south of Olympia and three miles east of I-5 at exit 95 on Tilley Rd. SW
Web Site: www.parks.wa.gov
Days/Hours: Daily, dawn-dusk; overnight camping year-round
Wheelchair/Stroller Access: In most places

Millersvania is an 842-acre park with over 3,000 feet of freshwater shoreline. One end of the park has cabins with bunks, a swimming beach and well-groomed fields for outdoor recreational activities. It's a very popular spot for outdoor camping. At the other end, tent and RV campers utilize the area. A sandy beach, a fishing dock and benches are available. Deep Lake Resort nearby (within walking distance) offers pedalboats and bikes for rent, or you can play a round of miniature golf. If you're inclined, there are interpretive trail walks lead by local naturalists during the summer months. Call to reserve your place. The park is rich with old-growth timber and much wildlife. There are signs of a narrow-gauge railroad and several skid roads that were used in the 1800s by the logging industry.

OLYMPIA FARMER'S MARKET   360-352-9096
   Location: 700 N Capitol Way
   Web Site: www.farmer-market.org
   Days/Hours: April–October; Thursday–Sunday, 10am–3pm. November–
      December, Saturday and Sunday, 10am–3pm
   Wheelchair/Stroller Access: Yes

Located on the waterfront, you can shop for almost anything here and enjoy some gorgeous views as well. Lots of free parking.

TUMWATER FALLS PARK   360-943-2550
   Location: Just north of the old Olympia Brewery. Southbound on I-5;
      take exit 103; go straight on 2nd Ave. through the stop sign; turn left
      onto Custer Way and cross the bridge; take the first right (Boston
      St.); turn left onto Deschutes Way and left again on C St.
   Days/Hours: Usually daily, 8am–4:30pm, but hours will change season-
      ally.
   Wheelchair/Stroller Access: In some areas. There is a steep gravely
      trail leading to the park with no barriers between it and the De-
      schutes river.

This is a privately-owned park in a beautiful natural setting. The concrete gunboats and pirate ships planted in the sand are magnets to children. Once down there, you'll discover more playground apparatus at adjacent Tumwater Historical Park. There is a half-mile of walking trails and good restrooms. In spawning season, a fish ladder and holding ponds are also attractions. The geese and ducks here are primed for handouts, so be prepared.

WASHINGTON STATE CAPITOL GROUNDS AND CONSERVATORY
                                             360-586-8687 (information)
   Location: Capitol Way and 14th St.
   Days/Hours: Conservatory is open weekdays, 9am–3pm.
   Admission: Free
   Wheelchair/Stroller Access: Yes

There is much to see on the grounds of our state capitol including a sunken garden filled with perennials and roses and a glass conservatory containing tropical and subtropical plants. The horticultural staff is quite creative on holidays; look for a splendid Fourth of July display (although budget cuts have affected some of their work). There are restrooms available.

WOLF HAVEN INTERNATIONAL   800-448-9653; 360-264-4695
  Location: 3111 Offut Lake Rd., Tenino. Take I-5 to exit 99 (93rd Ave.
    – just south of Olympia) and head east. Follow the brown and white
    signs; Wolf Haven is seven miles southeast of the freeway.
  Web Site: www.wolfhaven.org
  Days/Hours: April and October: 10am–4pm, closed on Tuesdays; guided
    walking tours every hour until 3pm. March, November, December
    and January; Saturday and Sunday only; 10am–4pm (last tour at
    3pm). May–September: 10am–5pm; guided walking tours every hour
    till 4pm. Closed in February.
  Admission: Daytime tours:$7/adults; $5/ages 3–12; $6/seniors. Howl-ins:
    $10/adults; $8/ages 3–12. Children under 3 always free.
  Wheelchair/Stroller Access: Yes

There are no big, bad wolves here, just animals that are revered and respected. More than three dozen wolves, coyotes and foxes are living in this sanctuary. This is not a hands-on place, rather hands-off, but the guides are well-versed in stories and anecdotes about the wolves' relationships and behavior. The Friday and Saturday Howl-Ins have become a very popular event in the Puget Sound area, plus they have summer programs, sleep-overs and youth day camp—all designed to bring you closer to them. For those who want to know more and get closer to an experience with wolves, you can "adopt a wolf" or join the pack.

YASHIRO JAPANESE GARDEN   360-753-8380
                                                        (Parks and Recreation Dept.)
  Location: Ninth and Plum Streets
  Web Site: www.ci.olympia.wa.us
  Days/Hours: 10am–dusk
  Admission: Free
  Tours: Call the Parks and Recreation Dept for guided tours
  Wheelchair/Stroller Access: Yes

Planned and created to honor Yashiro, Olympia's sister city in Japan, this garden bespeaks tranquility. Spring is an ideal time to visit this delightful little park to enjoy a quiet stroll and the pristine landscape, when the flowering cherry trees are in bloom. This park is a good example of the "hill and pond" style of classic Japanese gardens. The serenity of the garden is heightened by the calming influence of the waterfall. Japanese lanterns lend texture to the scene.

Lewis, Cowlitz and Clark Counties

Chehalis and Centralia

I.P. CALLISON & SONS   360-748-3315
Location: 799 N National Ave., Chehalis
Web Site: www.ipcallison.com
Days/Hours: Call for an appointment
Admission: Tours are free
Wheelchair/Stroller Access: Yes

I.P. Callison has been a part of the Chehalis landscape for many years. While there's not a lot of "action" as you tour the factory, there is lots to smell! For those who appreciate the fragrance of mint, this is an amazing experience. They process nine kinds of peppermint and eight kinds of spearmint; from these varieties they create flavors and fragrances for confections (candy), gum and cosmetic lotions. The mint oil industry produces crops worth up to $160 million in farm value each year, which translates into a $5 billion impact in the domestic market. Who ever thought that smelling good would be so important? But it is, and the quality of the crop is critical; their guidelines are quite strict. Peppermint is one of the most popular oils for gum, toothpaste and mouthwash. After this tour, you'll know most of what there is to know about the growing, harvesting and refinement, especially the mint distillation process. Keeping their technology and machinery current and in mint (sorry about that) condition is one of the challenges they face here. Today, the Pacific Northwest is the center in world production for peppermint and spearmint oil, due to the I.P. Callison "family."

CHEHALIS-CENTRALIA RAILROAD   360-748-9593
Location: 1101 SW Sylvenus St., Chehalis
Web Site: www.ccra.com/schedule
Days/Hours: Weekends from Memorial Day through September. Rides
    Saturdays, Sundays, Memorial Day and Labor Day; 1:00pm and
    3:00pm (13-mile roundtrip). Rides Saturdays ONLY, 5:00 pm (18 mile
    roundtrip).
Admission: For the 1:00 and 3:00 pm rides: $8/adults; $7/seniors;
    $5/children 4–15; 3 and under/free. For the 5:00pm ride: $11/adults;
    $10.00/seniors; $8/children 4–15; 3 and under/free.
Note: Dinner trains are scheduled on select Saturdays at 5:00pm; cost
    is $39.95 per person and a special children's menu (for 10 and under)
    at $20.00 per child. Call number above for schedule and information.
Wheelchair/Stroller Access: Yes. Reservations are not necessary, but
    they request that you call ahead if wheelchair access is needed.
Driving Directions: From I-5, take Exit 77; go west a short distance to

Riverside. Turn left; travel about a half mile to Sylvenus, turn left again and the train will be directly ahead.

You can ride this vintage 90-ton locomotive for a 13- or 18-mile round trip through the Chehalis countryside and a get a flavor of the journey made years ago when rail crews were bringing logs to the mill. There's something magical about a train, no matter where it goes. Here you can enjoy the signs and sounds of steam railroading the way it used to be.

FORT BORST PARK   360-330-7688
  Location: West of I-5 at Exit 82
  Web Site: www.centralia.com/cityhall.htm
  Days/Hours: Park is open daily, 7am–10pm. Borst House is open Memo-
    rial Day–Labor Day and in December on Saturdays and Sundays
    from 2–4:30pm.
  Admission: For Borst House $2/adults, $1/5–12; $10/family rate.
  Tours: Yes for Borst House. Allow two weeks; call number listed above.
  Wheelchair/Stroller Access: Yes

Fort Borst Park is named for a military fort built in 1856 on land once owned by pioneer Joseph Borst. A history panel tells the story; you"ll learn more if you tour Borst House, located on the grounds. The grounds have a forest-like environment with trees that are 75 to 100 years old, both deciduous and evergreen. It's a great place for hide and seek. There is lots to do here, with a playground, picnic area and walking trails; nearby is a major sports complex for Centralia's youth sports teams. On the west side of Borst House is a newly opened schoolhouse, complete with a wood stove, slate blackboard, and the original schoolhouse desks; the schoolhouse is open at the same time as Borst House.

ROTARY RIVERSIDE PARK   360-330-7688
  Location: Off Harrison Ave. at Exit 82, along the Skookumchuck River
  Web Site: www. www.centralia.com/cityhall.htm
  Days/Hours: Dawn to dusk, year-round
  Wheelchair/Stroller Access: Yes

This park has all the usual activities—horseshoes, trails, picnic areas, but adjacent to the park is a major attraction for teens and preteens—a skate board park. Managed by the city, there are some strict rules for usage, but it's a great opportunity for the kids who "have boards, will travel." Call the number above for guidelines; if you drive to the park, the rules and hours are posted.

COLDWATER RIDGE VISITORS CENTER   360-274-2114
  Location: On Hwy 504; Take I-5 exit 49 at Castle Rock; drive 43 miles
  east
  Web Site: www.fs.fed.us/gpnf/mshnvm
  Days/Hours: May–October; open daily, 10am–6pm. November–April;
  open Thursday–Monday, 10am–4pm. Closed New Year's Day, Thanks-
  giving and Christmas
  Admission: Fees are subject to change. Call or check Web site for cur-
  rent info.
  Wheelchair/Stroller Access: Yes, including the quarter-mile Winds of
  Change Trail

The Mount St. Helens crater is less than eight miles away, and the view from
the highway is amazing, including some spectacular spans. The Visitors Center
has a hands-on ecology lesson for both children and adults. It's literally the
"after" part of a remarkable story, for here the wildlife and wildflowers have
refurbished the blast zone, bringing new life and vibrant color to what was a
very dead area. You'll find computer games where youngster can "become" an
animal and try to live in the blast zone. There are exhibits with buttons to push
and drawers to pull out, designed with children in mind. If you want to do
some walking or mini-hiking, the Winds of Change Trail is a paved path with
some moderate grades; it leaves from the Visitors Center and offers mountain
and valley views.

JOHNSON RIDGE OBSERVATORY   360-274-2140
  Location: On Hwy 504; mile marker 51
  Web Site: www. fs.fed.us/gpnf/mshnvm
  Days/Hours: mid-May to October; open, 10am–6pm. Closes for winter in
  late October.
  Admission: Fees subject to change. Call for information.
  Wheelchair/Stroller Access: Yes, including the half-mile Eruption Trail
  (paved with some steep grades)

At Johnson Ridge, the focus is on geological aspects of the mountain. A sixteen-
minute movie depicts the eruption as it would have appeared from this site. A
relief model, with thousands of colorful lights depicting the eruptive events, is
a magnet for kids. By jumping up and down in front of a seismograph, kids can
try to create their own earthquake. The walk back to your car on the Eruption
Trail has some great views of the crater, lava dome and pumice plain.

Mount St. Helens Monument: Fees here subject to change. Call for current information: 360-274-2131; 360-274-2114.

FOREST LEARNING CENTER   **360-414-3439**
   Location: About 33 miles east of I-5 at exit 49 on the North Fork ridge
      of Spirit Lake Memorial Hwy 504
   Web Site: www.mountsthelens.weyerhaeuser.com
   Days/Hours: Open daily from mid-May to mid-October. Mid-May–Sep-
      tember, 10am–6pm; October, 10am–5pm. Closed remainder of year.
   Admission: Free
   Wheelchair/Stroller Access: Yes

Weyerhaeuser was the largest private land-owner affected by the May 18, eruption, losing 68,000 acres in the blast. The Forest Learning Center focuses on
forestry and the stories of before and after the eruption. You'll see a miniature working railroad, reminiscent of the ones that used to work around the
mountain. You'll also see a one-seat helicopter that youngsters can sit in, and
videos in the "Destruction Chamber" depicting the May 18, 1980 eruption, and
telescopes for viewing the Toutle Valley. All this is part of the story before
the mountain blew. Today, of course, most of the land has been reforested
by Weyerhaeuser; they operate the forest center with the State Department
of Transportation. Outside, the children's playground is definitely thematic: a
"crater" to climb inside of, and a "mudflow" to slide down. A small picnic area
is nearby; hiking trails made of recycled rubber tires are easy to walk on.

SILVER LAKE/MOUNT ST. HELENS VISITOR CENTER
                                    360-274-0962; 360-274-2102 (TDD)
   Location: Five miles east of I-5 at Mount St. Helens
   Web Site: www.parks.wa.gov
   Days/Hours: Summer: open daily, 9am–5pm. Winter: open daily,
      9am–4pm. Closed New Year's, Thanksgiving and Christmas.
   Wheelchair/Stroller Access: Yes
   Admission: This is subject to change; please call for current fee sched-
      ule.

Mount St. Helens Visitor Center focuses on the historical and cultural impacts
of volcanic eruptions in the Pacific Northwest. Two different movies are interesting: The Fire Below Us covers the 1980 eruption from survivors' perspectives;
Fire Mountains of the West takes you on a tour of some Cascade volcanoes in
our area. In the exhibit hall you can explore the inside of a volcano or make
your own earthquake on scientific monitoring stations, and learn more about
historic figures from Mt. St. Helens' past or which volcanoes in the world have
erupted in the last 200,000 years. Outside and east of the building, a one-mile
wetlands boardwalk trail takes you through the forest and marshy shores of
Silver Lake. It's a first-hand look at a Pacific Northwest ecosystem.

WINDY RIDGE   360-449-7800
                                          (MSH National Monument Headquarters)
   Location: A drive-up viewpoint overlooking pumice plain with views
      of the mountain on the monument's east side
   Web Site: www. fs.fed.us/gpnf/mshnvm
   Days/Hours: June–mid-October, daylight hours. Closed in winter due to
      snow.
   Admission: Northwest Forest Pass, $5/vehicle; fees subject to change.
   Wheelchair/Stroller Access: Yes; viewpoint is accessible but no trail
      available.

On a clear day, park here to enjoy a view of the mountain and Spirit Lake. Kids
like to hike up the steep staircase to the top of the hill; from here you can see
panoramic views of the blast zone. Good for camera buffs. A restaurant and
gift shop are located six miles east of windy ridge, open mid-June–September.

LEWIS COUNTY HISTORICAL MUSEUM   360-748-0831
   Location: 599 NW Front Way, Chehalis
   Web Site: www.lewiscountymuseum.org
   Admission: $5/families; $2/adults; $1.50/seniors; $1/children 6–18. Mem-
      bers and children under 6/free.
   Days/Hours: Tuesday–Saturday, 9am–5pm. Sunday, 1:00–5:00pm.
      Closed Mondays and holidays
   Tours: Yes. Call the number listed above for information and reserva-
      tions.
   Wheelchair/Stroller Access: Yes
   Driving Directions: From I-5, take Exit 79 and follow the signs to the
      museum.

Located in the old railroad depot in downtown Chehalis (now on the National
Register of Historic Places), they've kept the flavor of the building while focusing
on the history of the people and activities that have flourished in Chehalis. Local
Native American tribes were an important part of the early days; farming, logging and mining were major industries. There are four galleries of exhibits and
displays; these exhibits change throughout the year. A children's "hands-on"
area encourages youngsters to use the artifacts and be creative at the activity
table. The vignettes are permanent (although some will be changed as they enhance the Main Street exhibit that is currently a "work in progress"). This will
become five "house" rooms showcasing a late Victorian period. The Museum's
home was built in 1912 for the Northern Pacific Railway. Of special interest is
Gallery III which features indigenous Native American artifacts and a diorama
with a miniature longhouse depicting the lifestyle of the early natives. Cedar
was a primary ingredient in their culture (used for ropes, clothes, baskets and
the logs with which they built their dwellings). The small white dogs playing
around the longhouse were critical to the natives, who combed the dogs' hair

and had several uses for it in their daily life (blankets and floor coverings for example).

Places to Eat

MARKET STREET BAKERY AND CAFÉ   360-748-0875
   Location: 492 N Market St., Chehalis
   Days/Hours: Monday–Friday, 8:30am–5:30pm
   Wheelchair/Stroller Access: Yes

It's such fun to discover a great place to eat, and Market Street Bakery is right around the corner (kind of) from the Lewis County Historical Museum, so if you're hungry, it's a good stopping point. They have a high chair, a kid-size table and chairs near the window for preschoolers, and a changing shelf in the restroom. All breads and pastries are baked right there; come early (9am is a good time) and you can watch the baker mixing dough in the BIG mixer, rolling out pastries and working hard to be ready for the morning coffee trade. For lunch, the kids' menu has a half sandwich (cheese or pb&j), a drink (soda or milk), and chips for $3.95. The grownups' menu includes hot and cold salads, generous sandwiches, soups and some great cookies (macaroons, Death by Chocolate or White Peaks, which consists of shortbread and almonds dipped in white chocolate). Take a few for later; you'll be glad you did.

BURGERVILLE USA   360-736-5212
   Location: 818 Harrison Ave., Centralia
   Days/Hours: Open daily, 7am–10pm except Fridays when they're open
       until 11pm
   Wheelchair/Stroller Access: Yes

The southwest Washington (and Oregon) burger chain has outlets in the Vancouver area as well. They're popular for their sundaes and milkshakes, especially the green shamrock shakes on St. Patrick's Day. Another attraction is their fenced-in outdoor playground for toddlers and young children, including a slide, merry-go-round and bouncing rides. Kids also receive a free eight-page activity and coloring book.

Clark County

APE CAVE   **360-449-7800 (MSH National Monument Headquarters)**
  Location: From I-5, take exit 21 at Woodland; drive 27 miles east to
  Cougar, then eight miles beyond. Turn left on Forest Rd. 83; go two
  miles to Forest Rd. 8303. Ape Cave is a mile ahead on the right. On
  the map, Ape Cave is in Skamania County, but access is through
  Cowlitz County.
  Web Site: www. fs.fed.us/gpnf/mshnvm
  Days/Hours: Daily year-round. No parking at site from late-Octo-
  ber–May due to snow. Park at the Trail of Two Forests and hike in.
  Forest Rd. 8303 is gated and closed three-quarters of a mile from the
  cave entrance in winter. In summer, the cave is open sunrise to sunset. Lantern rental building is open mid-June to Labor Day, 10am–
  5pm. Tours: Daily from end of June–Labor Day; 10:30am–3:30pm.
  Self-guided tours allowed; guided tours are forty-five minutes
  offered throughout the day. Lantern rental: $3.50; last rental at 4pm,
  must be returned by 5:30pm.
  Wheelchair/Stroller Access: To cave entrance; not into the cave

This is the longest intact lava tube in the continental United States and, no, there are no apes here. The tube was named for some adventurers who called themselves the St. Helens Apes. The cave itself was created by Mount St. Helens' eruption 1900 years ago. Today the three-quarter mile lower cave is the best choice for exploring. Please note the following: in one area it's a tight fit (not the best place for the claustrophobic), but for the most part this is a great cave for first timers. It's chilly and dark year-round, warm sweaters or jackets and sturdy shoes advised, lights are required (can't explore without them) and the floor is uneven and contains sharp places. Flashlights or lanterns definitely recommended for everyone in the group (see lantern rental above). Guided tours are really helpful here; youngsters under 5 might find this tough going.

Vancouver

ESTHER SHORT PARK   **360-619-1111**
  Location: West Columbia and 8th Streets
  Web Site: www.ci.vancouver.wa.us
  Days/Hours: Daily, 5am–10pm. Closed from 10pm to 5 am. Park is
  patrolled after hours.
  Wheelchair/Stroller Access: Yes

The Esther Short Park is clearly one of the spectacular places in downtown Vancouver. Conceived and created by one of Vancouver's pioneers, the park was first planned as a town square in 1853 and gifted to the city when Short died in 1862, the first public park in the Pacific Northwest. It was the center of Vancouver's public activities for the first hundred years and then deteriorated through the late 1970s. In 1998, the city decided to revitalize its downtown area and brought the park back to life. Today a beautiful pavilion houses concerts, the rose garden and other landscaping delights horticulturists, the children's playground with Victorian-style equipment and rubberized matting (for soft landings) is a special corner, and the walkways allow for pleasant strolling. Lots of green grass and tall redwoods for kids to run around. Another stopping place is the Community Square and Carillon Tower with its stunning basalt columns and sculptures depicting the salmon's "circle of life." Inscriptions on the columns tell the Native Americans' story. Some beautiful sculptures throughout the park add to the ambiance. Note: Dogs must be on a leash.

WALKING ALONG THE COLUMBIA RIVER;
From the Esther Short Park it's a quick three-block walk to the river's edge, where the walking path, the Waterfront Renaissance Trail, extends for three miles. There's a path down to the beach, but the upper path follows the roadway, from which you can admire the ever-changing water patterns and scenery. Warning: Some of the path does not have guard rails; holding hands with young children is recommended.

FRENCHMAN'S BAR PARK   **360-619-1111**
   Location: 9612 NW Lower River Rd., Vancouver
   Web Site: www.ci.vancouver.wa.us/parks
   Days/Hours: 7am–dusk
   Wheelchair/Stroller Access: Yes

It's a great park for kids and families. With 120 acres on the Columbia River, there's a wide variety of activities available, including sand volleyball courts, play equipment and picnic sites. Parking is free to walkers and bicyclists, but there's a nominal charge for various vehicles (see Web site). The Frenchman's Bar Trail is about two and half miles and connects to Vancouver Lake Park. Both parks are located on the west side of the city.

VANCOUVER LAKE PARK   **360-619-1111**
   Location: 6801 NW Lower River Rd., Vancouver
   Web Site: www.ci.vancouver.wa.us/parks
   Days/Hours: 7am–dusk
   Wheelchair/Stroller Access: Yes

Like so many of the parks bordering lakes and rivers, Vancouver Lake Park has a special "richness" about it. The park rims the lake for about two and half miles, and there's a reserved swimming area but no lifeguards are on duty. Sculling and rowing competitions take place here; people enjoy watching from the park.

Lots of windsurfing, kayaking and canoeing here, especially good for beginners. The mountains in the distance and a wetlands are a haven for wildlife, and birds make this a good spot for kicking back for a while. If you're planning a picnic, you might need a reservation. Call the number listed above.

PEARSON AIR MUSEUM   360-694-7026
Location: 1115 E 5th St.
Web Site: www.pearsonairmuseum.org
Days/Hours: Tuesday–Sunday, 10am–5pm
Admission: $5/adults; $4/seniors 55 and up; $3/ages 12–18; $2/ages 6–12; members and those 5 and under/free. Family Fun Day once a month; kids are free.
Tours: Yes; reservations recommended; call ahead, allow at least one week
Driving Directions: From downtown Vancouver, go north on Columbia

The 16-year-old Museum is located next to Pearson Field, the oldest totally operating airfield in the United States. Anyone of any age intrigued by air flight, airplanes and the mechanics and physics of the world of aeronautics will enjoy this museum. In the main gallery are at least six full-scale vintage aircraft (still flight capable) on the floor and numerous small models are suspended from the ceiling. Exhibits tell the story of flight, from the Early Birds (1905–1916) to the Pioneers of Flight, World War I, the Golden Age of Flight, the Army Air Corps, Civilian Aviation, and Russian Transpolar Flights along with several short videos. Exhibits of interest: Leah Hing, the first Chinese American woman pilot in America, the Tuskegee Airmen and other Women in Flight. In the hands-on area, there's a Fluid Tunnel, The Forces of Flight and The Basics—Gravity and Air—six different exhibits displaying the physics of air. In the Restoration Room, test your skills at the USS Pearson Carrier Command —a simulated aircraft carrier landing. Kids at least 4 feet tall can take their turn on a Thrustmaster F-16 Flight Simulator; they can spend anywhere from ten to thirty minutes (with an instructor).

In the theater, you'll see Eyewitness Flight, an excellent history of flight. The first attempts at flight began in 1000 BC, through the evolution of birds—to balloons and, finally, man's successful attempts.

There are two good opportunities for kids to get more involved here.

One is Summer Aviation Camp, five hours a day for five days for $45. Includes two flights, building ribs for a plane, learning about weather forecasting; must be 12 and older. The second, also for 12 and older, is a building program, Kids Build Planes, on Saturdays during which they work on building a ground taxi trainer, comprised of a small spruce air frame covered with traditional linen and dope finish. Drop-ins welcome. A visit to the museum can easily encompass several hours. There are snacks in the gift shop if anyone gets too hungry, plus a myriad of flight-related items.

FORT VANCOUVER NATIONAL HISTORIC SITE   360-696-7659, ext. 14
   Location: 1501 E Evergreen Blvd. From I-5, take the Mill Plain exit and
      head east. Turn south onto Fort Vancouver Way. At the traffic circle,
      go east on Evergreen Blvd; follow signs to Fort Vancouver Visitor
      Center. The reconstructed fort site is south of the Visitor Center; fol-
      low the park road which connects the visitor center parking lot to
      the Fort parking lot.
   Web Site: www.vancouverusa.com; www.nps/fova//home
   Days/Hours: Daily, 9am–4pm
   Admission: Summer months: $3/adults; $5/family; 16 and under/free.
      Remainder of year, free.
   Tours: Yes. Groups of less than 15 may take public tours; check sched-
      ule at the Visitor Center. Groups of 15 or more require two weeks'
      notice; call the number above for reservations or more information.
   Wheelchair/Stroller Access: Yes

Fort Vancouver was the main supply depot and headquarters for the Hudson's
Bay Company's fur trading operations. When American immigrants arrived
during the 1830s and 40s, the Fort was their main source for supplies to build
their new settlements. Today, the stockade and nine major buildings have been
reconstructed in their original locations. The fifteen-minute video at the Visitor Center is a good starting place. Tours are short (maybe thirty minutes) and
very enlightening. Of special interest to kids is the bastion tower where they
can watch for intruders. They'll also watch a pioneer baker baking bread or a
blacksmith working on horseshoes. If you're there in October, don't miss the
Candlelight event.

HAZEL DELL GOLF-O-RAMA   360-694-4719 (golf); 360-694-3421
                                   (the Steakburger restaurant next door)
   Location: 7120 NE Hwy 99 (Vancouver's Hazel Dell community). Take I-5
      to exit 4 at NE 78th St.
   Days/Hours: Open daily at 6:30am. Friday and Saturday until 9:30pm;
      Sunday–Thursday until 8:30pm
   Admission: Prices vary for 18 and 36 holes. Call ahead.

Sinking a hole-in-one on the 18th hole wins you a prize here. There are two
well-lit eighteen-hole courses to play on, and The Steakburger restaurant to
console the troops if you don't play as well as you thought you should!

LEWISVILLE PARK
Location: 26411 NE Lewisville Hwy (north of Battle Ground)
Days/Hours: Daily, dawn to dusk
Wheelchair/Stroller Acess: Yes

This park is so spread out it may feel as if it's several parks. As Clark County's oldest park, there are 154 acres with a variety of opportunities for families to spend the day. Nearly all areas have picnic shelters; some have a wealth of children's play equipment, baseball fields, swimming and more. The park is especially popular.

MARINE PARK 360-619-1111
Location: SE Marine Park Way, south of Hwy 14, near Vancouver's
Blandford Dr. intersection
Web Site: www.ci.vancouver.wa.us/parks

Vancouver's largest park is stretched along the north edge of the Columbia River. Its ninety acres of trails are ideal for bikes and in-line skating, and there is delightful playground equipment for younger ones. Tables and restrooms are on hand for picnics; parking is free for the park, but there's a modest charge at the boat launch area.

The Ft. Lewis Military Museum Guest House.

Photo courtesy Ft. Lewis Museum

TEARS OF JOY THEATER   360-695-3050; 800-332-8692
    Location: 400 W Evergreen Blvd, Columbia Arts Center, downtown
    Vancouver
    Web Site: www.tojt.com
    Days/Hours: Season runs November–April; call ahead for performance
    schedules.
    Admission: $14/adults; $10/children. For subscription packages, con-
    tact office.
    Wheelchair/Stroller Access: Yes

This award-winning puppetry troupe is at home in Vancouver, but travels to Portland to perform as well. Using shadow, stick and hand puppets, they tell their multicultural stories to children of all ages. You'll usually find the parents as enraptured as their offspring; somehow puppets seem to have a life of their own.

WATER RESOURCES EDUCATION CENTER 360-696-8478
    Location: 4600 Columbia Way
    Web Site: www.ci.vancouver.wa.us/parks
    Days/Hours: Monday–Saturday, 9am–noon
    Admission: Free
    Tours: Yes. Public visits are self-guided; school tours by
    reservation.
    Wheelchair/Stroller Access: Yes

Driving Directions: From I-5 northbound or southbound, take the Camas Hwy 14 exit; within a quarter of a mile, take Exit 1 South. Travel under the railroad berm; at the traffic signal, turn east onto Columbia Way. Travel to the end of the road; turn north at the traffic circle and follow the drive around the fountain to the center parking lot.

They've worked hard to make this Center an interesting and challenging place for kids. There's a nature walk through some of the wetlands (the Center overlooks 48 acres of wetlands and the Columbia River), and numerous opportunities for learning and challenges with interactive exhibits, computer games and the multimedia theater, the Sturgeon Aquarium and more. During your visit, the kids can test their strength lifting and pushing a "virtual" water pump and taste the differences in various treated waters. That's a challenge for your palate. There's even a toddler's area with water-related games and activities specific to that age group. Check their brochure or ask at the front desk regarding the many programs, classes and events they sponsor throughout the year.

CLARK COUNTY HISTORICAL MUSEUM   360-993-5679
    Location: 1511 Main St., Vancouver
    Web Site: www.lcbo.net/clark.htm
    Days/Hours: Tuesday–Saturday, 11:00am– 4:00pm
    Admission: Free
    Tours: By request

Don't let the rumor that this museum has a ghost deter you! You may not meet up with her (a little girl that resides in the train museum room and occasionally calls for help!) but you will see artifacts dating from the mid-1200s through World War II. The building itself dates from 1909 and because the land was the site of the original Hidden Brick Company, the building is entirely Hidden brick. Just as other Washington museums celebrate our Native American heritage, here, too you'll find Native American exhibits featuring stone, bone, clothing and baskets. Early American settlements and the Hudson's Bay fur trade play a significant role in the museum, also. The Seattle-Portland & Spokane Railway Museum collection is also interesting. Here is another opportunity to understand our state's roots and beginnings.

PENDLETON WOOLEN MILLS   800-568-2480; 360-835-1118
    Location: 2 17th St., Washougal. From I-5 or 205, take Hwy 14 east to
      the 15th St/Washougal exit. Turn left; go one block north to A St.;
      turn right and go two blocks to 17th St. Turn right; Pendleton's
      parking lot is there. From Vancouver, take Hwy 14 and travel ap-
      proximately 16 miles to the traffic light at 15th St.; turn left and
      follow signs to the Mill.
    Web Site: www.pendletonmillstore.com
    Days/Hours: Store hours: Monday–Friday, 8am–5pm; Saturday, 9am–
      5pm; Sunday, 1–5pm. The mill closes down completely for two weeks
      in December and August.
    Admission: Tours and store, free
    Wheelchair/Stroller Access: Limited

Pendleton Woolen Mills and their excellent woolen products has been a Northwest "staple" since 1863, but few realize that the mills have been in the same family for over 100 years. The original mill in Salem, Oregon, dates back to 1863 and is now a museum. The Washougal mill was built in 1906 and is the busiest place in town. The products are among the highest quality in the industry, due to stringent quality control. Touring the factory takes about forty-five minutes; you're asked to be aware of the yellow "traffic" lane, which keeps your group within safe areas. Visitors will see the entire process from start to finish. The clean wool arrives in large bales, some weighing over 300 lbs (the shearing and scouring happens at the primary source). At the mill, the processes include dyeing, carding and spinning. The weaving looms are some of the most interesting; here the wool yarn becomes fabric before your eyes (often in colorful patterns), to be used for blankets, women's and men's apparel, and home furnishings. Your visit will conclude in the Pendleton store with shopping opportunities.

POMEROY HOUSE/LIVING HISTORY FARM   360-868-3537
   Location: 20902 NE Lucia Falls Rd. in Yacolt; 30 miles northeast of
      Vancouver.
   Web Site: www.pacifier.com/~pomeroy/all ^ farm
   Days/Hours: The Farm: open to general public first full weekend of every
      month; Saturday, 11am–5pm; Sunday, 1–5pm. Carriage House Tea
      Room: Wednesday–Saturday, 11:30am–3pm (except major holidays).
      Gift shop (under the Tea Room): Monday–Saturday, 10am–5pm; Sunday
      1–5pm (closed major holidays).
   Admission: For public tours: $5/adults; $3/children 3–11; free/chil-
      dren 2 and under
   Wheelchair/Stroller Access: Possible but difficult

It's always surprising how intriguing it is to look back at the way things used to be. The Farm depicts life as it was in an agrarian community in the 1920s. There are organized visits (groups, school, etc.) and open house for the general public (see above). Here, children can try their hands at grinding coffee, churning butter, spinning and weaving wool. It requires a little muscle, but they can also use a cross-cut saw, make rope, and pump water. Younger ones can feed the chickens. Look for cider pressing, hayrides and harvest fun on fall weekends. For a different atmosphere, sip tea and enjoy the special Tea Plate in the Tea room. A typical serving includes finger sandwiches, scones, soup, fruit, sorbet and dessert for around $8.

HELPFUL PHONE NUMBERS
   Chambers of Commerce:
   Battle Ground: 360-687-1510
   Gig Harbor/Peninsula: 253-834-2472
   Lakewood Area: 253-582-9400
   Longview/Kelso: 360-423-8400
   Puyallup: 253-845-6755
   Tumwater: 360-357-5153

VISITOR INFORMATION SERVICES:
   Olympia: 360-357-3362
   Eatonville: 360-832-4000
   Lewis County: 360-736-7132
   Mount Rainier Disabled Visitor: 360-569-2211, ext 2304
   Mount Rainier TDD: 360-569-2177
   State Capitol: 360-586-3460
   Tacoma/Pierce County Visitor and Convention Bureau: 800-272-2662
   Southwest Washington Visitor/Convention Bureau: 877-600-0800; 360-750-1553

OTHER RESOURCES:
   Metropolitan Park District: 253-305-1000

Southeast and South Central Washington

Celebrating Law Enforcement Day in Kennewick.

Photo: courtesy of the City of Kennewick

Early in the Columbia River's travels through Washington, the powerful waterway moves through the triangle known as the Tri-Cities—Kennewick, Pasco and Richland—where the sun shines nearly 300 days a year. The cities are nestled at the convergence of three major rivers; the Columbia is joined by the Yakima and the Snake. This makes for some major water sports activities, including water-skiing, jet-ski riding, fishing, and jet boat tours. About 50 miles east is Walla Walla; farther north is Pullman. The Blue Mountains and Umatilla National Forest are great hiking, fishing and camping destinations; the Snake, Touchet and Tucannon rivers offer river-rafting adventures. This interesting landscape of mountains and rivers challenges and tempts families who love the outdoors. Mixed into this landscape is a fertile wheat land known as the Palouse. More than just a regional and agricultural resource, the Palouse has inspired artists for years.

Moving right along via U.S. 195 to Hwy 270, you'll come to Pullman, home of Washington State University and source of one of the state's major rivalries. The Apple Cup pits the WSU Cougars (who went to the Rose Bowl in 1997 after a very long dry spell) against the Washington Huskies. Emotions and loyalties run very high at this annual football frolic.

TRI-CITIES: Once considered a secret city, Richland today is a leader in nuclear energy production and waste disposal. Pasco and Kennewick have historical significance related to the Lewis and Clark exploration. In 1805, Meriwether Lewis and William Clark camped in Pasco on their trek west and passed through what is now Kennewick, which means "winter haven" in the Chemanpum Native American language.

WALLA WALLA: Walla Walla is 50 miles east of the Tri-Cities on U.S. 12 and hovers on the Idaho border. In Native American language it means "many waters," and its fame centers around the fields of Walla Walla sweet onions. The harvest season is a busy one and somewhat brief, but the onions are incredibly popular across the country. The weather here has been described as "tongue-sticking cold" in the winter, but families who love the outdoors will feel at home. The mountains are home to elk, deer, bighorn sheep, black bear and cougar, and assorted collections of phenomenal wildflowers.

SOUTH CENTRAL WASHINGTON: Some of Washington's most fertile country is to be found here. From Ellensburg, moving southeast through the Yakima Valley on to Toppenish, the crops are abundant and delicious, from apples to asparagus. There's a rich ethnic blend of people, too. An emerging Hispanic population in Yakima has created the Hispanic Chamber of Commerce, and Native American history is celebrated in a number of areas. The cities are equally mysterious: Zillah, Wapato, Toppenish, Yakima, Naches and Selah. Past volcanic activity plus the Yakima and Columbia rivers are responsible for this opulent landscape.

Southeast Washington

Tri-Cities (Kennewick-Richland-Pasco)

Kennewick

Places to Eat

T S CATTLE CO. STEAKHOUSE 509-783-8251
 Location: 6515 W Clearwater Ave., Kennewick
 Days/Hours: Sunday, Monday–Thursday, 4:30–9:00pm, Friday and Saturday, 4:30– 10:00 pm
 Wheelchair/Stroller Access: Yes

Pretty casual here. The sign on the door tells you the whole story—"NO TIES! You wear 'em, we cut 'em!" And the display on the wall says it's true. Food is ample here, and the "young'ns" menu is aimed right at the small cowpokes. Steaks, ribs, hamburgers, fish and chips, chicken strips and grilled cheese—all kids' meals include a salad, fries and a small drink (and a small menu with crayons to color). Boosters and high chairs available; "boot" glasses to drink from. Kids really enjoy the music on Wednesday and Sunday evenings (6:30– 9:00 pm) and the dance floor invites them to cut loose. It's fun here!!! Save room for dessert—hot fudge sundaes, cowpies or apple dumplings a la mode.

Places to Go

COLUMBIA PARK
 Location: On the Columbia River banks
 Days/Hours: Dawn to dusk
 Wheelchair/Stroller Access: Yes

Like other Washington cities banked on the Columbia, Kennewick has made the most of this aquatic treasure. There's a Bike and Hike Trail, various small play areas with play equipment, a boat launch, lots of free parking. Look for the large hydroplane, mounted on a platform. In the main park area, a Water Play area just for kids is pure entertainment in warm weather. The Water Play hours are 10am–8pm. The "flooring" is rubberized; the jets spurt out, drenching anyone in the way; the water just runs right off into drains and the kids can dance around, turning water spigots on, usually with great glee. No pets allowed in the play area; in the Tot Lot there's a hydroplane, rubber tire walk (from VERY large vehicles), a tire crawl thru and more. Look for the mechanical garbage-eating goat; he'll take almost anything. Late in 2003, arsonists destroyed much of the playground area, but community-minded citizens went right to work rebuilding. By the time you read this, the new structures should be close to completion.

THE GOLF CLUB (formerly Longest Drive/Shortest Putt) 509-735-6072
  Location: 6311 W Clearwater Ave., Kennewick
  Days/Hours: Daily; 9am–8pm
  Admission: $3.50 per person for basketball: $4/per person for mini-golf;
    kids 4 and under play mini-golf free.
  Wheelchair/Stroller Access: The facility proper is accessible; also one of
    the miniature golf courses and the Bankshot Basketball.

The Golf Club can accommodate multi-talented families. The driving range is
covered and heated in winter, misted in summer. There are two eighteen-hole
miniature golf courses, and for the basketball addicts, an eighteen-station basketball course called Bankshot Basketball. Each station increases in difficulty.
The club provides one of the most fully-equipped pro shops in Southeast Washington.

TRI-CITY AMERICANS 509-736-0606
  Location: 7000 W Grandridge Blvd., Kennewick
  Web Site: www.amshockey.com
  Days/Hours: Season is September–March with 36 home games; starting
    at 7pm except for Sunday at 6pm.
  Admission: Call for current information.
  Wheelchair/Stroller Access: Yes

Hockey's the game here, and the team is part of the Western Hockey League.
Composed mainly of older teens with their eyes on the National Hockey League,
the competition is quite exciting. They skate hard and love what they do. The
Americans are closest thing to a professional sports team in this area, and it's
a popular family spectator sport.

Pasco

SACAJAWEA STATE PARK/SACAJAWEA INTERPRETIVE CENTER
                                                        509-545-2361
  Location: Tank Farm Rd. Take Hwy 12; four miles southeast of Pasco,
    you'll turn southwest onto Tank Farm Rd.; go one more mile and,
    at the Y-intersection, follow the road east for another mile. Parking
    nearby.
  Web Site: www.parks.wa.gov
  Days/Hours: 6:30am–dusk. Day use only. Closed from October 31 to
    March 25.
  Wheelchair/Stroller Access: Yes

Named after the courageous Shoshone woman who played such a critical role
in the Lewis and Clark expedition, the park and center offer much of interest to families. In the park, play spaces, swimming, water-skiing, fishing and

boating abound. In the Interpretive Center, videos about the expedition tell the extraordinary story. Elsewhere exhibits tell the story of the local Native Americans' lifestyle through tools, bowls and other artifacts.

ICE HARBOR DAM AND LOCKS   509-547-7781

    Location: On Snake River and Lake Sacajawea; from Pasco, take Hwy 12 across the Snake River Bridge about 10 miles; turn onto Hwy 124.

    Web Site: www.usace.army.mil

    Days/Hours: Dam open year round. Visitors Center: April–September; daily, 9am–5pm. Call ahead; they may be closed due to security measures.

    Admission: Free

    Tours: Self-guided

    Wheelchair/Stroller Access: Limited

Built in the 1950s, Ice Harbor Dam houses one of the largest navigational locks in the world. The dam retains the Snake River which, in turn, forms Lake Sacajawea. While the tours are self-guided, there's interesting history about the dam and its impact on hydroelectric power. You can stop inside the powerhouse and watch fish jumping up the ladder, in season. Near the dam, you'll find a small Native American petroglyph; it marks the tribal grounds inundated by the lake when the dam was built.

Richland

Places to Go

CREHST – COLUMBIA RIVER EXHIBITION OF HISTORY, SCIENCE AND TECHNOLOGY   509-943-9000

    Location: 95 Lee Blvd., Richland

    Web Site: www.crehst.org

    Days/Hours: Monday–Saturday, 10am–5pm; Sunday, noon–5pm. Closed Christmas and New Year's.

    Admission: $3.50/adults; $2.75/seniors 62 and older; $2.50/children 7–16; Free/children 6 and under.

    Tours: Yes

    Wheelchair/Stroller Access: Yes

Formerly Hanford Museum, this is now CREHST and a museum on the move. Considered a museum and science center, the focus here is the dynamic story of the Columbia Basin, the Hanford site and the history of Hanford Reach. With a new building coming, they will soon have additional space to expand their permanent exhibits as well as accommodate traveling exhibits. When Hanford, a nuclear fuel facility, was built, it was a secret city; the CREHST displays tell in great detail how Richland's people, the culture and the environment have been impacted. You'll learn much about the natural history of the region; other exhibits tell stories about "Where Does Natural Radiation Occur?" and the extraordinary actions of Richland and Tri-Cities citizens during times of crisis. Youngsters are particularly interested in the K Reactor Model and the active seismograph that tracks earthquakes worldwide. Plan to spend a couple hours here, and don't miss the gift shop. There's a good collection of books for both beginners and advanced readers who want to learn more about the science and technology. Note: CREHST shares the parking lot with the Three Rivers Children's Museum.

THREE RIVERS CHILDREN'S MUSEUM   **509-943-5437**
    Location: 650 George Washington Way, Richland
    Web Site: www.owt.com/trcm/
    Days/Hours: Tuesday–Saturday, 10am–5pm
    Admission: $3/ person. Members and children under 1/free. Adults
        must accompany all children.
    Tours: Yes; minimum of 10 people; $2.50 per person. Reserve one week
        in advance.
    Wheelchair/Stroller Access: Yes

A group of parents opened this museum in 1991, and it's been popular ever since. Children may step into outer space, dress up in costume, put on plays in the theatre, go to the Farmer's Market, pop into the Star Lab—all it takes is imagination. Exhibits here change periodically. Bring a birthday party to the Lunch Room (microwave available) and let the children have a ball. Good for ages 1–10 (especially the toddler climbing area).

Walla Walla

Places to Go

FORT WALLA WALLA MUSEUM   **509-525-7203; 509-525-7703 (tours)**
    Location: 755 Myra Rd. in Fort Walla Walla Park (west side of Walla
        Walla near College Place)
    Web Site: www.fortwallawallamuseum.org
    Days/Hours: Open daily, April 1–October 31. Closed remainder of year.
    Admission: $7/adults; $6/seniors and students; $3/children 6–12; Free/
        under six
    Tours: Yes, by appointment only for both general and school tours.
        Regular admission price charged for group tours; school tours free
        (sponsored by Boise Paper Solutions Wallula Mill).
    Wheelchair/Stroller Access: Strollers, yes; difficult in places for wheel-
        chairs. Golf cart transportation is usable here; they have cement trails.

A visit to Walla Walla is significant to the historically-minded. Walla Walla is the oldest city in Washington and was once considered the capital. Fort Walla Walla Museum is recognized as one of Washington's historic sites and received national attention from TIME magazine as being one of the 11 sites to visit to experience the Lewis and Clark Trail.

In the museum there are several opportunities for hands-on learning experiences for kids. When they try to pack a doll-house-size wagon with miniature versions of pioneer necessities, they quickly realize how challenging it was for Northwest settlers to pack their covered wagons. There's a Pioneer Village with 17 buildings, including an 1867 schoolhouse, an 1859 log cabin, an 1888 railroad depot and two reproductions. You'll also find an Italian Heritage Farmstead complete with vineyards. Other displays feature a full-size combine with a Shenandoah hitch and 33 life-size mules. Exhibits in other nearby buildings tell stories about the Marcus and Narcissa Whitman missionary party, local Native Americans, and early farming in the region. During special events, pioneer craftspeople and tradespeople are busy working, blacksmithing and baking. If you're going to be in the area during June and July, you might want to know about their kids' camps: Lewis and Clark Kids Camp and Pioneer Kids Camp. Each is a one-day event for which you can apply online.

WHITMAN MISSION   **509-522-6357**
   Location: 328 Whitman Mission Rd. off Hwy 12, seven miles west of
      Walla Walla
   Web Site: www.nps.gov/whmi
   Days/Hours: Open daily, 8am–4:30 pm. Closed Thanksgiving, Christmas and New Year's Day.
   Admission: $3/person; $5/family; Free/children under 17 and to those
      with Golden Age passports. National Park and Whitman Mission
      passes honored.
   Wheelchair/Stroller Access: Yes, except at approach to the
      monument

One of the earliest settlements on the Oregon Trail, the mission (Whitman Mission National Historic Site) is now a memorial to United States missionaries and settlers killed by a group of Cayuse Indian people during a measles epidemic in 1847. If time allows, hike up to the monument on the hill and watch the sunset.

During the summer, living history demonstrations are scheduled for visitors; call for a schedule of events. Rangers are available for school field trips.

Places to Eat

ICE BURG DRIVE-IN 509-529-1793
Location: 616 W Birch St. (corner of W Birch and Ninth Streets)
Days/Hours: Monday–Thursday, 8:00am–9pm; Friday, 8am–10pm; Saturday, 11am–10pm; Sunday, 11:30am–9pm.
Wheelchair/Stroller Access: Drive-in only

Nothing changes here, including the marvelous milkshakes made with fresh, seasonal fruits. In summer and fall, strawberry, cherry and blackberry are good choices; in other months, banana or pineapple. Of course we prefer chocolate. Locals claim these are the best burgers in the Northwest, but the local paper recently claimed that Ice Burg serves the best milkshakes in the world. It is possible—you'll have to see for yourself!

Clarkston and Pullman

Places to Go

CHIEF TIMOTHY STATE PARK/ALPOWAL INTERPRETIVE CENTER
877-444-6777 (National Reservation Service)
Location: Take Hwy 12; eight miles west of Clarkston, turn north onto Silvott Rd. cross the bridge onto the island in Lower Granite Lake.
Web Site: www.parks.wa.gov
Days/Hours: Open from May 15–September 2
Wheelchair/Stroller Access: Yes

The Lower Granite/Snake River behind the Lower Granite Dam offers a graduated sandy beach, safe for wading and swimming. The children's play and picnic tables nearby are tree-shaded for summer comfort. The Alpowai Interpretive Center tells the story of the Nez Perce Native Americans who lived here. On display are artifacts recovered from archaeological digs before the dam's waters flooded the area. Chief Timothy and the Nez Perce played an important role in the Lewis and Clark expedition.

FERDINAND'S 509-335-2141 (for tours)
Location: In the Food Quality Building on WSU Campus (South Fairway), Pullman
Web Site: www.wsu.edu/creamery
Days/Hours: Monday–Friday, 9:30am–4:30pm
Tours: Self-guided tours anytime. Guided tours are thirty minutes, offered from 10:30am–12:30pm. Reservations required; allow one to two weeks.
Wheelchair/Stroller Access: Yes

This is indeed a working university, and Ferdinand's is an important part of the campus. Stop here for delicious ice cream, milk shakes and Cougar Gold cheese made in their own dairy. In fact, you can watch the process via a video and window in the Observation Room. You can take the self-guided tour anytime, which might include just the video. On the guided tours, you will see the cheese being made, and their marvelous antique milk bottle display. Tours of the dairy farm are also available with advance planning.

PALOUSE FALLS/LYONS FERRY STATE PARK

877-444-6777 (National Reservation Service)

Location: Lyons Ferry State Park is west of Pullman, north of Walla Walla, 17 miles southeast of Washtucna, just off Hwy 261 and eight miles northwest of Starbuck. Palouse Falls is six miles north of Lyons Ferry on Palouse Falls Road.

Web Site: www.parks.wa.gov

Days/Hours: Summer; 6:30am–dusk. Winter; 8am–dusk. Open yearround for day use. For camping, closes September 22, reopens March 12.

Wheelchair/Stroller Access: No

A great adventure occurs here. As the 198-foot Palouse River waterfall rushes to the Snake River through hardened lava flows, the rising mist creates a mysterious but colorful aura. If you want to hike up the hillside, which is layered with columns of basalt, ask a ranger about the best climbing route, as the steep hike is daunting for younger children. Nearby, Lyons Ferry State Park offers 52 camping sites, located on the west side of Hwy 261. The park's waterfront activities are on the east side of the highway. A roped-off swimming beach is protected by a breakwater. The fishing dock is actually the old open-deck Lyons Ferry, used for river crossings more than 35 years ago. North of the breakwater, a dirt road takes you to a one-mile gravel path leading to a historical overlook. A nearby Native American burial site contains prehistoric human bones known as Marmes Man, thought to be at least 10,000 years old.

WASHINGTON STATE UNIVERSITY

509-335-3581

Location: in Pullman

Web Site: www.wsu.edu

Tours: Offered when school is open, Monday–Friday at 1pm. Tours are free; the one-hour guided tours start at Room 442, French Administration Building.

Wheelchair/Stroller Access: Yes

The tours are a great opportunity to climb the hills and see this popular campus. You'll stop inside the Conner Museum, which has the largest collection of birds and mammals in the Pacific Northwest. Next, the WSU Museum of

Art, and then the Webster Physical Sciences Building where you'll see the Jacklin Collection, one of the world's largest petrified wood assemblages. If you're there during the week, a swing by Ferdinand's in the Food Quality Building is a must. One of WSU's strong points is the vast number of students whose parents are alumni.

South Central Washington

Skamania and Klickitat Counties

Places to Go

COLUMBIA GORGE INTERPRETIVE CENTER MUSEUM   509-427-8210
  Location: 990 SW Rock Creek Dr.; off Hwy 14 in Stevenson
  Web Site: www.columbiagorge.org
  Days/Hours: Daily, 10am–5pm except New Year's Day, Thanksgiving
    and Christmas
  Admission: $6/adults; $5/seniors; $5/students 13 and older; $4/children
    6–12; Free/children under 5
  Wheelchair/Stroller Access: Yes

This $10.5 million center houses displays and exhibits that tell the story of the people and activity that shaped the Columbia Gorge. It's an important historical saga for our state: the Native Americans and white pioneers, the industries (fishing and forestry) and the geological events. There are centuries-old artifacts and a Corliss Steam engine that operated a saw mill, a 1917 Jenny bi-plane and a restored 1957 locomotive. Children particularly enjoy the nine-project slide show with the potent sounds dramatizing the floods, lava flows and other geologic forces that shaped the gorge, and the replica of a Native American fishing platform next to an indoor working waterfall. Youngsters 10 and older are most receptive to the history to be learned here.

GOLDENDALE OBSERVATORY STATE PARK
AND INTERPRETIVE CENTER   509-773-3141
  Location: 1602 Observatory Dr. in Goldendale on Hwy 142. Turn north
    on N Columbus Ave. at the light, drive one mile to the Y intersection,
    turn right, then follow the road up the hill for another mile.
  Web Site: www.parks.wa.gov
  Days/Hours: Park: April–September, Wednesday–Sunday, 2–5pm and
    8pm–midnight. October–March; Saturday, 1–5pm and 7–9pm; Sunday, 1–5pm; Wednesday–Friday by appointment.
  Wheelchair/Stroller Access: No

The telescope sits in a metal dome on top of the hill. The scope peers through a rotating opening. It's a 24-and-a-half inch reflecting Cassegrain, one of the largest of its type accessible to the United States public. You can see planets and stars in daylight, but evening viewing is by far the best experience.

COLUMBIA HILLS (formerly Horsethief Lake) STATE PARK

509-767-1159

Location: On Hwy 14, two miles east of Hwy 7, 33 miles west of Goldendale
Web Site: www.parks.wa.gov
Days/Hours: Overnight camping April–October; closed remainder of
year
Tours: Guided tours on Friday and Saturday at 10am. Reservations
required. Tour is about one and a half hours with about a half-mile
mild elevation gain.
Wheelchair/Stroller Access: No

Years ago, coastal and interior Native American tribes gathered here to trade and socialize. Tribal members created pictographs and petroglyphs, still visible on the basalt cliffs along the river, next to the trail west of the south parking lot. (Today that trail is closed due to vandalism.) Later, in the 1800s, Lewis and Clark passed through, camped at the village and described its wooden houses in one of their journals. Today there are 16 campsites for campers (eight with water and power) and a lake full of trout beckoning to fisherpersons. The lake and butte were nicknamed by the U.S. Army Corps of Engineers (COE) workers stationed in the area during the construction of The Dalles dam. The butte and the subsequently flooded canyon below had all the looks of a horse hide-out from the Hollywood western movies popular during the 1940s and 1950s. However, descendants from early settlers have passed more colorful stories on to the park staff.

ICE CAVES AT GIFFORD PINCHOT FOREST

509-395-3400

Location: On Forest Road 24, about six miles west of Trout Lake
Web Site: www.fs.fed.us/gpnf/
Days/Hours: Daily until they are snowed out (or in)
Tours: Self-guided. Stop at the Mount Adams Ranger Station in Trout
Lake for maps and information sheets.
Wheelchair/Stroller Access: No

It's the maze of ice stalactites dripping from the ceiling and stalagmites grow-ing from the floor in the Trout Lake Ice Cave that keep children entranced as they climb up and down basalt boulders. It takes an agile climber to maneuver through these slick and uneven passages. Most visitors are 9 and older. The eerie sight is something they won't soon forget. Inside the cave the atmosphere is cold and dark. Come equipped with flashlights, warm jackets and sturdy shoes. A staircase descends from the surface to an underground level that can be explored for 300 feet. The cave is a lava tube formed by basalt flows from an ancient volcano. Ice formations are most interesting during late spring and early summer. Above ground, there are picnic facilities nestled among the tall fir trees.

MARYHILL MUSEUM   509-773-3733
Location: 35 Maryhill Museum Dr.; off Hwy 14, south of Goldendale
Web Site: www.maryhillmuseum.org
Days/Hours: Mid-march to mid-November: daily, 9am–5pm
Admission: $7/general; $6/seniors 65 and older; $2/children 6–16; Free/ members. Groups are welcome; reservations are recommended.
Tours: Groups of 10 or more may reserve a tour; includes a fifteen-minute orientation. A one-hour tour with curator requires a fee (which varies).
Wheelchair/Stroller Access: Yes

It's amazing to find this extraordinary museum tucked away in the south central corner of our state, but here are permanent collections of great value, as well as a variety of special exhibitions. Originally it was to be the home of entrepreneur Sam Hill, who envisioned a 7,000 acre Quaker community on the property. When his personal vision failed to attract enough followers, the home became the museum. After his death, the museum was completed through the efforts of Alma Spreckels of the San Francisco sugar family. Among the permanent collections at the museum: the Auguste Rodin Sculpture and drawings; the Queen Marie Gallery containing memorabilia and the possessions of the Romanian Queen; the miniature Theatre de la Mode of French fashion mannequins; the Native American collections with rare prehistoric rock carvings; and (especially popular with youngsters) the Chess Set collection with over 100 antique and unusual sets from around the world. The Museum's Eye See Resource Room has educational art toys and projects for kids of all ages; it's open daily and free with admission. The Café Maryhill offers lunch and light refreshment from 10am–4pm. Children also enjoy exploring the landscaped grounds and sculpture gardens filled with wild peacocks.

Three miles east of Maryhill, just off Hwy 14, is Stonehenge, the first monument in the country to honor the dead of World War I. A replica of England's famous memorial, this monument was also built by Sam Hill as a tribute to the men of Klickitat County.

MARYHILL STATE PARK   509-773-5007
Location: On Hwy 97, 12 miles south of Goldendale
Web Site: www.parks.wa.gov

Days/Hours: Open year-round for overnight camping.
Wheelchair/Stroller Access: Yes

Only three miles east of the Maryhill Museum, overlooking the Columbia River, the park has two stone breakwaters creating a sheltered swimming area with a gravel beach. From here you can watch the adventurous (and skilled) wind-surfers as they catch a breeze and skim across the river on their sailboards. It's a tricky sport at best, but looks like fun! Nearby, there are 50 utility campsites and 20 tent sites for overnights, plus a boat launch and an adjacent fish-cleaning station at the park. Note: There is no running water here during winter months.

Places to Eat

BIG RIVER GRILL   **509-427-4888**
   Location: 192 SW Second St., Stevenson
   Web Site: www.bigrivergrill.us/
   Days/Hours: Open daily, 11:30am–9pm
   Wheelchair/Stroller Access: Yes

This is a good place to dine with kids. It's a non-smoking facility with boosters and high chairs, but kids don't care about that. They'll like the kids' menu, with hot dogs, spaghetti, cheeseburgers, grilled cheese, even a kid-size quesadilla. Plenty to choose from on the drink menu, including apple juice and hot chocolate. But the root beer floats or a Brownie McGee may be their favorite. For adults, the Friday special—homemade salmon chowder in a bread bowl is hugely popular here. Lots of atmosphere and interesting décor—you can count the license plates while you're waiting. (No, we won't tell you what a Brownie McGee is. You'll have to discover that for yourself.)

Ellensburg

Places to Go

CENTRAL WASHINGTON UNIVERSITY   **509-963-1215**
   Location: 400 E 8th Ave. Enter campus at the corner of 8th and D
   Streets.
   Web Site: www.ewu.edu
   Tours: Reservations necessary. To go into classrooms, make the
   request when you call for reservations; they will need to make ar-
   rangements. Tours are forty-five minutes.
   Wheelchair/Stroller Access: Yes

Usually teens are most interested in this, especially if they're considering Central as their next educational challenge. The tour is an outdoor walk past some fairly modern structures: the library, fine arts building and dormitories. But just off campus, you'll see the more historical side of Ellensburg in turn-of-the-century homes. Of special interest here is the "Chimposiums," one-hour educational workshops involving the university's well-known signing chimpanzees. Four primates—Washoe, Loulis, Moja Dar and Tatu—have learned to sign using the ASL (American Sign Language) vocabularies. The Chimposiums take place on Saturdays at 9:15am and 10:45am, and Sundays at 12:30pm and 2:00pm, March through November. Prepaid reservations are recommended (call 509-963-2244); fee is $10 per adult, $7.50 per student (CWU students and youth under 18). The CHCI facility is located at the corner of Nicholson Blvd. and D St. The program began in 1966 and is the longest running research project of its kind.

CHILDREN'S ACTIVITY MUSEUM   509-925-6789
   Location: 400 N Main
   Web Site: www.televar.com/~cam4kids/about.html
   Days/Hours: Wednesday–Friday, 10am–3pm; Friday evening, 6:30–
      8:30pm; Saturday, 10am–4pm; Sunday, 1–4pm. First Friday evening
      of every month is free.
   Admission: $3.50/each for everyone 1 and older. Family pass is $12.50
   Wheelchair/Stroller Access: Yes.

Toddlers love to come here just to play on Old McToddler's Farm. Older children spend their time trying on costumes and performing on a stage in the theatre. Other intriguing areas include the Curiosity Cabinet, Paddy Wagon, Fire Truck, and Spellbound Wall. After shopping at the Fine Foods Market, you can take your groceries to the kitchen and start play cooking! The whole family can get involved in the Forest and Lookout Tower or be challenged with the Math Brainteasers. Birthday parties here include a chance to explore the museum. Call for more information.

DICK AND JANE'S SPOT
   Location: First and Pearl Streets
   Days/Hours: It's there year-round; weather dependent
   Admission: None
   Tours: No
   Wheelchair/Stroller Access: Yes

Once in a great while, we come across something that almost leaves us speechless. Dick and Jane's Spot does that. Dick and Jane's Spot is "out of the box," a garden filled with imagination, created by two talented artists and some of their friends. Children will totally love this place. But so will most grown-ups. You can only view this garden from the street-side; peeking over the fence is quite legitimate here. Totems made of bicycle wheels, reflectors, license plates and insulators, fence posts that look like giant crayons and pencils. Sculptures that might defy definition but delight the spirit. Start at the alley on the side of the house and simply walk around, but do it slowly, you don't want to miss anything. Take your time—there are all sorts of little surprises in corners, on steps. What happens to the footsteps from the can of spilled paint? In summer months, Jane's garden is ablaze. In fall and winter, the colorful art in the garden will lift your spirits. And best of all, your child(ren) will come away with a new way of thinking about (and looking at) art.

Special Note: Please respect their guest statement; "Although we are not open to the public, we hope you enjoy viewing our Spot. What you see from outside the fence is what you see. The rest is our private yard, so please respect the fences." Enjoy!

KITTITAS COUNTY FARMER'S MARKET   509-929-0612
   Location: 4th St. and Pearl St.
   Web Site: www.kcfmellensburgwa.us
   Days/Hours: Saturday, 9am–1pm; May through October
   Wheelchair/Stroller Access: Yes

Nothing's more fun than a down-home farmer's market, with fresh veggies, fresh baked goodies and some local entertainment. There's a little bit of everything here: fruits and vegetables, plants, jams and jellies, pottery, woodworking, soaps, jewelry—the list goes on. And you can wander around exploring.

ELLENSBURG RODEO   800-637-2444
   Location:609 N Main St., Ellensburg. It's about ninety minutes east of
      Seattle; take exits 102 or 109.
   Web Site: www.ellensburgrodeo.com
   Days/Hours: Labor Day weekend; from Friday at 6:45pm to Monday's
      Finals at noon. Kittitas County Fair opens 10am–10pm.
   Admission: Tickets range from $10–$35; all seats reserved. Senior,
      group and family package discounts available for Friday and Monday
      performances only. Rodeo tickets cover fair admission for that day.
   Wheelchair/Stroller Access: Special seating for wheelchair users; special parking for strollers outside the arena.

One of Washington's oldest and best-known weekend winners, the Ellensburg Rodeo began in 1923 and celebrated its Diamond Jubilee in 1997. It's a uniquely American sport featuring some of the finest ropers, racers, wrestlers and riders in the county, and a great family getaway. You can count on fireworks, barrel racing, bull-riding and lots of hard riding. Participants come from as far away as Mexico, Australia and Canada. Accommodations are available through

Central Washington University (call 800-925-2204); free shuttles from the university and Ellensburg High School make getting there easy. Save time for the fair, with its prize-winning animal exhibits, carnival rides and good old-fashioned food.

HIGH COUNTRY OUTFITTERS/CAMP WAHOO, INC.

509-674-4903; 888-235-0111

Location: Teanaway Valley, Wenatchee National Forest
Web Site: www.highcountry-outfitters.com
Days/Hours: Varies. Call for schedules and required reservations.
Wheelchair/Stroller Access: No, but horseback riding is available for
 people with certain disabilities.

Summer trail rides, overnight and extended pack trips are the focal point of High Country in Cle Elum. Deep in the Wenatchee National Forest, Cle Elum means fresh air, sunshine, scenery and solitude in the High Cascades. It's a challenging way for families with children ages 8 and older to test their skills and endurance while spending quality time together.

Camp Wahoo, a summer horse camp in the wilderness, is for youth ages 10–16. Each camper is assigned a horse to care for and ride for the week. They learn to handle, saddle and bridle a horse; advanced work is available for those with experience. Half-day, full-day and overnight pack trips are offered. Outdoor living skills, how to build a shelter, use a compass, read a map, build a cooking fire and prepare meals on the trail. All are part of this outdoor experience.

FLYING HORSESHOE RANCH

509-674-2366

Location: 3190 Red Bridge Rd. Easy ninety-minute drive from Seattle.
 Take exit 85 just past Cle Elum; continue east about four miles on
 Hwy 970. The ranch is on your left.
Web Site: www.flyinghorseshoeranch.com
Days/Hours: Open year-round (some areas on the ranch are weather-de-
 pendent). Call ahead for reservations.
Wheelchair/Stroller Access: Yes

The Blackburn family has been in the "entertainment" business for 48 years. For 46 years they offered summer camps for groups of all ages. Today, they entertain families and groups, host wedding and birthday events and parties, and generally cater to anyone looking for a great get-away experience. For families, here's a perfect opportunity to "kick back" and play together. Sleeping accommodations here include sleeping cabins, a Log Cabin for six, Wrangler Cabin for four, tents for two, and the Tipi Encampment (Sioux-style tipi, sleeps four). On the grounds there's a heated swimming pool (from mid-May to mid-October), a cookhouse for meals (with a barbecue and campfire pit next to the cookhouse), and a large lawn for games and running around. Two-hour trail rides into the surrounding pine forest and meadows are exhilarating. Before the trail rides, your guide (wrangler) will teach you how to saddle your horse and give you a basic lesson in horsemanship and safety. Jeans and boots are required; they will loan boots for children and provide riding helmets (also required). Nearby the Teanaway River offers fishing and swimming. Bring your bikes and take an easy ride on the Back County Road. There's even a hammock for napping! Just a half-hour from Ellensburg, you can stay here and "do" the Rodeo as well. For families that like to vacation together, this is a great experience.

GINGKO PETRIFIED FOREST STATE PARK

509-856-2700; 888-226-7688 (campsite reservations)
Location: Near Vantage, 30 miles east of Ellensburg
Web Site: www.parks.wa.gov
Days/Hours: Summer: 6:30am–dusk. Winter: 8am–dusk. Ginkgo Petrified Forest day-use area: open weekends and holidays only November 6–March 25. Wanapum area open to camping and day use: weekends and holidays only November 3–March 25.
Wheelchair/Stroller Access: In some areas, but it's difficult.

It's not a rock band or a space alien or a UFO. It's a prehistoric tree, now a living fossil, that dates back about 200 million years to the Triassic period. In those days, they grew abundantly near Vantage until a lava flow destroyed them. Today visitors can still find pieces of petrified wood from the ginkgo. In the Interpretive Center, you'll find information about the gingko, other minerals and the basic geology of Washington State. Outside, an interpretive trail two miles west of the center leads you through a desert marked with fossil recoveries.

OLMSTED PLACE STATE PARK   509-925-1943

Location: At the end of North Ferguson Rd., four miles east of Ellensburg
Web Site: www. parks.wa.gov
Days/Hours: Park open year-round for day use; dawn-dusk.
Tours: Both guided and self-guided. Reservations needed for guided tours; fee is $1/per person or $36/thirty people (school groups).
Wheelchair/Stroller Access: No

If you're browsing on your own, you can visit a vintage 1875 cabin and a neighboring home built in 1908 that still contains most of its original furniture. The guided tours do offer more information and usually prove to be more interesting to children. The tours include a visit to a turn-of-the-century schoolhouse, an overview of early farm equipment still in working condition, and a ride in a covered wagon. The Olmsted brothers have been responsible for numerous well-known parks and recreational areas both within the state and elsewhere in the country. The land for this park was left to the state by the Olmsted granddaughters years ago. The park is now the site for several popular annual family events.

Place to Eat

SWEET MEMORIES BAKERY   **509-925-4783**
   Location: 319 Pearl St., Ellensburg
   Days/Hours: Monday–Friday, 7am–5:30pm; Saturday, 8am–4:30pm
   Wheelchair/Stroller Access: Yes

The fragrance of fresh sourdough and cheese breadsticks will lead you around the corner to the bakery. Located close to the Children's Activity Museum, sandwiches are made to order here and pb&j is a priority. High chairs available.

HELPFUL PHONE NUMBERS
   Chambers of Commerce:
   Asotin/Clarkston: 800-933-2128; 509-758-7712
   Dayton: 800-882-6299; 509-382-4825
   Ellensburg: 509-925-3137
   Goldendale: 509-773-3400
   Greater Yakima: 509-248-2021
   Hispanic Chamber of Commerce of Greater Yakima: 509-248-6751; 509-453-2050
   Prosser: 509-786-3177
   Pullman: 509-334-3565
   Selah: 509-697-5545
   Skamania County: 509-427-8911
   Toppenish: 509-865-3262
   Walla Walla: 509-525-0850; 877-998-4748
   Wapato: 509-877-9906

OTHER RESOURCES
   Klickitat County Visitor Information Center: 509-493-3630
   Tri-Cities Visitor and Convention Bureau: 509-735-8486
   Umatilla National Forest's Walla Walla Ranger District: 509-522-6290
   Yakima Valley Visitor and Convention Bureau: 509-575-3101
   Reservations Northwest: 800-452-5687 (to reserve campsites)

Spokane

Spokane—a great family place!

Photo: courtesy of Spokane Chamber/dominic az bonuccelli azfoto.com

Greater Spokane

It's been called the "Heart of the Inland Northwest" and its Native American name, "Spokan" comes from a Native American tribe of the same name, meaning "Children of the Sun." The city can claim some impressive "firsts": among them, the site of the first white settlement in the Northwest and the smallest city to host a World's Fair. Riverfront Park was the Expo '74 Fair site; today it offers a sparkling selection of family-oriented activities, not the least of which is the Looff Carousel (see Riverfront Park write-up later). Popular annual events here include the Lilac Festival and the Bloomsday Run, early in May, and the Hoopfest in June. Whatever else you do, take time to stroll or walk the Centennial Trail, which takes you over the Don Kardong Bridge (he's the Bloomsday Run founder) onto the Gonzaga campus. The Trail is a 39-mile long paved path (up to 12 feet wide) that begins at the confluence of the Spokane and Little Spokane Rivers, runs east through downtown Spokane and Spokane Valley, ending at the Washington/Idaho border. The path is a favorite for walkers, joggers, runners and bikers (no motorized vehicles here). Spokane enjoys four seasons, with the geography to take full advantage of the climate. Active people are happy here— there's lots of indoor and outdoor activities available. High on the list: kayaking, canoeing, recreational running, cross-country skiing, biking, walking, camping, golfing (Spokane has 19 public courses within a forty-five minute drive), fishing and horseback riding. There's literally something for everyone here.

Places to Go

AUDUBON PARK   509-625-6200 (Park Department)
  Location: W 3000 Audubon St.
  Days/Hours: Daily, dawn to dusk
  Wheelchair/Stroller Access: Yes

Shade's the magic word here, and there's lots of it. It's a spacious park with some grand old trees that provide welcome relief on hot summer days. For kids, there's a wading pool and play equipment, plus baseball fields and tennis courts. Note: Restrooms are closed after Labor Day.

MANITO PARK   509-625-6200 (Park Dept)
  Location: Grand Blvd. and 18th St.
  Days/Hours: Park open daily, dawn to dusk; Conservatory, 8am–4pm;
    admission is free.
  Wheelchair/Stroller Access: In most places

There are several "rooms" in this park, different gardens with lots of running space. The rose garden and Japanese garden are favorites, with their highly aromatic flowers and plantings. Inside the Gaiser Conservatory, displays will vary seasonally. The big hill makes for some terrific sledding in the winter months. At the duck pond you'll be expected to share bread crumbs.

MOUNT SPOKANE STATE PARK   509-238-4258
   Location: Thirty miles northeast of Spokane. Drive north on Hwy 2; at
   Hwy 206 turn east; drive another 16 miles.
   Days/Hours: Closed to camping in winter months when it becomes a
   snow park. Summer hours: 6:30am– dusk. Overnight camping ac-
   commodations June–September
   Wheelchair/Stroller Access: In some places

After camping shuts down, Mount Spokane is a major ski destination. There
are 32 runs with five chairlifts for the downhill addicts, and 25 kilometers
of groomed cross-country trails, plus several miles of groomed snowmobile
routes. Sports equipment can be rented nearby. During summer months, 50
miles of park trails are shared by hikers and horseback riders.

RIVERSIDE STATE PARK   509-465-5064 (park);
                                              509-0466-4747 (Spokane House);
                                      800-452-5687 (camping reservations)
   Location: Six miles northwest of Spokane
   Web Site: www.riversidestatepark.org
   Days/Hours: April 1–September 30: daily, 6:30am–dusk. October
   1–March 31: daily, 8am–dusk. Year-round overnight camping accom-
   modations available by reservations. For Spokane House: Mid-May–
   Labor Day; Wednesday–Sunday, 10am–6pm
   Admission: Free
   Wheelchair/Stroller Access: No

Driving Directions: From I-90, take exit 281 to Hwy 2 (Division St.); continue to
Hwy 291, turning west on Rifle Club Rd.; go half a mile and turn south on A.L.
White Parkway. Riverside is about two miles away.

Two centuries ago the Spokane River area was the meeting place for Native
Americans and white fur traders negotiating business. Today, 101 campsites,
great hiking trails, bicycling, canoeing, rafting and horseback riding attract
active families. The Park is nearly 10,000 acres and has over 30 miles of shoreline. The view of the gorge is wonderful, but the Bowl and Pitcher area of the
river is a deceptive place, with a very strong and dangerous undercurrent and
treacherous rapids nearby. Much more harmless and definitely still interesting
is the park's Spokane House Interpretive Center. Exhibits include displays from
local archaeological digs regarding life before white settlers arrived, and a
diorama showcasing the story of the thriving 1810 fur trading post that eventually lost its business to Kettle Falls. East of the Center, off Rutter Parkway,
is Indian Painted Rocks, colored traces of petroglyphs. Kids can stretch their
imagination trying to decipher the messages. Visitors can explore fossil beds in
the Deep Creek canyon area. In winter, cross-country skiing and sledding are
popular activities.

CAT TALES   509-238-4126
   Location: N 17020 Newport Hwy
   Web Site: www.zooschool.org
   Days/Hours: Tuesday–Sunday: May–September, 10am–6pm; October–
      April, 10am–4pm.
     Admission: $5/per person (prices may change)
   Wheelchair/Stroller Access: Yes
   Tours: Yes. Call for reservations and arrangements.
   Driving Directions: Cat Tales is 15 miles north of downtown Spokane.
     If you are entering Spokane on I-90 from the west, take the Division
     St. exit and travel north to the separation point of Hwy 395 and Hwy
     2 (the "Y"). Follow Hwy 2 for six miles; turn right on Carney Rd and
     you're there!

What a great place for a birthday party! But beware: the signs on the fences mean business: NO RUNNING—you look like food. NO SHOUTING—don't want to startle the animals. NO HANGING OR CLIMBING ON FENCES—for obvious reasons. This is a zoological park. The animals at Cat Tales are either rescued or retired. It's also a learning/teaching facility, where future zookeepers, veterinarians and zoo workers can learn their professions from the ground up, so to speak.

At first glance, the large Royal White Bengal tiger sleeping on his back with his paws in the air looks just like your favorite pet sleeping peacefully at home. But scratching his tummy is not an option. All Whites are born in captivity today; the last wild White came out of the jungle in 1952 and there are only 500 in the world today. They are magnificent creatures, and at Cat Tales they have a good home. There are many other cats as well, including servals and bobcats. You can picnic on the grounds, right next to the toddlers' playground (pick up a picnic lunch from The Picnic Company, just down the road). Little ones will enjoy the small petting zoo (ducks and geese, a goat and bunnies).

Downtown Spokane

CHILDREN'S MUSEUM OF SPOKANE   509-624-KIDS (5437)
   Location: Lower level; River Park Square
   Web Site: www.childrensmuseum.net
   Days/Hours: Summer, call for hours. Other months: Tuesday–Saturday,
     10am–5 pm.
     Admission: $3.75/general; Free/under 1
   Wheelchair/Stroller Access: Yes

They offer school field trips, birthday parties and group tours. Considered the largest hands-on learning facility for children in Washington's inland. They are moving to a larger facility in 2004; best to call for updated information.

RIVERFRONT PARK   **509-625-6600; 509-625-6601;**
509-456-4FUN (recording); 509-625-6632 (administration)
Location: 507 N Howard St.
Web Site: www.spokaneriverfrontpark.com
Days/Hours: Varies with each venue; call ahead for information.
Admission: Park is free; each activity has its own fee. Winter Day or
    Season Passes available at Guest Services/Gift Shop.
Wheelchair/Stroller Access: Yes

As the site for the 1974 World's Fair, Riverfront Park enhanced its reputation as a family destination. Regardless of weather, there's much to do. The IMAX Theatre has a six-channel sound system and a screen five stories high. The Looff Carousel is a grand experience, with 54 prancing horses, plus a tiger, a giraffe and four Chinese dragons. Each of the animals was hand carved by Looff himself and each is just a little different; there are only three Looff carousels left in the United States. You can read about the Looff's history on the nearby wall poster. Elsewhere in the Park, the Ice Palace is a mecca for budding Olympic beginners (it closes January to March for annual maintenance). For quiet or reflective time, you can feed the ducks on the steps next to the river or relax on benches along the Centennial Trail where some charming sculptures tell a little history. In summer months the Spokane Symphony presents free outdoor concerts; some performances take place on the anchored stage floating in the river. For updated and in-depth information about each of the Park's activities, check the Web site listed above.

SPOKANE RIVER CENTENNIAL TRAIL 509-456-3964
Location: East from the Opera House at Riverfront Park to the Idaho
    border; west from Riverfront to Carlson Rd. near Nine Mile Bridge
Days/Hours: Daily
Wheelchair/Stroller Access: Yes

The trail was dedicated in 1989 to celebrate Washington's 100th anniversary of statehood. Stretching for more than 37 miles, the paved route is ideal for children learning to bike or skate, for parents pushing strollers, for walkers, joggers, bicyclists. The trail passes Gonzaga University and continues north along the river through Mission Park. The jogging path will follow the river bank while the bike route stays near the road shoulder. Benches along the way are restful stopping points; the trail stretches across the Washington-Idaho border. It's a lovely walk, well utilized by the locals.

SPOKANE CHILDREN'S THEATRE   509-328-4886 (box office)
   Location: 315 W Mission St.; main ticket office
   Web Site: www.spokanechildrenstheatre.org
   Days/Hours: May vary with performance; usually at 1, 4 and 7pm.
   Admission: Usually around $5. Tickets can be purchased at the box of-
      fice or online. Box office hours: Monday–Friday, 9am–2pm.
   Wheelchair/Stroller Access: Yes

They usually offer a season of five plays, all dedicated to the interest of their audience. Performances are offered in the Spokane Civic Theatre and the Metropolitan Performing Arts Center. It's an entertaining series and a great way to introduce children to theatre.

SPOKANE SYMPHONY FAMILY CONCERTS   509-624-1200
   Location: Spokane Falls Blvd. and Washington St.
   Web Site: www.spokanesymphony.org
   Days/Hours: Youth Exploration Series takes place on Friday evenings
   Admission: You can purchase four concerts for $100; includes tickets
      for one adult and one child (ages 8–14). Additional series tickets are
      $36/per child, $64/per adult.
   Wheelchair/Stroller Access: Yes

The Spokane Symphony offers several musical events for children. The Youth Exploration Series (mentioned above) targets youngsters 8–14. The Holiday Pops Concert and Nutcracker can appeal to all ages. If a parent (or family) purchases a Series ticket, the child will also receive a free classical music CD designed to introduce him/her to the orchestra. If you show your membership card at the concert, you will also receive a free gift.

SPOKANE CHIEFS   509-328-0450; 509-535-7825 (tickets)
   Location: Spokane Veterans Memorial Arena; W 701 Mallon
   Web Site: www.spokanechiefs.com
   Days/Hours: Game time is usually 6 or 7pm
      Admission: From $7–$14
   Wheelchair/Stroller Access: Yes

Ice hockey is a BIG sport in this city and the Chiefs are THE hockey club. They play against cross-state rivals, the Seattle Thunderbirds and several other Northwest and Canadian teams. They cater to kids through birthday party specials and other activities. The team also gets involved with community activities such as visiting children in local hospitals and working with local elementary schools to support children's reading programs.

SPOKANE INDIANS 509-535-2922
  Location: Avista Stadium, Interstate Fairgrounds,
    N 602 Havana St.
  Web Site: www.spokaneindiansbaseball.com
  Days/Hours: Season is June–September; game times vary
    Admission: Varies; call or go online for specific information.
  Wheelchair/Stroller Access: Yes

The Indians are part of the cross-state baseball rivalries and play in the same league with the Everett Aquasox (Class A farm team for the Mariners). Because the closest big league team is many miles away in Seattle, local enthusiasm for the home team is high. It's a great family thing so bring your mitt because you never know when one of those foul balls might drop in your lap for a souvenir.

BUMPERS FUN CENTERS (two locations) 509-489-4000 (North Town);
  509-624-6678 (Riverfront)
  Location: 4750 N Division at North Town Mall; Riverfront Park
  Days/Hours: Riverfront Park open seasonally, May–September, 11am–
    9pm. North Town: daily, 11am–9pm except Sunday, 11am–6pm
  Admission: Entry is free; miniature golf is $5/ages 11 and older; $3/
    ages 10 and under
  Wheelchair/Stroller Access: Yes

It's called the Enchanted Forest, a medieval-style fun forest with fountains and greenery with an eighteen-hole miniature golf course and bumper cars nearby. Parties are a big deal here, with two party rooms to accommodate groups, and two different party packages. Party details must be arranged in advance and your group must have a minimum of six people. One package is $7.95 per child; the other, the Ultimate, is $9.95 per child. Call for details.

WONDERLAND GOLF AND GAMES 509-469-4386
  Location: N 10515 Division St.
  Web Site: www.wonderlandusa.com
  Days/Hours: Open daily year-round except for Thanksgiving and
    Christmas. Monday–Thursday, 11am–10pm; Friday, 11am–midnight;
    Saturday, 10am–midnight; Sunday, 11am–10pm
    Admission: Free; each activity has a separate cost.
  Wheelchair/Stroller Access: Yes, at the outdoor miniature golf site; not
    inside
  Driving Directions: From I-90, take the exit to Hwy2/Division St.; con-
    tinue for seven miles.

Wonderland offers activities for kids ages 2–18 in any kind of weather. The miniature golf course is enhanced with castles, shipwrecks and mysterious old mansions. Indoors there's another mini-putt, plus softball and baseball batting cages, over 100 video and skill games and Laser Tag. The climbing wall is for all ages (no harnesses provided). If you're hungry, the restaurant has kid-friendly food. It's a great place for birthday parties and other special events. For younger ones, the Rock-a-Fire Explosion Pizza Theater has animated, mechanical animals performing while you munch on pizza.

NORTHWEST MUSEUM OF ART 509-456-3931
 Location: 2316 W First Ave. in historic Browne's Addition
 Web Site: www.northwestmuseum.org
 Days/Hours: Museum and store: 11am–5pm, Tuesday–Sunday. Closed most Mondays (except Martin Luther King Day and President's Day) and most major holidays (except New Year's Day).
 Admission: $7/adults; $5/seniors 62 and older; $5/students over 18 with valid ID; Free/children 5 and under and museum members. Special rates for adult groups of 15 or more, school groups K-12. First Friday of each month by donation. A visit to Campbell House is included with your admission fee.
 Tours: Self-guided and guided. With the self-guided tour, you'll be escorted to Admissions, then be off on your own. Group rates for 15 or more: $5/adults, $4/seniors 62 and older and students with ID. Nongroup rate: $7/adults; $5/seniors and students. Note: Please leave your personal items outside or in a storage locker provided by the museum (25 cent charge).
 Wheelchair/Stroller Access: Yes, in the museum; no, at the Campbell House

The Campbell House was built many years before wheelchair access was an issue, and they have elected to keep the House in its pristine, original form. A visit to the Campbell House is included in the regular Museum admission; it's open during regular museum hours (see above). Formerly called Cheney-Cowles Museum, the MAC reopened in 2001 after a massive expansion that more than doubled the size of the facility. For dining, Café MAC is open Tuesday–Saturday from 7am–3pm. The new facility is quite family-friendly, featuring interactive exhibits and programs on regional history, Native American and other cultures, and visual arts. Look for some whimsical outdoor sculpture as well. They've scheduled some annual children's' programs you may want to watch for: Family MACFest is the second Saturday of every month from October through March; Spring Break at the MAC is in the spring but those dates will vary; and ArtFest is on Memorial Day Weekend. Call for information or check their colorful Web site for events.

Places to Eat

AZTECA   **509-456-0350**
Location: 200 W Spokane Falls Blvd.
Days/Hours: Monday–Thursday, 11am–10:30pm; Friday–Saturday,
   11am–11:30pm; Sunday, 11am–10pm.
Wheelchair/Stroller Access: Yes

The best deal here is Sunday, when kids' menu items are just 95 cents. The
meals come with rice, beans and a choice of enchilada, taco or burrito. Their
"Little Amigos" menu has other choices, too. At the table, crayons and place
mats to color can stave off hungry energy, along with tortilla chips and salsa.
High chairs and boosters are available.

THE ONION (two locations)   **509-747-3852 (Riverside);**
                                                      509-482-6100 (Northgate)
Location: W 302 Riverside; 7522 N Division St.
Web Site: www.Landmark-Restaurants.com
Days/Hours: Sunday–Thursday, 11:00am–11:30pm; Friday and Satur-
   day, 11:15am–1:00am (both locations)
Wheelchair/Stroller Access: Yes

If the food doesn't keep you busy, reading the menu will. And don't miss the
fabulous 1937 Harley-Davidson suspended from the ceiling at the N Division
St. restaurant. Proper dress is expected here; that means "feather boas and
sneakers optional." Kids get balloons, along with kid-type fare and their own
placemats with puzzles and crayons. All kids' meals are $3.99. Adults have
almost too much to choose from—and "outlandish desserts" finish your meal
in fine style. Free refills on all soft drinks. The building itself has historical
significance. The Onion is just plain fun.

OLD SPAGHETTI FACTORY   **509-624-8916**
Location: 152 S Monroe St.
Web Site: www.osf.com
Days/Hours: Sunday–Thursday, 4:30–9:30pm; Friday and Saturday,
   4:30– 10:30pm
Wheelchair/Stroller Access: Yes, into the building, but not into the
   restrooms

Tables can't be reserved here, but when you arrive, ask if you can be seated at a
table in the train. That, plus the hardwood floors and vintage collectibles on the
walls give this restaurant an entertaining ambiance. Children can order off the
menu with smaller portions for a few dollars less.

PICNIC COMPANY GOURMET CAFÉ   **509-467-0123**
  Location: 9326 N Division St.
  Web Site: www.picnic-company.com
  Days/Hours: Open Monday–Saturday, 10am–5pm; closed Sunday
  Wheelchair/Stroller Access: Yes

Boosters and high chairs are available here; you can even "rent" a basket for a picnic. They deliver daily from 10am–3pm. There are lots of treats for kids; the cookies are baked fresh daily and some of the bars are big! The Kids' special for $2.50 includes a pb&J sandwich, a cookie and milk or soda. Also on the menu are soups and salads. The "Unique" sandwiches can be ordered whole only (with 19 kinds from which to choose), but picnic sandwiches are whole or half. Yogurt, yogurt floats, shakes or a cookie sundae are the toppers. This place is fun and friendly. Even going to the restroom is fun—you can play hopscotch or track the ants. If you're running on up to Cat Tales, take a picnic and enjoy the sunshine.

HELPFUL PHONE NUMBERS:
  City of Spokane Parks and Recreation Department: 509-625-6200
  Spokane Visitor Information Center: 800-248-3230; 509-747-3250

North Cascades and North Central Washington

Success! at the Kennewick Fishing Derby.

Photo courtesy Kennewick Chamber of Commerce

The North Cascades Highway Loop is just one of the links between western and eastern Washington, but probably the most scenic, especially in fall when trees burst into glorious autumn colors. The Loop began in 1896 as two separate wagon roads inching their way twelve miles up on both sides of the mountain. Today those roads are Highway 20 and Highway 2, well over 168 miles long, and the two highways link northwest Washington to northeast Washington. The Cascade Highway Loop hooks through Stevens Pass, the Wenatchee Valley,

Chelan country and the Methow Valley; some of the most popular stops are the towns of Leavenworth, Wenatchee, Lake Chelan and Winthrop. If you're looking for spectacular views, going east on the North Cascade Highway just before Newhalem is the best way to see Diablo and Ross Lakes, descending from the pass. Traveling west, watch for the signed lookouts to catch this scenery. An average trip over the Loop is two to four days, but you can take as much or as little time as you want to take in all the sights. Note: One of winter's most enjoyable family trips is a pilgrimage to Leavenworth for the Christmas Lights Festival.

NORTH CENTRAL WASHINGTON: Coulee Country has its own distinct and fascinating culture. Odessa is located in Lincoln County. This little town honors its German heritage with "Deutschesfest," a three-day festival famous for its authentic sausages and polka music. Soap Lake, just west of Odessa, is perhaps best known for the medicinal and curative powers of the lake itself (from high alkaline content), but is also popular on Memorial Day weekend for the Greek Panayiri Festival. Moses Lake is a mecca for water activities - skiing, boating, fishing, swimming and camping.

OKANOGAN COUNTY: Almost completely surrounded by a national forest and a state range, the Methow Valley has a four-season climate. It is a hugely popular destination for a multitude of activities: mountain biking, horseback riding, hiking, cross-country skiing, snowshoeing, helicopter skiing and river rafting, to name a few! In summer, swimming, camping, tennis and golf are primary attractions as well. In Winthrop, the wooden sidewalks and western-style turn-of-the-century buildings here qualify the town for "fascinating," if not quaint. One of the tourist attractions here is the Shafer Museum, previously a log cabin in which author Owen Wister wrote his famous novel, The Virginian.

NORTHEASTERN WASHINGTON: The northeast corner of the state seems remote and the towns are small, but the range of activities is big! The counties here are Ferry, Stevens and Pend Oreille (pronounced Pend-o-ray), and this is the destination for those who love the wild, unspoiled outdoors. This is home to a major moose population, grizzly bears, bighorn sheep and woodland caribou. It may be remote, but the beauty of the country commends it to families looking for a unique experience. Do bring your binoculars.

North Cascades

LAKE CHELAN BOAT COMPANY   **509-682-2224 (recording);**
509-682-4584 (reservations for groups of 15 or more);
509-682-4494 (reservations for the North Cascades and Stehekin Lodge)
Location: One mile south of downtown Chelan, off Hwy 907A
Web Site: www.ladyofthelake.com; www.stehekin.com (for lodge
reservations)

Days/Hours: Varies with choice of trip
Admission: Also varies with choice of trip
Wheelchair/Stroller Access: Yes

Whichever cruise you select, the trip will be rich with scenery and natural beauty. There are three ships from which to choose, and a multitude of options; it's best to go to their Web site (listed above) and see what suits your timeframe. The Lady of the Lake II holds 350 passengers; her destination is Stehekin, usually a three-hour trip with several stops. There are bathrooms on board, and food service is offered on both boats, but you are welcome to pack along some food and beverage. The Lady Express, a smaller vessel, holds 150 passengers, makes fewer stops and arrives at Stehekin in about half the time. Reservations are recommended for both boats. Or you might choose the Lady Cat, the newest and fastest boat in the fleet, and she'll get you there (to Stehekin) in just over an hour. One of the boats will be running year-round, regardless of the weather. If your plan is an overnight trip, adults can carry up to 75 pounds of gear, children up to 40. Bicycles can be transported for an additional $13. Ask about their overnight snowshoe package from the lodge; it's a must for outdoor enthusiasts.

LAKE CHELAN NATIONAL RECREATION AREA   360-856-5700,
ext 340, then ext 14

Location: Golden West Visitors Center, Stehekin
Web Site: www.nps.gov/lach; www.nps.gov/noca
Days/Hours: Recreation area is open year-round. Visitors Center: open
   on days that the Lake Chelan Boat Company provides ferry service to
   Stehekin.
Wheelchair/Stroller Access: In some areas; there is a wheelchair eleva-
   tor to the lodge and from there, access to the restaurant, store and
   rooms. The Golden West Visitor Center has a ramp and an elevator.

If you're looking for wilderness or a remote getaway, Stehekin is the place. Situated at the headwaters at the north end of Lake Chelan and the south end of the North Cascades National Service Complex (Park), you can only reach it by boat or floatplane; there are NO road connections beyond the Stehekin Valley. There are a number of accommodations (bed and breakfast inns, cabins or the North Cascades Stehekin Lodge); call 509-682-4494 for more information. Camping families pitch their tents in the more remote areas of the park or at campgrounds along the Stehekin Valley Road. Day hikes and backpacking trips for preteens and teens and short jaunts for younger ones are all part of the attraction here.

LAKE CHELAN PARASAILING   509-687-7245
Location: The ticket office is at the Lake Chelan Marina (across the

street from Slidewaters).

Days/Hours: Memorial Day – Labor Day; daily, 9am–dusk. Reservations advised.

With good weather, they'll be open into September.

Wheelchair/Stroller Access: Wheelchairs and strollers must be left on the dock.

Parasailing is actually a great experience for kids. Children can ride the wind over Lake Chelan beneath a colorful parachute, sailing behind the boats towing their lines. There must be at least 80 pounds in the harness, so lightweight youngsters must accompany another child rider or an adult; the maximum combined weight is 250 pounds. The view is glorious and riders never get wet, they tell us, even when the boat slows down in order for parasailors to experience the "atomic drop." Rates are about $39.95 for single riders, $69.95 for tandems. The Boat-Load Special (six people) is $35.95 each—everybody gets a turn!

NORTH CASCADES NATIONAL PARK VISITORS CENTER
206-386-4495 ext 515

Location: In Newhalem. Take I-5 to exit 232 to Hwy 20; drive east for about 60 miles

Web Site: www.nps.gov/noca

Days/Hours: Mid-April – mid-November; daily, 9am–dusk. Other months, weekends only; 9am–5pm.

Wheelchair/Stroller Access: Yes

You'll be delighted to find this family-friendly visitor's center; they provide an excellent educational introduction to the North Cascades National Park. There's a twenty-five-minute film presentation and a twenty-minute slide presentation, each with a different focus and message. The exhibit room is designed to take you through each life zone of the forest. The hands-on displays for kids include dark cubbyholes to feel (and identify) some animal hide or fur. Fortunately, nothing bites back. There are Junior Ranger Programs offered at the center, and campground programs daily in the summer. Ask about their kid-friendly trails.

SEATTLE CITY LIGHT SKAGIT DAM TOUR
206-684-3030 (Skagit Tour Desk);
206-233-2709 (Diablo office)

Location: In Newhalem, three hours northeast of Seattle. Take I-5 to exit 232 (Cook Rd./Sedro Woolley, near Mount Vernon); head east through the first stoplight close to the exit off-ramp, continue east on Cook Rd for 4.5 miles until you reach a second stoplight; turn left onto the North Cascades/Hwy 20. Continue for approximately 40 miles, through the town of Marblemount. Newhalem is 15 miles east of Marblemount; look for the black and blue sign, "Welcome to the Skagit River Hydroelectric Project and for Train Engine "Old Number 6" parked adjacent to the highway. Parking available on the north side of the highway.

Web Site: www.SkagitTours.com

Days/Hours: Tours run June through September. Weekends only in June and September; Thursday – Monday in July and August.

Admission: Two and a half hour tour; $17/ages 12 and older; $15/seniors over 62; $12/ages 6–11; Free/children 5 and younger. Group discounts available. Reservations strongly recommended.

Wheelchair/Stroller Access: Accommodations are available with advance request.

If your kids have ever wondered where the power for their video games, television and boom boxes comes from, this tour explains it quite well. Set in the spectacular alpine wilderness, the Diablo Lake Tour brings together natural and cultural history of the North Cascades with local stories and legends. A one-hour cruise of remote Diablo Lake brings many "face-to-face" with glaciers for the first time. The "company town" of Newhalem offers many opportunities for some new experiences. Climb aboard Engine Old Number 6 and ring the bell; this announces your arrival! You can pick up snacks and souvenirs at the Skagit General Store (listed on the National Register of Historic Places). Nearby, there are old growth forest trails and pedestrian suspension bridges crossing the mighty Skagit River. If you've taken the Dam Tour previously and wonder about the changes, they've had to change the procedure due to heightened restrictions as a result of security. Even with these changes, this is an extraordinary experience. Call ahead for new information.

SLIDEWATERS 509-682-5751; 206-821-1796 (in winter)

Location: 102 Waterslide Dr., Chelan

Web Site: www.slidewaters.com

Days/Hours: Memorial Day–Labor Day, 10am–7pm daily (some 6pm closings weekdays from late May–mid-June).

Admission: For all-day passes: $14/those over 4 feet tall; $11/those under 4 feet; Free/2 years and under. From 4pm–7pm; $11/over 4 feet; $8/under 4 feet; free/2 years and under.

Wheelchair/Stroller Access: For observation only

You won't have far to look to find Slidewaters; it's just up the hill as you enter town. The water park features 10 waterslides and a Kids' Aqua Zoo, plus a 60-person spa. Those 7 and younger must have an adult along. Shower rooms and lockers available, as well as outside picnic areas.

SUN MOUNTAIN LODGE   800-572-0493; 509-996-2211
  Location: 604 Patterson Lake Rd., seven miles west of Hwy 20
  Web Site: www.sunmountainlodge.com
  Days/Hours: Overnight accommodations available year-round. Two-
    night minimum on weekends; three-night minimum on holidays
  Wheelchair/Stroller Access: Yes

Located on the east side of the North Cascades, there is a plethora of family-type activities to be enjoyed here. Not the least of these are horseback riding, whitewater rafting trips on the Methow River, mountain bike tours, guided hikes and fly fishing classes. There are special programs for kids during summer months and on holidays. You'll also find tennis courts, two playgrounds, a swimming pool and a hot tub. In winter months, more than 50 miles of cross-country ski trails start just outside the lodge's front door. On Patterson Lake there are 13 cabins with cooking facilities, which are very popular with families: five are two-bedroom, seven are one-bedroom.

Leavenworth

Places to Go

ICICLE JUNCTION FAMILY FUN CENTER AND ENTERTAINMENT PARK
     800-538-2438, ext. 428; 509-548-2400
  Location: 565 Hwy 2
  Web Site: www.iciclejunction.com
  Days/Hours: November–March, open daily; Monday–Friday, 3pm–9pm,
    Saturday and Sunday, 10am–9pm. April–October, open daily,
    10am–10pm.
  Admission: Park itself is free; each activity has a separate admission
    fee.
  Wheelchair/Stroller Access: Yes

Icicle Junction is a welcome addition to this delightful town – a place dedicated to kids of all ages. There are kiddie rides for toddlers in the plaza, an eighteen-hole miniature golf course (with a Bavarian church, castle and barn), a Bumper Boat Lagoon with remote control boats, and an Excursion Train that runs around the outskirts of the amusement center (to the delight of those on board). The train runs over a small trestle and a fish pond with koi waiting to be fed (ask for fish food before you climb on board). For the older kids there's an indoor Interactive Game Center and Indoor Jumpshot Basketball; for the whole family, a small theater with movies you can all watch. Snack bar and concessions, too. You can test your rock climbing skills at the 25-foot Pinnacle; safety gear is provided. Wander around—there's a lot to see. If you're looking for getaways, ask about their overnight packages with the Icicle Inn next door (800-538-2438). Note: Pets are not welcome here.

LEAVENWORTH NATIONAL FISH HATCHERY
Location: 12790 Fish Hatchery Rd. At the west edge of Leavenworth, turn south from Hwy 2 onto Icicle Road; continue for one and half miles; turn left at the fish hatchery sign.
Web Site: www.leavenworth.fws.gov/
Days/Hours: Daily, 8am–4pm
Wheelchair/Stroller Access: Yes

The adult salmon return to the hatchery in June and July; spawning takes place from late August through early September, and the young salmon are released in April. Displays in the hatchery lobby describe the salmon's environmental needs. In good weather, try the Icicle Creek Interpretive Trail, a one-mile loop that explores the history, environment and wildlife of the hatchery and the creek. Watch for the Wenatchee River Salmon Festival in September.

THE HAT SHOP
Location: 719 Front St., next to the Wood Shop
Days/Hours: Seasonal; hours vary
Wheelchair/Stroller Access: Yes, but very narrow aisles here

If you have a thing for hats, you can get lost in here, with over 1,000 to browse through, including one that is the Cat in the Hat. There's lots for kids to choose from on the back wall, but be sure to look up—that's where the surprises are!

THE NUTCRACKER MUSEUM   509-548-4573; 800-892-3989
Location: 735 Front St.
Web Site: www.nutcrackermuseum.com
Days/Hours: May 1–October 31; daily, 2pm–5pm. November 1–April 30; weekends only; 2pm–5pm
Admission: $2.50/adults; $1/students; Free/5 and under
Tours: For groups of 10 or more, $2 each (guides and drivers free). Groups larger than 25 will need special arrangements.
Wheelchair/Stroller Access: Yes; look for the lift as you enter at the street level.

Some people miss this phenomenal museum simply because it's not on street level, but up a flight of stairs. Don't miss it—it's an amazing collection of over 5,000 nutcrackers from around the world, from six-foot Karl to the tiny carving on the head of a matchstick. An interesting fifteen-minute video tells about the world of nutcrackers, their history and success. The oldest nutcracker dates from 1569 and depicts Francis I; the oldest known nutcracker is a stone believed to be between 4000 and 8000 years old. If you're in a buying mood, there are some for sale. Your host is Arlene Wagner; she knows everything there is to know about nutcrackers!

Places to Eat

ROCKY MOUNTAIN CHOCOLATE SHOP
Location: 636 Front St.
Days/Hours: Varies from winter to summer
Tours: Yes, mostly weekends, some weekdays. Reservations requested; call at least one week in advance. No age minimum; groups up to 20. Families welcome.
Wheelchair/Stroller Access: Yes

They make 40 percent of their fudge, but caramel apples are a big favorite here with flavors such as apple pie, apple with cinnamon and sugar, white chocolate, Rocky Road and more. On the tour, the kids get to help make fudge and then taste it! For little ones, they'll find other activities to enjoy. Look for the chocolate bears here—dark, milk and white—and their peanut-butter bucket.

THE SOUP CELLAR   509-548-6300
Location: 725 Front St.
Days/Hours: Daily for lunch and dinner; Sunday–Thursday, 11am–3pm, Friday and Saturday, 11am–8pm.
Wheelchair/Stroller Access: No; access is down a steep stairway

A good stopping place for something quick and hot (or in summer, something cool). They have soup and salad combos and sandwiches, with German potato salad and German sausage. But the specialty here is white chili. The Child's Plate can be a hot dog or pb&j with chips, applesauce and carrot sticks for those 12 and under. A real curiosity here is the dollar bills on the beams, over 5,000 of them, mostly written on. If you're sitting in a booth, the story of the bills is on the wall over your table. Service is cafeteria style.

THE TAFFY SHOP 509-548-4857
Location: 725 Front St.
Days/Hours: Seasonal; hours vary
Wheelchair/Stroller Access: Yes

If you time it just right, the taffy-pulling machine in the window pulls the sweet stuff while you watch. There are barrels and barrels of saltwater taffy, and buckets of other sweets. If you're looking for decorated cans and tins, there's shelves full with all shapes and sizes. Some are replicas of bygone food labels and well-known food purveyors. Perfect for gifts.

MORE OUTDOOR FUN
Art in the Park: In downtown Leavenworth, from May to October, the ongoing art festival brings out some pretty amazing talent.

Blackbird Island: This is where the locals go swimming in summer. No life-guard here, just common sense. Also enjoy an easy two and a half mile walk along the Wenatchee River. Driving directions: Drive west from town on Hwy 2; turn left at the yellow blinking light. Turn right on Commercial St; go two blocks to the parking lot.

EAGLE CREEK RANCH 509-548-7798; 800-221-7433
Location: Eagle Creek Rd; call for driving directions.
Web Site: www.eaglecreek.ws
Days/Hours: Open year-round
Admission: Four-mile horse ride/$25.93 per person; Six-mile ride/$38.88 per person; Four-hour ride/$69.45 per person (some experience needed). Wagon rides: $15/adults; $7.50/ages 3–12; Free/2 and under. Sleigh rides: $14.82/adults; children 12 and under/half price; 2 and under/free. Ask about their packages and discounts for larger groups.

Horseback riding is the appeal here; you can take guided trail rides in spring, summer and fall. The four-mile ride is approximately an hour and twenty minutes, good for ages 6 years and up, no experience necessary. The six-mile ride is for ages 10 and up, and the biggie, the four-hour ride, requires you to have some experience and be able to mount your horse unassisted. There is an all-day ride for the more experienced. The longer rides will take you several thousand feet above the ranch into alpine terrain with some spectacular views. The wagon rides around the ranch (for the less adventurous) are only for groups of 10 or more. Sleigh rides in winter months here are another "specialty of the house"—see the information above. They also offer hourly sleigh rides from 10am–4pm. Hot spiced cider is waiting at the end of the ride.

RED TAIL CANYON FARM 509-548-4512; 800-678-4512
Location: Two and half miles north of Leavenworth. From downtown Leavenworth, take Chumstick Hwy 209 to the left, turn on Freund Canyon Road. Turn right at Red-Tail Canyon Farm sign.
Web Site: www.redtailcanyonfarm.com
Days/Hours: Open daily by reservation
Wheelchair/Stroller Access: Yes

This is a working Belgian Draft horse farm; they offer old-fashioned horse-drawn hayrides and sleigh rides taking you "over the meadow and through the woods" (their words). They can accommodate a family of four or up to groups of 44. In cold months, November to March, you'll enjoy a hot chocolate after the ride. In the summer months, you can relax by a bonfire and enjoy a homecooked barbecue, served inside a large Indian tipi. If you want to stay overnight, their Guest House sleeps up to eight; stay right on the farm and help with the chores if you'd like! Their Western Birthday Party comes complete with cowboy hat and rope you make yourself.

OTHER RESOURCES
Icicle Outfitters and Guides; 509-763-3647 or 669-4909. Open from May 1–September 30, they offer two-mile guided trail rides for $16/person and five-mile rides for $32/person. Please call for special prices for kids or families.

Mountain Springs Lodge: 509-763-2713; 800-858-2270. They offer guided trail rides, priced individually. Winter sleigh rides offered daily, December through February. A wagon-ride requires a minimum of 10 people; you must reserve in advance. For a two-mile, 40-minute trail ride, the fee is $16/person, kids must be 8 or older. Guides are provided.

Wenatchee

LAKE WENATCHEE STATE PARK
509-763-3101;
888-CAMPOUT (campsite reservations)
Location 21588A Hwy 207; 22 miles north of Leavenworth, 20 miles east of Stevens Pass
Web Site: www.parks.wa.gov
Days/Hours: 8am–dusk; overnight camping accommodations year-round
Wheelchair/Stroller Access: Yes
Driving Directions: From Hwy 2 turn north on Hwy 207 North. Drive another four miles to the park.

This park offers an incredible variety of activities year-round. In winter, cross-country skiers, snowshoers and snowboarders take over. Come spring, horseback riding, camping, hiking and the picnickers come roaring in. At the lake's southeast corner, there's swimming, water-skiing, fishing both from boats and the bank, scuba diving and windsurfing. Warning: Bring mosquito repellent for the summer months.

LINCOLN ROCK STATE PARK
509-884-8702;
888-CAMPOUT (campsite reservations)
Location: 13253 St. Rte. 2; seven miles north of East Wenatchee, on the eastern bank of Lake Entiat
Web Site: www.parks.wa.gov
Days/Hours: Closes October 20; reopens March 12; during season, open daily, 6:30am–dusk
Wheelchair/Stroller Access: Yes

Outdoor activities for everyone makes this one of the 10 most popular parks in the state. There are baseball and soccer fields for older kids, play equipment for the younger ones. Lake Entiat, created from the Columbia River by the building of Rocky Reach Dam, offers water-skiing, a swimming area with a shallow wading section, and picnic tables nearby. Within walking distance of the water are three loops with close to 90 campsites. Someone with a good imagination thought the nearby basalt cliffs look like Abraham Lincoln (thus the park's name). Do you agree?

MISSION RIDGE   509-663-6543
Location: Twelve miles southwest of Wenatchee
Web Site: www.missionridge.com
Days/Hours: Open from December 6 to April 4; daily, 9am–4pm. Can be earlier depending on snow conditions.
Wheelchair/Stroller Access: Yes

Located on the eastern slope of the Cascade Mountains and easily one of the state's most popular ski and snowboarding areas, Mission ridge offers 35 designated ski runs; most are at least one mile or more, the longest nearly three miles. Their Kids' Club Ski School is for ages 4–12 and is considered one of the best in the state. Programs are designed for both half-day and full-day activities; prices range from $38 up. For skiing parents, there is childcare for ages 3 months to 6 years; call for current fees. There is a safe ski zone for beginners. Inside the Lodge, you can get hot lunches and après ski snacks.

Wenatchee is so close that there are a number of good lodging and skiing packages to choose from; many of the lodging properties allow children 12 and under to stay free. A new Terrain Park (the B24) for skiers and snowboarders has been opened at the top of Katsuk off Chair 2, complete with rails and jumps.

WENATCHEE VALLEY MUSEUM AND CULTURAL CENTER 509-664-3340
Location: 127 S Mission St., in downtown Wenatchee
Web Site: www.wenatcheevalleymuseum.com
Days/Hours: Open year-round, except for some holidays. Tuesday – Saturday, 10am-4pm. The first Friday of the month is free to the public (donations always welcomed).
Admission: $3/adults; $2/seniors; $1/students
Wheelchair/Stroller Access: Yes; there is a ramp from the loading dock between the two buildings and a ramp behind the annex leading into the Apple Exhibit. A buzzer at the back door of the main building alerts the front desk to visitors waiting at the dock.
Tours: Guided group tours available for 10 or more; call ahead for reservations

The Museum is actually housed in two buildings (formerly post offices), with a sky bridge linking the main museum to an annex featuring art exhibits and the marvelous Apple Industry Heritage display. This is where kids will want to spend most of their time; the apple sorter, part of the 1920s vintage packing line, delights them. This is how the apple industry prepared their product for market in the early days, starting with the wiper which cleans the apples. In those days they were still spraying with arsenic. On the sorting table the apples (the display as authentic as possible, they are weighted differently to depict how an actual apple would weigh based on its water content and size); today it's all done by computers and specialized technology. The catapult shoots the apples into the appropriate bin. The guide explains the entire process, taking the apples from orchard to shipping. With all the improvements made in this process, it's no wonder our apples arrive at market in such good condition.

Elsewhere in the museum you'll find displays that "walk" you through a pioneer home with turn-of-the-century furnishings, a pioneer workshop and a trading store. Look for the certificate that declares that as of November 10, 1997, Wenatchee holds the record for the world's largest apple pie (weighing in at over 34,000 pounds). Another great attraction here is the coin-operated miniature Great Northern Railway. Don't miss this excellent museum when you visit Wenatchee—you'll learn some amazing things about this part of the state.

OHME GARDENS   509-662-5785
   Location: 3327 Ohme, right near the junction of Hwy 2 and
      Hwy 97
   Web Site: www.ohmegardens.com
   Days/Hours: April 15–October 15, 9am–7pm; other, 9am–6pm
      Admission: $6/adults; $3/ages 7–17; 6 and under/free.
   Wheelchair/Stroller Access: No

Herman Ohme created a lush, bountiful, green abundance on a hillside dramatic for its stark, natural earth tones. The garden walk is 400 feet short of a mile and takes about an hour, but it is taxing in places and the stone benches and rest facilities are opportune. The emphasis is on greenery, with trees, plants and existing rock formations creating small environments, from a lush rain forest and shaded fern retreat. In 1939, the gardens were opened to the public and belong now to the state of Washington. The spectacular view of the valley, the Cascade Mountains and the Columbia River is ample reason to return here often.

Note: No food and no pets, please.

RIVERFRONT PARK   509-664-3396 (Ice Arena)
   Location: 2 Fifth St., downtown Wenatchee
   Days/Hours: Park is open year-round. Ice Arena: October–April; Monday and Wednesday, 4pm–5:30pm; Tuesday and Thursday, 11:30am–1pm; adults only, 7pm–8:30pm; Friday, 7pm–10pm; Saturday and Sunday, 1pm–3pm, 7pm–9pm. Admission: Park is free. Ice Arena: $4/adults and children over 4; $2/seniors and children 3 and under; skate rental/$2. Family rate (immediate only): $20 limit (includes skate rental).
   Wheelchair/Stroller Access: Yes
   Driving Directions: Going north on Wenatchee Ave., turn right on Fifth St. It runs right into the park. There is ample parking.

If a city has a jewel in its crown, Riverfront is Wenatchee's. This glorious park belongs to everyone, and everyone enjoys it. There are people of all ages from moms with toddlers to students working at picnic tables to very active seniors briskly walking the Trail – but there are quiet and reflective places, too. Bordering the Columbia River, the scenery is captivating and the river provides ever-changing scenery as well. The Xeriscape, a low-water-use demonstration garden, is an excellent example of how to plant a beautiful garden while saving up to 80% in landscape water use. The Farmer's Market is open Wednesday and Saturday from 8am–noon. The Ice Arena located in the park is open from October until April (see above). The grand old maples have some huge limbs, great for low-level climbing. You might have a conversation with Captain Alexander Griggs; his statue depicts him walking from home to work (his shipyard was located nearby on the river). The "thumbs up" means it's a good day to sail. There are two foot bridges into the park from Northern Ave. If you're hungry, stop at the Petriola Bread Company for sustenance (see Places to Eat).

The park's pathways link to two bridges spanning the Columbia River, offering a 15-mile trail loop (for biking, skating or walking). If you've brought along a watercraft, the park has a large boat ramp for river access. In season, 40 lb king salmon have been caught just off the park.

WENATCHEE RIVERFRONT RAILWAY   509-664-3340
   Location: 155 N Worthen St.
   Days/Hours: Runs 1–5pm on weekends, weather permitting; April through October, once in December and on selected holidays. Admission: $1 donation
   Wheelchair/Stroller Access: Difficult for wheelchairs; kids can be lifted out of strollers to sit on a parent's lap.

It's a five-minute run around a 500-foot (approximate) track with an authentic engine pulling the railcars on this mini-train trip. Birthday Runs are available by arrangement; call Dave at 509-889-0929 or Sid at 509-663-4495 to book your party.

ROCKY REACH DAM   509-663-8121 ext 6645, weekdays;
                                        509-663-7522, weekends

Location: On Hwy 97A, seven miles north of Wenatchee on the Columbia River

Web Site: www.chelanpud.org

Days/Hours: February 15 – November 30; 8:15am – 5:45pm

Admission: Free

Tours: Self-guided at all times. Guided tours for groups during May through September. Please call ahead to make arrangements for groups of 10 or more.

Wheelchair/Stroller Access: Yes

Rocky Reach is a fascinating place with several areas of interest you don't want to miss. Beginning at the "bottom" or downstairs, the Fish Ladder allows you to view large fish swimming in river water as they make their way through the Columbia River project on their way upstream to spawn. You'll see eels and other marine life, as well. The four types of fish most commonly seen here are Coho, sockeye, Chinook and steelhead trout. The best times to see them are: steelhead in September, Chinook in May and August, sockeye in July. You can watch videos in the theater; most are about ten minutes. New is the juvenile fish bypass system designed to help young fish work their way safely downstream past the dam. On the fourth floor of the powerhouse, the Gallery of the Columbia depicts early life along the Columbia, and exhibits explain aspects of hydropower. Walking from the Visitor Center to the powerhouse, the outlook from the walkway is spectacular. You'll overlook the grounds, the river, the dam and surrounding scenery. If you want to picnic on the grounds, shelters are available by reservation (call ahead).

Notes: No pets allowed; no food or drink allowed in the powerhouse but there is a café in the Visitor Center that is open seasonally. Leave personal items securely in your vehicle. Large bags, backpacks, umbrellas and weapons are prohibited. With new security provisions in place, you will pass through a metal detector in the Visitor Center.

Places to Eat

PETRIOLA BREAD COMPANY   509-664-9079

Location: One 5th St. #160. At the end of 5th St. in the Riverfront Center

Days/Hours: Monday–Friday, 7am–5:30pm; Saturday, 7am–4pm. Closed Sunday

Wheelchair/Stroller Access: Yes

PETRIOLA means reward, and the freshly baked bread and pretzels here are definitely a reward for hungry mouths. A sample of one of their fresh breads awaits you; butter is handy if you want. Except for a few specialty breads, most are made without oils, fats or eggs, so indulging can be healthy! If you want to picnic, sandwiches, soups and salads and some great cookies are on the menu. A cinnamon roll and a steaming espresso after a morning stroll ....enough said.

Cashmere

APLETS AND COTLETS CANDY KITCHEN   509-782-4088
   Location: 17 Mission St., one block off Cottage Ave., about 10 miles east
      of Leavenworth, off Hwy 2
   Web Site: www.libertyorchards.com
   Days/Hours: April – December: Monday–Friday, 8am–4:30pm; Saturday
      and Sunday, 10am–4pm. January – March: Monday – Friday, 8:30am–
      4:30pm
   Wheelchair/Stroller Access: Yes
   Tours: Every twenty minutes

Two Armenian immigrants founded this Washington landmark. Known in the beginning as Turkish Delights, the first batch of Aplets and Cotlets were mixed in an aluminum kettle on their kitchen stove. Today there are more than 20 different flavors (some are nut-free and sugar-free), and the family's third generation is running the business. Tours start in the sorting room where the nuts are carefully culled. The candy is guaranteed 100% shell-free, so this is a key site. Huge kettles holding 256 pounds of candy are next; the hot mixture is poured onto wooden trays, rolled level and cooled for up to 10 hours, then cut into bite-size pieces. Rolling those pieces into powdered sugar is the final step, and, of course, you'll get a sample. Don't hesitate to ask questions! You can purchase products in the country store. If you tour on a weekend, you'll miss the production line.

THE WALKING ARBORETUM OF CASHMERE
This is a one-and-two-thirds-mile self-guided tour that begins and ends on Cottage Avenue. You'll see picturesque streets and homes, a mini-view of this charming town, with 60 different trees that can be identified. Pick up a "Walking Arboretum" brochure at the Visitors' Center or stores in town.

CASHMERE MUSEUM AND PIONEER VILLAGE   509-782-3230
   Location: 600 Cotlets Way
   Web Site: www.cashmeremuseum.com
   Days/Hours: March 1 – October 31: daily, 9:30am–4:30. Closed November thru February.

Admission: $4.50/adults; $3.50/seniors and students; $2.50/ages 5 – 12; under 5/free

Tours: Guided tours available; schedule with the museum via telephone or email (check Web site)

Wheelchair/Stroller Access: Yes

The admission is small, considering they are almost entirely self-supporting through the Chelan County Historical Society. Donations are much appreciated. Docents dressed in pioneer clothing lead the one-hour guided tours. Twelve cabins present a fascinating look back into their history. You may see an old print shop in action, or try your hand at using a goose-quill pen. You'll also see an 1891 waterwheel. They are now growing herbs and flowers on the grounds, as well. The museum has an extraordinary collection of Native American artifacts reflecting lifestyle and environment, some dating back 9,000 years. Look for their displays of semi-precious stones and other minerals from the surrounding area. The wildlife, geology and natural history of North Central Washington are illuminating. Don't miss this as you travel through.

North Central Washington and Coulee Country

GRANT COUNTY HISTORICAL MUSEUM AND VILLAGE   509-754-3334

Location: 742 Basin St. NW. From Seattle, take I-90 to exit 151 to Hwy 283 to Ephrata. From Spokane westbound, take I-90 to exit 179 (Hwy 17) to Ephrata.

Web Site: www.ohwy.com/wa/g/grachspv.htm

Days/Hours: Monday–Saturday, 10am–5pm, closed Wednesday; Sunday, 1pm–4pm

Admission: $2/adults; $1.50/children 6–15; Free/children 5 and under

Wheelchair/Stroller Access: Yes

On the second weekend of June and the last Saturday of September, this becomes a living museum, with pioneers plying their trades in the village's 28 cabins and public buildings. Some have been moved here from their original sites; the village includes a church, one-room school house, jail, bank, print shop, blacksmith, dress shop, even an old-time saloon, with a completely authentic pioneer homestead. You can wander in and out of the buildings at your leisure; grandparents can talk about the "good old days." On those weekends, there is also a petting zoo.

Okanogan County

Places to Go

OMAK STAMPEDE AND SUICIDE RACE   509-826-1002; 800-933-6625
  Location: Omak is 60 miles north of Chelan on Hwy 97, or 50 miles
    southwest of Grand Coulee Dam via Hwy 155.
  Web Site: www.omakstampede.org
  Days/Hours: Annually, second weekend in August
    Admission: Tickets required for many events; call ahead.
  Wheelchair/Stroller Access: In some areas

The Stampede is a week-long event featuring four performances by real cow-boys (members of the Professional Rodeo Cowboys Association), grand and kiddy parades, a carnival, 5K Run and a Native American encampment and trib-al dance competition. And, of course, the well-publicized, electrifying Suicide Race. Whatever your personal attitude, it's a colorful and unusual experience. Visitors are welcome to browse around the teepees at the Native American village. The quaint little town of Omak is within walking distance. There are nearly 1,000 campsites at nearby Omak Eastside Park.

Lincoln County

Places to Go

GRAND COULEE DAM   509-633-3074 (Chamber of Commerce);
                                          509-633-9265
  Location: Ninety miles west of Spokane on Hwy 2 and Hwys. 174 and
    155; 90 miles northeast of George from I-90 on Hwys. 283, 28, 27 and
    155.
  Web Site: www.grandcouleedam.org; www.usbr.gov/pn/grandcoulee
  Days/Hours: Daily, 9am–5pm, except closed December and January.
    Nightly laser light shows during summer only
  Tours: Due to security enhancements after 9/11, there are no more reg-ularly scheduled guided tours. Call 509-633-9265 for tour schedule.
    Note: For security reasons, packs, purses, bags, cases and packages
    are not allowed in the Visitor Arrival Center or on tours.
  Wheelchair/Stroller Access: Yes

Perhaps the most memorable part of a Grand Coulee visit in summer months is the forty-minute laser light show that is projected nightly onto the dam's face. It starts at sunset, opening with a startling quiet as the blue lights illuminate the spillway and the water starts gushing downward. This 5,000-foot long dam seems to become a larger-than-life movie screen, complete with some animated cartoons during the show. There are some good choices for viewpoints of the display: in town, grab a bleacher seat across from the Coulee House motel or at the Visitor Arrival Center; or stake out a spot on the lawn below the Visitor Arrival Center; or watch from the parking lot at the third Powerhouse. All three have stereo systems which broadcast music synchronized with the light show.

For a good photo vantage point, the Crown Point Vista overlooks the dam, Lake Roosevelt and the town of Coulee Dam. You can see the laser show from here, also.

Tours of the dam are given periodically during the day. Call the Dam (509-633-9503) for further information. For those considering extended visits, you can rent a houseboat or camp on Lake Roosevelt, behind the Dam.

SUN LAKES STATE PARK AND
DRY FALLS INTERPRETIVE – VISITOR CENTER   509-632-5583 (park);
509-632-5214 (center);
888-CAMPOUT (campsite reservations)

Location: On Hwy 17, seven miles southwest of Coulee City
Web Site: www.parks.wa.gov
Days/Hours: Park opens daily, 6:30am–dusk; overnight camping year-round. Visitors Center is open mid-May through September, 10am–6pm, and by appointment in winter.
Admission: By donation
Wheelchair/Stroller Access: Yes

Spring, summer and fall months are most popular here. The desert-like environment is great for horseback riding, swimming, trout fishing and boating, although heavy winds are a possibility. The state operates the campground and swimming beach on Deep Lake and Dry Falls Lake; much of Park Lake is privately managed. For those who like some amenities, there's a golf course, laundromat, general store and concessions near by. The Visitor/Interpretive Center is located two miles north of the main park on Hwy 17. When it's open, Center naturalists give scheduled talks about the mammoth ice sheets that covered the land a million years ago, forcing the Columbia River to carve a new channel. On exhibit at the center is a fossilized baby rhinoceros trapped in a pre-Ice Age mudflow. Dry Falls, three-and-one-half miles wide with a 400-foot drop, is the skeleton of one of the greatest waterfalls in geologic history.

Places to Eat

ROCK 'N ROBIN DRIVE-IN   509-633-1290
Location: Bridgeport and Hwy 174 in Grand Coulee
Days/Hours: Summer: daily 10am–10pm. Winter: 10am–7pm
Wheelchair/Stroller Access: Yes

This place will push your nostalgia button. In summer months the servers come to your car window to take your order. Hamburgers, milkshakes and French fries are the main menu items here, but they've added subs, sandwiches and salads. Also available are buffalo burgers, a good choice.

Northeast Washington

Places to Go

GARDNER CAVE AT CRAWFORD STATE PARK   509-238-4258
Location: North of Metaline, take Hwy 31; turn west on Boundary Rd.; drive 12 miles.
Web Site: www.parks.wa.gov
Days/Hours: Summer: 9am–6pm. Winter: closed September–April.
Tours: Memorial Day–Labor Day; Thursday–Monday; 10am–noon, 2pm and 4pm
Wheelchair/Stroller Access: No

This 1,055-foot-long limestone cave has a story worth listening to, assuming it's true. Seems it once housed moonshine stills, but the owner/bootlegger lost the tunnel in a card game to a Metaline storekeeper who then gave the property to the state parks department. Only the upper 494 feet of the cave are explorable; steel walkways and stairs keep visitors away from the precious 9,000-year-old stalactites which grow only a half-inch a century. Natural oils in our hands would kill further growth, so no touching is allowed. The quiet drip, drip, drip you hear is water falling from the stalactites. It can get very cool (low 40s); warm clothing recommended.

MANRESA GROTTO   509-445-1147 (Tribal Center)
Location: Off LeClerc Rd., on the Kalispel Indian Reservation. Take Newport Hwy to Hwy 211; continue 17 miles, cross over the railroad tracks, cross the bridge and continue another six miles into Kalispel.
Days/Hours: Monday–Thursday, 7am–5pm
Wheelchair/Stroller Access; Yes, but difficult

This hillside cave was used for religious ceremonies by both the Kalispel Native Americans and settlers. Inside are a stone altar and pews, outside a wonderful view of the Pend Oreille Valley. On the third weekend in September, a priest celebrates mass with the public. For more information about the Kalispel Native Americans, call the Tribal Center (days and hours listed above).

PEND OREILLE VALLEY TRAIN RIDES   509-442-3397
**(this number is in operation two weeks
prior to first scheduled train ride)**
Location: Ione and Metaline Falls
Days/Hours: Weekends only; 11am, 1pm, 3pm. Trips are 90 minutes.
Admission: $12/ages 13–64; $7/ages 2–12; $7/over 64. Reservations
    strongly recommended
Wheelchair/Stroller Access: Yes, for wheelchairs; no, for strollers. Ba-
    bies and toddlers may be carried aboard.

Schedules do vary from year to year for this exhilarating excursion, but they generally start their season in mid-June and continue until mid-October. Most trips originate in Ione; there are both covered and open cars. If you want lots of fresh air and the wind in your hair, request an open car! The train winds along the Pend Oreille River and makes a breathtaking stop on the trestle at Box

Canyon Dam some 180 feet above the water. The autumn excursions are most popular for the brilliant fall colors along the way. Check the Web site for current schedules.

This is bigger than all of us!

Photo courtesy Great Harvest Bakery/M. Weissman

STONEROSE INTERPETIVE CENTER   **509-775-2295**
  Location: 15 Kean St., Republic, one block west of Main St.
  Web Site: www.stonerosefossil.org
  Days/Hours: May–October; Tuesday–Saturday, 10am–5pm. Mid-June to
    mid-September; Sunday, 10am–4pm. Center is closed on Mondays.
    Group and field trips by arrangement.
  Admission: $3/adults; $2/ages 12–18 and seniors 62 and older; Free/chil-
    dren under 12.
  Wheelchair/Stroller Access: Yes, but bumpy

About 10 million years after the dinosaurs roamed the earth, impressions of
plants, insects and fish were left in the ground at these fossil beds. The layers
of shale simply split apart "like pages in a book," telling the story of the Eo-
cene Epoch. Today you can see those fossils at the Stonerose Interpretive Center,
which draws almost 10,000 visitors annually. Or find some yourself by doing
your own digging. After registering at the center, you can go out to hunt for
your own organisms using your own tools (hammer and cold chisel) or renting
theirs ($3 plus tax for the day). The digging tools are usually hammers and cold
or nonwooden chisels but putty knives and screwdrivers work, too. Long pants
and goggles are suggested. You're limited to three pieces per person per day;
with a family that can add up to quite a collection. Please bring them back to
the center for identification and cataloging. Finding one to keep is a real treasure. Be advised that the center reserves the right to retain any fossil that is of
real scientific value or significance to the Stonerose collection.

HELPFUL PHONE NUMBERS:
  Chambers of Commerce:
  Wenatchee Valley: 509-662-2116
  Ephrata: 509-754-4656
  Grand Coulee Dam Area: 509-633-3074
  Leavenworth: 509-548-5807
  Marblemount: 360-873-2106
  Metaline and Metaline Falls: 509-446-4012
  Moses Lake: 509-765-7888; 800-992-6233 (Washington only)
  Chelan: 800-424-3526
  Newport: 509-447-5812
  Cashmere: 509-782-3513
  Soap Lake: 509-246-1821

OTHER RESOURCES
Colville National Forest: 509-684-3711
Douglas County: 800-245-3922, ext 2
Odessa Visitor Information Center: 509-982-0188
Okanogan National Forest: 509-826-3275
Okanogan Tourism Council: 800-225-6625
Omak Visitor Information Center: 800-225-6625
Republic City Hall: 509-775-3216

Olympic Peninsula, Hood Canal, Ocean Beaches

Getting together for a summer nature camp photo at the Dungeness River Audubon Center at Railroad Bridge Park.

Photo courtesy of Bob Boekelheide

Many visitors are surprised that much of the Olympic Peninsula is a rain forest, with up to 175 inches of precipitation annually. No wonder there are majestic trees and monster mosses. Even in summer, it's smart to bring a raincoat. But the rain doesn't slow anyone down! National Park Service naturalists host programs for both children and adults at Mora, Kalaloch, Hoh and Heart o' the

Hills. Other places to visit are Port Gamble, Port Townsend and Port Angeles; each has its individual attractions. But take note–Sequim and Port Townsend enjoy a "rain shadow" with up to half the annual rainfall in the Seattle area.

NORTH AND NORTH CENTRAL BEACHES: Washington's coast is rugged and often misty. Beachcombing is fun but challenging. The shoreline is not nearly as permissive as neighboring Oregon's, but the "catch" can be rewarding. Driftwood, rocks polished by the tides, and other finds become treasures. Lake Quinault and Kalaloch Lodges provide stopping and resting places for vacationers. There are also some good places to spot bald eagles. The 30-mile stretch between Moclips and Ocean Shores is razor-clam paradise, with a gentle coastline and sandy beaches. Be sure to check with authorities about the legal clam–digging seasons. Sand castles, tide pools and kite flying – all inviting activities for families who love to play on the beach.

SOUTH BEACHES: Grays Harbor, Aberdeen, Hoquiam: These waters are home to fishing charter boats, and oyster and crab catchers. From Grays Harbor to the mouth of the Columbia River, fishing is a high priority. Timber was once the primary industry, but has declined precipitously in past decades. Today, Westport is a great attraction for its recreational fishing. A major event down here is the migration of the gray whales as they move north along the Washington coast from Mexico, usually between late February and April. Long Beach is on state Hwy 103, about four miles north of U.S. Hwy 101, and 73 miles south of Aberdeen. It's a long day trip, and overnight accommodations are in short supply. Call the Visitors Bureau (see the end of the chapter) or AAA for recommendations.

Olympic Peninsula and Hood Canal

Between Hood Canal and Sequim

DEPOT AT DISCOVERY BAY   **360-385-9490**
  Location: 282023 Hwy 101
  Web Site: www.discobaydepot.com
  Days/Hours: Weekdays, 8am –6pm; weekends, 8am–8 pm
  Wheelchair/Stroller Access: No
  Driving Directions: After crossing the Hood Canal Bridge, go west toward Port Angeles on Hwy 104; take the 101 exit and go west three miles.
  Coming from Port Townsend, take Hwy 20 to the 101 interchange; take the right fork, go one mile—the train cars are there, on your right.

What could be more fun than climbing on up a train for an ice cream cone? Or candy snack! Also called the Railroad Park, there's a caboose and a yard engine from the 1950s converted into mini-diners. Parents be advised – kids climb the engine at their (or your) own risk. It's awfully tempting, too. Also tempting are the waffle cones, milk shakes and sandwiches (pb&j, tuna, turkey and hot dogs) in one car, major candy choices in the other. Candy choices include jelly bellies (great blue sharks, tropical fish), English toffee and chocolate cocoa clusters—all in all, about 150 varieties from which to choose. Sugar-free candy is available, too. Look for the cute party favors—candy trains made from candy bars, peppermint candy, kisses and more. You can eat on the deck overlooking Discovery Bay. On a nice day, it's quite a treat.

OLYMPIC MUSIC FESTIVAL   **206-527-8839**
  Location: Olympia Peninsula; 10 miles west of the Hood Canal Bridge,
    near Quilcene
  Web Site: www.olympicmusicfestival.org
  Days/Hours: June–September; Saturday and Sunday, 2pm
  Admission: $12–$24; special prices for children. Free/children under
    6. Season passes and group rates available. Advance reservations
    strongly recommended.
  Barn tickets are date-specific; lawn tickets are good for any concert.
  Wheelchair/Stroller Access: Yes

The Olympic Music Festival's "Concerts in the Barn" series is a summer highlight for many families. The chance to sit on bales of hay or just relax and stretch out on the grass outside the barn is both unique and enticing, and the music is exceptional. Inside the barn, you can sit on padded church pews or the hay bales; acoustics are really quite good. Families usually bring picnic lunches, but be sure to arrive early enough to picnic and stroll around, and pet the very friendly farm animals (no dogs except service dogs allowed). Concessions sell sandwiches, espresso and other beverages; gourmet lunch boxes can be ordered in advance (call the number above) and picnic tables are available. Save some time for the gift shop—it's fun to browse and they appreciate the sales.

Note: If you can't take sun, umbrellas are suggested.

Port Townsend

Places to Go

FORT WORDEN STATE PARK 360-385-4730
  Location: 200 Battery Way; one mile north of Port Townsend
  Web Site: www.olympus.net/ftworden
  Days/Hours: Daylight hours for day visitors; overnight camping and
    rental home accommodations year-round.
  Wheelchair/Stroller Access: Yes, in most places

Gun mounts and bunkers are just waiting for make-believe battles and war plans. Flashlights are an appropriate accessory here for playing inside the ammunitions bunkers. The beach outside is part of the park and a wonderful destination for exploring and sand architecture. There's lots of running around and biking space, too. If you're interested in Fort Worden history, visit the Commanding Officers' Quarters Museum, open daily from 1–5 pm, or the 248 Coastal Artillery Museum, open in May from noon–4pm on weekends, Memorial Day–Labor Day, 11am–4pm daily. There are 18 turn-of-the-century officers' quarters, furnished in an ornate Victorian style, which are available for overnight rental. These are quite popular, so allow two to four months advance planning. Call the number above or check their Web site. Warning: They do not accept credit cards. Do spend /some time learning about the rich and fascinating history of the Fort.

PORT TOWNSEND MARINE SCIENCE CENTER   **360-385-5582**
    Location: In Fort Worden State Park, at the end of the dock
    Web Site: www.plmsc.org
    Days/Hours: Marine exhibit: November 1–March 31 by appointment
        only. April 1–June 14; Saturday and Sunday, noon–4pm; June
        15–Labor Day, open Wednesday–Monday, 11am–5pm; from day after
        Labor Day–October 31, Saturday and Sunday, noon–4pmAdmission:
        $3/adults; $2/ages 6–17; 5 and under/free
    Wheelchair/Stroller Access: Yes

There's a live underwater video camera here that captures action under the pier, fascinating to both kids and parents. Indoors, there are touch tanks with underwater sea creatures. "Touch" means do just that—poke your fingers in to see what the creatures feel like. The Center offers interpretive programs daily, and day and overnight camps dedicated to hands-on marine science.

Places to Eat and Stay

ELEVATED ICE CREAM PARLOR & CANDY SHOP   **360-385-1156**
    Location: 627 and 631 Water St., Port Townsend
    Web Site: www.elevatedicecream.com
    Days/Hours: Open daily, 10am–10pm
    Wheelchair/Stroller Access: Yes

From a tiny shop so small it fit into an unused Victorian elevator car, this wonderful ice-cream boutique has "elevated" itself to a popular place that can accommodate the many visitors looking for delicious homemade ice cream. They've added a candy shop (which shouldn't disappoint anyone!) and homemade desserts, espresso, Italian ices, sherbet and frozen yogurt. Many of their flavors are made with local Sequim strawberries or Olympic Peninsula raspberries. The scoops of ice cream and Italian ice are sold by weight, so you can "customize" your portion. Enjoy!

PORT LUDLOW RESORT 360-437-2222(resort);
800-732-1239 (reservations; front desk open twenty-four hours)
  Location: 9483 Oak Bay Rd.
  Web Site: www.ludlowbayresort.com
  Days/Hours: Overnight accommodations year-round.
  Wheelchair/Stroller Access: Yes, by ferry; on-site, some units are accessible.

Most folks prefer to cruise up to the marina, which holds up to 300 boats comfortably. Others will arrive by small plane, but the ferry is the usual mode of transportation. There's lots to do here: golf, tennis, bicycling, strolling, maybe just relaxing and enjoying some spectacular views. There are 38 rooms with the usual amenities (each has a fireplace and oversize Jacuzzi tub). Children under 12 are free in their parents' room.

Sequim

Places to Eat

101 DINER 360-683-3388
  Location: 392 W Washington St.
  Days/Hours: Daily, 6am–9pm
  Wheelchair/Stroller Access: Yes

Yes, it's noisy, but that's part of the fun here. The period décor pulls you in and the food is pretty good, with hamburgers and Chicago-style pizza as the specialties. There's a CD player tucked into the rear of a 1956 thunderbird, good for some very nostalgic music. Kids may not appreciate the tunes, but parents will.

CONEHEADS DRIVE-IN 360-683-1232
  Location: 3rd and Washington St.Hours: Daily, 6am–8pm

The kids will want to stop and see the eye-popper on this drive-thru; it's the front end of a shiny, years-old car bursting through the second-storywindow! But down below they've serving kid-size mac 'n cheese sandwiches or Sabrett hot dogs. For dessert, try a soft ice-cream cone; choose from two of eight flavors for the swirled confection. They're located just next to the Oak Table.

THE OAK TABLE
  Location: Third and Bell Sts.
  Web Site: www.oaktablecafe.com
  Days/Hours: Breakfast and lunch daily, 7am–3pm. Sunday, breakfast only.

Wheelchair/Stroller Access: Yes

Yes, the tables are oak, and the tiffany lamps and stained glass panels lend a charming air to this constantly popular landmark in Sequim, there since 1981. They're known for their apple pancakes that are more like a soufflé, three inches high and filled with fresh apples. Easy for two people, a challenge for one. They serve breakfast from an extensive menu all day, lunch from 11 am. Dessert could be an ice cream crepe or a yogurt granola parfait. On weekends, go early or expect a moderate wait.

THE THREE CRABS   **360-683-4262**
    Location: 11 Three Crabs Rd., Sequim
    Days/Hours: Summer: daily, 11:30am except Saturday until 10 pm. Winter: daily, 11:30am, except Saturday until 9pm. Closed Thanksgiving and Christmas. Reservations recommended for parties of six or more.
    Wheelchair Access: Yes, but no strollers, please. High chairs available.

Once listed in USA TODAY as one of the top 10 restaurants for seafood by the seashore, they specialize in seafood of course and hold a Dungeness Crabfest in October that includes special events for children. Tops on the children's menu here is the fish or clam basket, grilled cheese sandwich or a cheeseburger. Young guests also receive a favor when they dine here.

Places to Go

RAILROAD BRIDGE PARK
    Location: At the end of Hendrickson Rd. From Washington St. in downtown Sequim, turn left on to Sequim-Dungeness Rd. to Hendrickson Rd., turn left and follow Hendrickson to the park.
    Hours: Dawn to dusk; no overnight camping or parking
    Wheelchair/Stroller Access: Yes in the park, not up to the bridge

DUNGENESS RIVER AUDUBON CENTER 360-681-4076
    Location: Railroad Bridge Park, 2151 W Hendrickson Rd, SequimWeb Site: www.dungenessrivercenter.org
    Days/Hours: Open year-round. Tuesday–Saturday, 10am–4pm; Sunday, noon–4pm
    Wheelchair/Stroller Access: Yes

Part of the Olympic Discovery Trail, Railroad Bridge Park's highlight is the 1500 foot-long River Trestle. The bridge was built in 1915 by what was later the Milwaukee Railroad. Their goal was to link Port Angeles to Port Townsend by rail, and the trains ran (by tides, not timetables) until 1985. Kids enjoy running from one end to the other, and gazing over the railing to the river below and surrounding woods. Considering the low rainfall in Sequim, the forest is surprisingly green and verdant; just notice the lack of moss (as compared to the rain forest). The Center is located in Railroad Bridge Park, quite near the historic bridge and trestle, with a gift shop and learning center. Their classes are devoted to teaching people about Northwest birds, fish, and other natural history of the north Olympic Peninsula. There are many interesting displays about animals, the Dungeness River, and the history of the area. Note: If you're interested in birds, don't miss the Whatcom County Museum's fabulous collection in Bellingham.

OLYMPIC GAME FARM 800-778-4295; 360-683-4295

Location: 1423 Ward Rd.; about ten minutes outside of town. From Washington St. in downtown Sequim, turn left onto Dungeness Rd.; follow the main road to Woodcock Rd.; turn left and continue to Ward Rd. Turn right (follow the signs) to the end of the road.

Days/Hours: Driving tour: mid-May to mid-September, daily; 9am–6pm. Remainder of year: 9am–3pm.

Walking tour: mid-May to mid-September, 9am–3pm. Closed remainder of year.Admission:

Driving tour: call for current information.

Wheelchair/Stroller Access: Not on walking tour.

There are 56 species of animals here and you can view most of them,especially on the driving tour, which takes about forty-five minutes. Note the strict warnings about remaining in your car. The animal population is down now, but the Farm is lively with wolves, big bison, bears, even a lion and lioness. There's a vast variety of other wildlife on this 90-acre preserve. The bunnies on the walking tour are very friendly. Many of the animals are retired from film and television. There's a small petting farm near the entrance with very amiable goats and some miniature farm buildings to crawl through and play inside. Be aware that all animals on the walking tour are in cages with small outside pens. The larger animals run free on the preserve.

ROOSEVELT ELK HERD

Location: Foothills of the Dungeness River As you drive into Sequim, you'll notice a prominent metal elk mounted on the welcome sign. The Roosevelt elk herd is a familiar site in these parts. Native to the Olympic Peninsula, there are approximately 100 in the herd comprised of bulls and cows, with calves appearing in the spring. The herd moves about the foothills east of the Dungeness River, south to Blyn, east of Sequim and north to Port Williams Road. Their favorite spots are along Happy Valley Rd. and the hills, West Sequim Bay Rd., Palo Alto Rd. and north toward Port Williams Rd. If you are fortunate enough to spot them, be advised that they are NOT tame and will usually move away when approached. The Roosevelt elk is a magnificent animal; imposing to watch if you can find them.

MUSEUM & ARTS CENTER 360-683-8110
Location: 175 W Cedar St.; from Washington St. turn left on Sequim-
Dungeness Rd. and left again on Cedar. The Museum is in the middle
of the block; parking is in the back.
Hours: Tuesday–Saturday, 8am–4pm
Admission: Free; donations appreciated
Wheelchair/Stroller Access: Yes

Founded in 1976, the museum has been in the process of renovation and plans
to complete a new exhibit by the time you read this. Several years ago, a phenomenal find of mastodon bones several miles away in Happy Valley was a
huge occurrence. The bones are now in the museum, which will mount them
on a mural for display. Kids can stand next to the mural and see how they compare in height and size to these enormous creatures. On exhibit now is a 1907
REO—the first car in the Sequim Dungeness Valley, a bedroom with furnishings belonging to an early Sequim pioneer whose great-grandfather was the
first governor of the Oregon Territories in 1849. The furniture is of bird's eye
maple and came around the Horn in the 1800s. Models of passenger steamers
that plied Puget Sound are interesting; both the Alice Gertrude and Rosalie
steamers have stories to tell. They were the transportation from Seattle to Port
Angeles and Port Townsend in the early 1900s.

DUNGENESS SPIT NATIONAL WILDLIFE REFUGE   **360-457-8451**
Location: Just off Hwy 101, take Kitchen-Dick Rd., which becomes
Lotzgesell Rd. Follow the directional signs to Voice of America Rd.
Web Site: www.dungeness.com/refuge/
Days/Hours: Daily, sunrise to sunset
Admission: $3 per family; those with Federal Recreation Passes admit-
ted free.
Wheelchair/Stroller Access: Very difficult

This rugged, windswept spit reaches for over five miles into the Strait of Juan
de Fuca. The longest sand spit in the United States, its beauty lies in the stark
yet fertile beach and cliffs. There's much to see here—a peaceful bay, sandy
and rocky beaches, tide flats, and a short but steep half-mile trail to reach the
cliff. There's great bird-watching (over 250 species) and clam–digging (check
first with the Refuge or Clallam Bay Recreation Area rangers regarding conditions). Another point of interest is the New Dungeness Lighthouse at the end
of the spit; it's a 10-mile round-trip hike out there, but the lighthouse keepers
(all volunteers from the U.S. Lighthouse Association) will lead tours for those
interested (usually between 10am–4pm daily). The Lighthouse history is rich;
the light went on, on December 1, 1857, making it the first to be lit in the Strait
of Juan de Fuca-Puget Sound area.

Port Angeles

Places to Go

ARTHUR D. FEIRO MARINE LABORATORY 360-417-6254
  Location: Adjacent to the Port Angeles city pier, at the intersection of
  Lincoln St. and Railroad Ave.
  Web Site: www.olympen.com/feirolab
  Days/Hours: Memorial Day–Labor Day, 10am–5pm. After Labor Day;
  Saturday and Sunday, noon–4pm. Pre-arranged tours for groups
  available by appointment; call 360-452-9277, ext. 264.Admission:
  $2.50/adults; $1/ages 6–12 and seniors; Free/members and children 5
  and under with parent.
  Wheelchair/Stroller Access: Yes

This is an ideal place for children to learn about the marine creatures of the
Washington coast—and not get wet. Take some time to walk around the pier,
as well. At the front of the building, a sculpture of cormorants graces the
area. On the side of the building, a marvelous mural depicting an early Native
American Indians' long house and a mural of early Port Angeles and a 1750
scene of Klallam Village tells pictorial stories.

ON THE PORT ANGELES CITY PIER: The pier is good for strolling, with a great
view of the water and the huge container ships and tankers that are waiting
or loading. Look for the octopus topiary and the climbing boat. Also on the pier,
a 50-foot Climbing Tower with wide stairways. Next to the Pier, Hollywood
Beach has a sandy beach for playing and a waterfront walkway; nearby there's
a mile-long waterfront walking path. The estuary nearby is full of seabirds in
constant motion.

HURRICANE RIDGE 360-565-3130 (visitors' center);
  360-565-3131 (24-hour recorded road and weather information)
  Location: Seventeen miles south of Port Angeles
  Web Site: www.nps.gov.olym
  Days/Hours: Road is open 24 hours a day from mid-May to mid-October
  (weather dependent); road closes at night after these dates due to
  overnight snowstorms. Road openings depend on weather and staff
  availability. Call Visitor Center or recorded information for updates.
  Admission: $10 for park entry fee per car; call visitor center or re-
  corded information for road status.
  Hurricane Ridge Visitor Center: Summer, open 9am–4pm. Snack
  bar/gift shop open daily, 10am–6pm from May through September.
  Winter: If the road is open, the Center is open. From mid-December
  through late March, the snack bar, gift shop and ski/snowshoe

rental shop is open 10am–4pm only on weekends and holidays that
fall on a Monday.
Wheelchair/Stroller Access: Some degree of accessibility on short
trails adjacent to Visitors Center. Handouts available with detailed
information.

The 17-mile drive up the Ridge on the only paved road to the mountains takes
approximately thirty to forty minutes; the view is worth all of that and more.
Explorers on an expedition there in 1855 took nearly a month. There are over
600 miles of trail in the park, including numerous options for day hikes; many
are very forgiving for less experienced hikers. The Hurricane Hill Trail is 1.6
miles (paved) to the summit with a 360-degree view. Black tailed deer, black
bears, Olympic marmots, chipmunks, golden eagles, snowshoe hares and other
wildlife share the woods with you. If you make it to the top, on a clear day
you'll see the Straits of Juan de Fuca and the surrounding Olympic mountain
peaks —the view (and the climb) takes your breath away. Snow can linger on
mountain trails well into July, so check at the Visitor Center for current conditions.

Playing in the snow, sightseeing, cross-country skiing, snowshoeing and inner
tubing or sledding are big attractions. There is also a small downhill ski operation (two rope tows and a poma lift, 10am–4pm, weekends only) during its ski
school weeks, usually early January to mid-March.

OLYMPIC PARK INSTITUTE   **800-775-3720; 360-928-3720**
Location: 111 Barnes Point Rd., Port Angeles
Web Site: www.OlympicParkInstitute.org
Days/Hours: Office hours: 8:30am–4:30pm, Monday–Friday. April–Octo-
ber: weekend family learning vacations, Lake Crescent family camp,
Elderhostel programs, teen outdoor adventure program, private
events and retreats. February–November: science field trips for
teachers and students.
Admission: $20–$64
Wheelchair/Stroller Access: Yes

Families can chose from guided hikes through the lush forest of Olympic National Park exploring Lake Crescent in giant Montreal canoes, learn about
orienteering (compass and map-reading), and attend workshops on tool-build-
ing and fire-making. All have expert instructors in a safe environment. You'll
stay overnight in rustic cabins, eat your meals in the dining hall and enjoy
campfires.

OLYMPIC NATIONAL PARK VISITORS' CENTER

360-565-3130 (information);
360-565-3130 (recorded information);
800-833-6388 (TTY)

Location: 600 E Park Ave., Port Angeles
Web Site: www.nps.gov/olym/pphtm
Days/Hours: Open year-round, 9am–4pm
Wheelchair/Stroller Access: Yes

The Olympic National Park is an amazing destination, even in our state. You'll find snow-capped mountains, a coastline for marine activity, and a temperate rain forest. Ninety-five percent of the Park is designated wilderness; there's no end of opportunities for almost any recreational activity you enjoy, including hiking, mountaineering, fishing, skiing, camping, horseback riding–you get the idea.

The Visitors' Center is dedicated to making the Park accessible to you, and this is an education center that really mixes it up. In the Discovery Room, drawers around the room are full of activities (you'll need a key to access them). A tray full of artifacts to play with includes shells, rocks, bark, pieces of skeleton, even antlers. In the Discovery Ranger Station there are stunning murals of the Olympic National Forest, plus a Circle of Life puzzle in large scale, a Water Cycle puzzle and a Migrating Salmon Maze. Don't miss the Roosevelt elk in the corner, and The Canoe, filled with necessary implements once used for whale hunts. There's an excellent book collection in the gift shop. They have a complete catalogue of activities available to families, for example, "Birds, Bats and Bugs." Ask at the desk; they can answer any question you may have.

SOL DUC HOT SPRINGS
360-327-3583

Location: On Hwy 101, a few miles past Lake Crescent; take Sol Duc road 12 miles to its end.
Web Site: www.northolympic.com/solduc/
Days/Hours: Open daily, April through October. Mineral Pools; 9am–dusk.Admission: $10/ages 13–61; $7.50/ages 4–12; $6.50/seniors 62 and older and those physically challenged; $3/ages 1–3; Free/children under 1.
Wheelchair/Stroller Access: Yes

The bubbling mineral waters of this natural hot springs can be as hot as 122 degrees, but by the time it reaches the three pools here, it cools to 100 to 107 degrees. There is a shallower, cooler pool for youngsters, and a large chlorinated swimming pool for everyone. For families, a resort area offers 32 cabins and 17 RV sites. The National Park Service has 80 camp sites within walking distance.

ERICKSEN MEMORIAL PARK
  Location: 4th & Race Sts.
  Web Site: www.ci.port-angeles.wa.us/menus/parks
  Days/Hours: 5am–11pm
  Wheelchair/Stroller Access: Yes, although it might be difficult to cross
    the grass in certain weather.

Apart from the extensive recreational opportunities here (sports fields and tennis courts), the "frosting" is the Dream Playground for ages 5–12. Adult supervision is required and this is a pet-free area. Memorial plaques signify the great community support in creating this park. They've thought of everything. There are swings of all kinds: rubber ropes, buckets, rubber tires. Kids can climb anywhere in this structure–around, over, under, through, up and down. There are slides, towers, and a vertical xylophone. Look for the colorful dragon that graces one of the towers–a gift from a friend in Japan. On the fences around the playground are tiles created by the schoolchildren. And still there is more. Adjacent to this playground is a smaller version created for the toddlers.

PORT ANGELES SLOT CARS   360-452-7264; 888-774-3227
  Location: 529 E First St.
  Web Site: www.gofastest.com/pascr/start
  Days/Hours: Wednesday and Thursday, 4pm–10pm; Friday, 3pm–10pm;
    Saturday, noon–10pm; Sunday, 2pm–8pm; closed Monday and Tues-
    dayAdmission: $2/15 minutes; $1/rent controller; $1/rent a car.
  Wheelchair/Stroller Access: Tight quarters here; no way to maneuver
    around the raceways

The only slot car site outside Tacoma, they have two racetracks here; one is 21 feet long and 13 feet wide, the other is 16 feet long and 8 feet wide. Kids as young as seven are intrigued by this sport and come here to use the track; the average age range is from 8–10 after school; adults come in the evening. The rules are strict; no smoking and no substance abuse allowed. And if there's no one to race with, the manager will happily race against you. They have over 1000 cars in stock, and over 100 in the cases to admire. On the 124 scale track, cars will hit 60 miles, which is a scale speed of 300 mph; on the 132 scale the real speed is 20–30 mile and the scale speed is 60–100 mph. If you purchase a 1/32 scale car, you'll get free track time for a month. It's competitive and an adrenaline boost. Easy to see why the kids enjoy it.

Places to Eat

THE OLYMPIC BAGEL CO.   360-452-9100
  Location: 802 E First St.
  Web Site: www.olympicbagel.com
  Days/Hours: Monday–Friday, 6am–4pm; Saturday and Sunday, 7am–
    3pm; closed some holidays
  Wheelchair/Stroller Access: Yes

They serve breakfast and lunch all day, with over 20 kinds of bagels and gourmet cream cheese, plus soups, salads, pizzas and calzones. Kids will love their smoothies or the rich, gourmet hot chocolate. You can eat there or take it to go.

FRUGALS   360-452-4320
  Location:1520 E Front St.
  Web Site: www.frugals.com
  Days/Hours: Summer months: daily, 10:30am–11pm. Winter months:
    Sunday–Thursday, 10:30am–10pm; Friday and Saturday, 10:30am–
    11pm
  Wheelchair/Stroller Access: Not relevant; no inside dining

A drive-up burger bar, they've won local and regional polls for the best "cheap eats" around, and they serve monster-sized buns and burgers. There are special burgers and shakes each week. It's a very convenient family stop.

North and North Central Beaches

Neah Bay, Ocean Shores

Places to Go

BJ'S FAMILY FUN CENTER   360-289-2702 (the center);
                    360-289-0752 (Peppermint Parlor, next door)
  Location: Point Brown Ave. across from Ocean Shores City Hall
  Days/Hours: After Labor Day, Friday to Monday, 11am–6pmAdmission:
    $4/bumper cars (doubles, $4.50); $4/boats and go-karts; $4/slick track
    ($5/doubles) (This is an oval track for go-karts that is watered.) Dis-
    counts for groups of 15 or more.
  Wheelchair/Stroller Access: Only for game-viewing

Kids must be at least 3 years old and within a designated height range to join the ranks of hot-rodders here. The Fast Cars are for those 16 years and older. The Center also has an arcade, a small Ferris wheel and an ice cream shop (with shakes and lattes).

MAKAH CULTURAL AND RESEARCH CENTER — 360-645-2711
Location: In Neah Bay, 75 miles west of Port Angeles
Web Site: mcrc@olypen.com
Days/Hours: Open daily, Memorial Day–September 15. September 16–Memorial Day weekend, open Wednesday–Sunday. Limited openings on Monday and Tuesday also.Admission: $5/adults; $4/seniors and students age 6 thru college; Free/Makah tribal members and youngsters 5 and under
Wheelchair/Stroller Access: Yes

The Makah Indians on Neah Bay can trace their ancestry back to 1000 B.C. History tells that a mudslide buried some Makah houses at a village called Ozette over 500 years ago. In 1970, after years of soil erosion, artifacts from that village began to appear, telling the Makah story. Those artifacts and more items recovered from an 11-year excavation are on display at this museum. There are replicas of whaling and sealing canoes, and a full-size longhouse.

NAN-SEA STABLES 360-289-0194
Location: 255 State Route 115, Ocean Shores
Web Site: www.horseplanet.com
Days/Hours: Open year-round, 10am–5pm, weather permitting
Admission: Prices vary, depending on rental times, hours of use; range is from $15 up.
Wheelchair/Stroller Access: Not equipped for disabled riders.

Trotting along the beach on horseback is an adventure you have to feel, rather than describe. The sensations are heightened if the sun is setting. Later, when you're not sore, it's a delicious memory. Whether you're experienced or a novice, you'll be accompanied by a guide. For the sunset rides, those over 6 may ride on their own; younger children will ride with an adult. Guidelines for children are: 6 and under, horse will be led by a staff member; 7 and older will be guided by a staff member.

Places to Eat and Stay

KALALOCH LODGE 360-962-2271; 866-525-2562 (toll-free)
Location: Olympic National Park on Hwy101 at milepost 157, 35 miles south of Forks
Web Site: www.visitkalaloch.com
Days/Hours: Overnight accommodations year-round
Wheelchair/Stroller Access: Yes, at the lodge; also, two of forty cabins are accessible

On a bluff overlooking the Pacific Ocean, Kalaloch Lodge offers a relaxing retreat from the city. Many families make this an annual vacation, no matter how brief. There are 40 cabins, some with kitchenettes, and the lodge for over-night visits. Children 5 and younger stay free, and the lodge's dining room features a children's menu and high chairs. It's a mecca for beachcombing; winter specials are more economical, and winter storms provide an ambiance all their own.

LAKE QUINAULT LODGE 360-288-2900; 800-562-6672

Location: Southwest of Port Angeles on Hwy101 at mile post 125; turn east onto South Shore Rd.

Web Site: www.visitlakequinault.com

Days/Hours: Overnight accommodations year-round

Wheelchair/Stroller Access: Yes

If ever there was a place to get away from it all, this is it. No television or tele-phones at this 70-year-old lodge, although both have been added in the lakeside building. For entertainment there are canoes, sea cycles, rowboats, badminton and croquet, reading in front of a hospitable brick fireplace, hiking trails that take you all the way to the rain forest, and walking and strolling around the grounds. Swimming in a heated pool is a favorite activity here. The lodge dining room serves breakfast, lunch and dinner daily; homemade cheesecake and stuffed trout are specialties, as well as cedar-planked salmon for two. Room rates will vary; children 5 and under stay free. Cribs and rooms with fireplaces are an option, and pets are allowed in boathouse rooms.

Shops to Browse

Kite Shops: one of the special delights around Ocean Shores is kite flying. To take the kids out onto the beach to indulge in this great family sport, you can buy or rent from either of the two shops listed below.

CLOUD NINE KITE SHOP   360-289-2221

Location: On Oyehut Rd., just outside north gates of Ocean Shores entrance

Days/Hours: Open daily, 10am–7pm. Winter hours will vary based on the time of sunset.

Wheelchair/Stroller Access: Yes

Also featured here is a grand selection of lighthouse and kite-flying prints.

CUTTING EDGE KITES   360-289-5682

Location: Nantucket Mall on Ocean Shores Blvd.

Web Site: www.cuttingedgekites.com

Days/Hours: Summer hours: March–October; Sunday–Thursday, 9am–7pm, Friday and Saturday, 9am–9pm. Winter hours: Novem-

ber–February will vary.
Wheelchair/Stroller Access: Yes

No end of choices here, from beginner's kites to stunt kites, windsocks, flags, windtoys, even yo-yos.

South Beaches

Grays Harbor, Aberdeen And Long Beach

GRAYS HARBOR HISTORIC SEAPORT AND LADY WASHINGTON

360-532-8611

Location: Heron St. in Aberdeen, where the Wishkah and Chehalis rivers meet
Web Site: www.ladywashington.org
Days/Hours: Varies; please call ahead.
Tours: $3/adults; $2/seniors and students; $1/12 and under; $7/family package (up to five). Tours are thirty minutes long. Cruises: $40/adults; $20/children 12 and under.
Wheelchair/Stroller Access: Special wheelchair lift available; not useful for strollers

This majestic eighteenth-century ship is docked here most of the year, but does visit other seaports. For those students studying Washington state history, this is a visual experience; see shipboard life as Capt. Robert Gray, commander of the exploration of the Columbia River and Grays Harbor, knew it. The Lady is a Tall Ship and was considered a merchant brig. Note: Wheelchairs can be lifted aboard by crane but there are no ramps on board.

Long Beach/Nahcotta/Ocean Park/Ilwaco

Long Beach, Nahcotta and Ocean Park are all "related," within a few miles of each other, and share a rich and vibrant history. There's a historic hotel (the Shelburne) and several motels at which to stay in Long Beach, and several inns and B&B's in the area, plus a popular camping site.

Long Beach can boast the longest beach in the continental United States and some of the best kite flying and sandcastle competitions on the West Coast.

Nahcotta is a small rural community located on the inland side of the Long Beach Peninsula, facing Willapa Bay, just south of Oysterville (once an important oyster-producing area until it got "picked out"). Ocean Park is another small community adjacent to both Long Beach and Nahcotta; everyone knows everyone here.

Places to Go – Things to Do

FUNLAND 360-642-2223
   Location: 200 Pacific Hwy S, Long Beach
   Days/Hours: May–August, daily, 9am–10pm; September–April, 10am–
      10pm
   Wheelchair/Stroller Access: Yes

The fact that this place has been around since pinball was the only game in town doesn't make it any less popular. Funland offers both old favorites and new attractions in the world of video games. This amusement arcade is one of the hot spots in town; winners get tickets that can be redeemed for stuffed animals and other souvenir prizes. There's even a supervised laser-tag arena for kids 6 years and older. This is a good place for the older kids.

LONG BEACH GO-KARTS   **360-642-2904**
   Location: Pacific and 10th Streets, Long Beach
   Days/Hours: Summer: open daily, 9am–5pm or whenever everyone
      leaves (they close at midnight). Winter:10am – whenever (weather-
      dependent)Admission: $3.50/three minutes
   Wheelchair/Stroller Access: Yes, for viewing

It's a pretty large go-cart track, as tracks go (considered the largest in south-west Washington). They even offer a senior track for those 12 and older and a junior track for those 5–11 years old. It's a fast blast around, taking all of three minutes.

WORLD KITE MUSEUM AND HALL OF FAME 360-642-4020
   Location: 112 3rd St. NW, Long Beach
   Web Site: worldkitemuseum.com
   Days/Hours: June–September, open daily, 11am–5pm. October–May,
      open Friday –Monday, 11am–5pm
   Admission: $3/adults; $2/kids and seniors; $8/family
   Wheelchair/Stroller Access: Yes

Their major exhibits change annually, and you can always count on seeing award-winning kites. There is a particular area in which children of all ages can spend some time making kites. One room is dedicated to the Washington State International Kite Festival. If you're planning a trip to Long Beach, check their Web site for special family events you'll want to know about.

MARSH'S FREE MUSEUM 360-642-2188
   Location: 409 S Pacific Ave.,Long Beach
   Days/Hours: Daily year-roundWheelchair/Stroller Access: Yes, but some
      of the aisles are narrow and congested

If you've ever been to the Olde Curiosity Shop in Seattle, you might think it's been transplanted. This is an amazing collection of everything, from very old player pianos to mounted (stuffed) animals to beach artifacts and shells of all kinds. You can "measure the passion of your kiss" (great for teenagers) for 10 cents or have your fortune told by Estrella (for only 25 cents), gawk at the skeleton in the case, or be mesmerized by some tantalizing electric lamps. The old Seeburg Orchestra has 10 tunes (plus a flute, violin, pipes, bass snare drum, triangle, cymbal, xylophone and more!) and still plays for $1.This is part of the charm of Long Beach—enjoy.

SANDSATIONS 800-451-2542

Location: On the beach at Long Beach
Web Site: www.funbeach.com
Days/Hours: This varies each year; best to call ahead. Much depends on the tides!
Wheelchair/Stroller Access: Tough on the sand, but viewing is great from the boardwalk

This annual sand-building competition gets a little wilder each year, but that's the fun of it! Families can team together for competition entries; children can create their own. The entrance fee depends on the level of expertise. The craziness starts at 8am on Saturday; judging is on Saturday only and takes place from noon–1pm. Prizes are awarded for all the events. After the competition, the sand architects team up to build a giant castle to compete with out-of-state challengers. Other activities take place over the weekend; best to check the Web Site or call ahead. Sandsations is a great excuse to come down to Long Beach; it's a fun getaway for families.

WASHINGTON STATE INTERNATIONAL KITE-FLYING FESTIVAL
800-451-2542

Location: On the beach, near the Long Beach boardwalk
Web Site: www.funbeach.com
Days/Hours: Third full week of August. Check the Web site for current info
Wheelchair/Stroller Access: Mostly on the boardwalk. Sand is hard packed in places but difficult to maneuver.

Kite flying is a major sport in this part of Washington. In 1997 the 16th annual World Kite Festival was celebrated here. The Washington State event is usually held mid-August and the town is filled to overflowing, so if you want to come down, make your reservations well in advance. Some of the participants come from other countries. At the festival, kites float to music, sail majestically on wind currents and even light up the night. The competition is open to novices and masters alike; there are special children's and seniors' days. This sport is addicting, and one that all ages in a family can share.

NAHCOTTA TIDELANDS INTERPRETIVE SITE
Location: Sandridge Rd. and 268th St., Nahcotta
Days/Hours: Open Friday, Saturday, Sunday and holidays, 10am–3pm
Wheelchair/Stroller Access: Yes

Is the red tide really red? What happens when a crab loses its claws? A five-panel interpretive display tells the story of Willapa Bay and its lusty oyster community. It's interesting to learn how this natural setting (assisted by local concern) continues to be a healthy and productive economic center.

JACK'S COUNTRY STORE   360-665-4989; 888-665-4989
Location: Bay Ave. and Hwy 103, Ocean Park
Web Site: www. jackscountrystore.com
Days/Hours: Open daily, 8am–8pm
Wheelchair/Stroller Access: Yes, although some aisles are narrower
than others

As you enter, the general market is disarming, but keep going, there's much to see here. If you live in the country, this IS your store. A part of the Nahcotta/Ocean Park scenery since 1885, they still carry wood-burning stoves, oil lanterns and kerosene lamps, an amazing assortment of knives and other essential implements, and more nuts and bolts than you could imagine. A big surprise is the little red wagon most kids have grown up with. There's now an all-terrain cargo version, several other sizes and styles, and even a three-wheeled kid's airplane to scoot around in. All in all, a delightful place to browse.

OYSTER U-PICK/NAHCOTTA OYSTER FARM
360-665-2926 (for reservations)
Location: 27008 Sandridge Rd, Nahcotta (next to the Nahcotta Post Office), about 12 miles from Long Beach on the bay side of the Peninsula
Days/Hours: Seasonal. Open September–June, closed July and August
Wheelchair/Stroller Access: Not really. If the ground is dry, you can
roll to the water's edge, but it requires caution.

Larry Warnberg is your host, and he welcomes families. The bay tide here is one hour later than the ocean tide; you'll have a three-hour window with one and half hours on either side for harvesting. Cost is $7 for a five-gallon bucket. Suggested equipment: coolers for transporting the little gems, good fitting knee-high boots, rubber gloves, and screwdrivers (to pry the oysters off the stakes they grow on). The u-pick flats are muddy and, to quote Larry, they'll "suck the boots right off you!" if your footwear doesn't fit well. Rain gear may be needed. Fresh oysters from Willapa Bay can be a delicious experience. Drop-ins are welcome, but scheduling in advance is recommended. Use the phone number listed above, or go online: warnberg@ pacifier.com

THE CRANBERRY MUSEUM 360-642-5553
  Location: 2907 Pioneer Rd., Long Beach
  Web Site: www.cranberrymuseum.org
  Days/Hours: April–December, 10am–5pm (museum and gift shop);
    8am–dusk (self-guided walking tour)
  Admission: Free, but donations gratefully accepted
  Tours: Self-guided at any time; group tours by arrangement (call number above or email info@cranberrymuseum.com).
  Wheelchair/Stroller Access: Museum and gift shop only; fields not easily accessible (dirt paths)

Cranberries have risen to a whole new height. Not only are they very good for us, it turns out they're interesting as well. Long before our history books take up the story, the Native Americans crushed cranberries and combined them with deer meat and melted fat to make pemmican, a substantial food for their lifestyle. Planting takes place here in April and May, with berries are ripening in September and harvested in October. Self-guided tours are at your own pace, but you'll probably learn more on a guided tour. Remember the berries grow in bogs, so dress accordingly. You'll get to know about the history of cranberry farming and see the current methods used in harvesting the berries, which are very seasonal. We see them fresh in the markets in November and December, and have to rely on the frozen version during the rest of the year. If you're a cranberry fancier, you'll love the museum and the gift shop.

Place to Eat

There are scads of kid-oriented eating establishments in Long Beach; pizza is high on the list. We've included one in Nahcotta that's a "cut above."

THE ARK   **360-665-4133**
  Location: Sandridge Rd., Nahcotta (about five miles from the town of Long Beach)
  Web Site: www.arkrestaurant.com
  Days/Hours: The restaurant is open for dinner year-round but hours change seasonally. They are open for brunch on most Sundays. Call ahead for current information or check their Web Site; reservations recommended.
  Wheelchair/Stroller Access: Yes

Located right on Willapa Bay (famous for their oysters), The Ark is a four-star restaurant that delights in introducing children to the fine art of dining. Good behavior is encouraged, of course, but they make it easier by providing a delightful Children's Menu with pictures to color, and an enticing selection of well-priced entrees, including fish and chips, a cheeseburger, baked salmon and barbecued chicken. Everything is baked fresh on the premises; take some bread home, but don't miss the oatmeal-raisin cookies baked with molasses. Dining at The Ark is a must for many Long Beach visitors. If you go during daylight hours, save time for the surrounding scenery—fishermen tending their boats at the dock, small mountains of oyster shells—and some great aromas in the air.

Ilwaco

Ilwaco is a small town in the southwest corner of Washington, a neighbor to Long Beach, and part of the Long Beach Peninsula.

ILWACO HERITAGE MUSEUM   360-642-3446
    Location: 115 SE Lake Street; one block south and a half-block east of the stoplight on Hwy 101
    Web Site: www.ilwacoheritagemuseum.org
    Days/Hours: Monday–Saturday, 10am–4pm; closed Sundays. Call for updates.
    Admission: $3/ages 18–54; $2.50/55 and over; $1/ages 6–11; under 6/free.
    Wheelchair/Stroller Access: Yes in most areas.

One guidebook calls this "a big city museum that just happens to be in a small town." They've worked hard to present an interesting picture of Ilwaco's local history, which tells us that in November of 1805, in his walk to the Pacific Ocean, William Clark walked across what is now the site of the museum. In commemoration, the museum has exhibits dedicated to Lewis and Clark that detail many pertinent aspects of the Corp of Discovery's 18 days in present-day Pacific County. But there's much more. Exhibits include the Land of the Canoe People and the Railroad that Ran by the Tide, and Life in a Seashore Village, among others. A Chinookan Utility Canoe is on display, as is the prow of an archaic Chinookan Utility Canoe that is dated at 800 years old. Did you know that cat tails were important in some Native Americans' diet? The tender greens were edible; the leaves could be woven or sewn into baskets, mats, floor coverings, emergency shelters and more. Of special interest is the story of one man's test against the ocean, Gerard D'Arborville, age 46, who single-handedly rowed a specially constructed 26-foot boat from Japan to Ilwaco in 1991. Capsizing four times and surviving a typhoon, his test of self is quite a story. You'll see a model of his boat, the Sector; video and descriptive displays tell his story. Upstairs is a not-to-be-missed model railroad. Outside, the Irregular Rambling and Never Get There Railroad, Chinook Railway Station and an engine from the Ilwaco Railway and Navigation Company (firmly anchored) are on display.

PACIFIC SALMON CHARTERS   360-642-3466; 800-831-2695
  Location: Port of Ilwaco
  Web Site: www.pacificsalmoncharters.com
  Days/Hours: January–October; call ahead for current times and dates.
  Wheelchair/Stroller Access: Three boats are equipped for wheelchairs

While they offer charters for fishing (salmon or sturgeon, regular bottom fish and deep-water fishing as well), you can also enjoy a two-hour scenic cruise on one of the boats during the summer. Deep-sea fishing is quite strenuous; they prefer youngsters over 10. Some of the larger fishing boats are designed to hold passengers as well, which is a great way to break in to this sport. The rise and fall of ocean swells is a totally new feeling for landlubbers.

Westport

TWIN HARBORS STATE PARK 360-268-9717
  Location: Three miles south of Westport on Hwy 105
  Web Site: www.parks.wa.gov
  Days/Hours: Summer: 6:30am–10pm. Winter: 8am–5pm. Open year-
    round for camping and day use.
  Wheelchair/Stroller Access: Yes

This is a 172-acre camping park with a saltwater shoreline that offers a multitude of activities, including beachcombing, kite flying, clamming and even surf fishing (for the adventurous teens, of course). From lookout sites (usually February and March) you might see gray whales migrating north. The park's north beach has designated areas for horseback riding. The Shifting Sands Nature Trail is interesting for its plants and wildlife; pick up a brochure for complete information. The one-mile trail does have tall beach grass that can be confusing; best not to let children wander here alone.

WESTPORT MARITIME MUSEUM 360-268-0078
  Location: 2201 Westhaven Dr., Westport
  Web Site: www.westportmuseum.org; www.westportmuseum.org/
    grays harbor_lighthouse.htm
  Days/Hours: Memorial Day–Labor Day; 10am–4pm. Winter; Thurs-
    day–Monday, noon–4pm. January–February; weekends and holidays,
    noon–4pm. Hours for the Museum and Lighthouse are same.
  Admission: $3/adults; $1/children 5–14; under 5/free.
  Tours: Yes; can be scheduled at any time. Call for information.
  Wheelchair/Stroller Access: Strollers only. Main museum not
    accessible; the two Whales Houses and Lens Building are.

The museum is located in a 64-year-old former Coast Guard station. In the main building are exhibits of Coast Guard history, ships and shipwrecks, and lots of information regarding fishing, cranberry-growing and timber. Separate buildings house whale and other sea creature skeletons and the 113-year-old operating lens from the Destruction Island Lighthouse. How these mammals were once hunted by fishermen is recounted in the exhibits; the Discovery Room is a "hands-on" experience for young visitors. The Ocean Community Room depicts the lifestyle of an ocean community in the early days.

GRAYS HARBOR LIGHTHOUSE   360-268-0078
Location: 2201 Westhaven Dr., Westport
Web Site: www.westportmuseum.org/grays_harbor_lighthouse.htm
Days/Hours: Memorial Day–Labor Day; 10am–4pm. Winter: Thursday–
   Monday, noon–4 pm. January–February; weekends and holidays,
   noon–4pm. Hours for the Museum and Lighthouse are same.
Tours: Yes; can be scheduled at any time. Coast Guard restrictions
   require children to be 7 years old and 42 inches tall. Tour fee: $3/per
   visitor.
Wheelchair/Stroller Access: No. It's a historical building.

This is a working lighthouse, located about one and a half miles from the museum, easily accessible by car. At 107 feet tall, it's the tallest lighthouse on the Washington and Oregon coast. It was built in 1898 as a harbor light for Westport, even then a busy fishing town, and a coastal light to help ships sailing between Willapa Bay and Destruction Island. Considered one of Washington's architectural highlights, photographers and artists are frequent visitors.

CAPE DISAPPOINTMENT STATE PARK AREA 360-642-3078
Location: About one and a half miles south of Ilwaco. On St. Rte 100,
   follow the signs.
Web Site: www.capedisapointment.org
Days/Hours: Daily, 8am–dusk.
Wheelchair/Stroller Access: Most of this area is soft ground, beach and
   unpaved trails; not hospitable to wheelchairs or strollers.

You'll find the Cape Disappointment Park area at the extreme southwest part of Washington. Within this park are Old Ft. Canby State Park, the Lewis and Clark Interpretive Center, North Head Lighthouse, Fort Columbia, Cape Disappointment Lighthouse and Leadbetter Point State Park.

CAPE DISAPPOINTMENT STATE PARK
Location: About one and a half miles south of Ilwaco; on St. Rte 100,
   follow the signs to the Park.

Within this park is Fort Canby State Park. There are over 250 overnight campsites, more than 20 furnished "yurt" cabins with heat and electricity (bring your own cook stove or barbeque). The camping fee is $38/night. The park has more than 11 miles of hiking trails and two lakes well-stocked with bass. Sixty sites have water, sewer and electricity; a nearby store sells camping supplies and groceries.

LEWIS AND CLARK INTERPETIVE CENTER 360-642-3029
 Location: Cape Disappointment (formerly Fort Canby) State Park. From the light in Ilwaco, go west on N Head Rd. for about five miles into Cape Disappointment State Park.
 Web Site: www.parks.wa.gov
 Days/Hours: Open daily, 10am–5pm.
 Admission: Donations welcome
 Tours: Yes; call to schedule.
 Wheelchair/Stroller Access: Yes

The Center is located on top of two silent gun emplacements that were located at the mouth of the Columbia River from 1905 through World War II. Lewis and Clark's unforgettable Corps of Discovery journey is recounted here in murals, paintings, photographs and entries from their original journals. From the viewing room, you'll see the Fresnel lighthouse lens that was used to warn the ships at sea; this stretch of sea was once known as the "Graveyard of the Pacific" and with good reason. It's a hugely interesting bit of historical nostalgia, and ties in perfectly with the continuing story-telling that surrounds the Lewis and Clark saga.

NORTH HEAD LIGHTHOUSE TOURS 360-642-3078
 Location: From the light in Ilwaco, go west on N Head Rd. for three miles; follow the signs to the North Head Lighthouse.
 Days/Hours: Lighthouse grounds are open year-round daily until dusk.
 Tours: Tours of the lighthouse are given seasonally; call for hours.
 Admission: $1

The North Head Lighthouse (still operational) was built to alert ships coming from the north who could not see the Cape Disappointment light. The 65-foot lighthouse, completed in 1898, sits on a solid basalt base more than 190 feet above sea level; "she" is white with a red cap and has the distinction of being the windiest lighthouse on the West Coast, third windiest nationally. Winds of 120 miles per hour have been recorded. You'll enjoy a breathtaking (perhaps literally!) view of the Peninsula and the Pacific Ocean.

FORT COLUMBIA 360-641-3078
  Location: Two miles east of Chinook, on Hwy 101
  Web Site: www.capedisappointment.org

Built on the historic Chinook Point promontory, within the Chinook community, the Fort had an unobstructed view of the Columbia and was designed to provide protection for the river, along with Forts Canby and Stevens. It took eight years to build, from 1896 to 1904, and was considered important for coast defense, including World Wars I and II. But not one shot was ever fired in anger. The Fort's interpretive center has displays of its military history as well as the Chinook Indian culture.Two rapid firing 6-inch guns are on display.

CAPE DISAPPOINTMENT LIGHTHOUSE
This is currently an active lighthouse, operated and maintained by the U.S. Coast Guard. You can reach the site from the south portion of Fort Canby State Park by hiking trail only. There are no public tours of the facility at this time because of security reasons.

LEADBETTER POINT STATE PARK
Coming up the coast from Ilwaco, there are several access points to the beach on the way to Leadbetter Point State Park. They are Long Beach, Loomis Lake State Park, Pacific Pines State Park and Oysterville. Leadbetter Point State Park is at the northern tip of the Long Beach/Willapa Bay Peninsula. The park offers a four-mile (round trip) beach walk to the north end and back. There are no overnight camping facilities here. Not accessible to wheelchairs and strollers.

HELPFUL PHONE NUMBERS

Chambers of Commerce:

Elma: 360-482-2212

Forks: 800-44-FORKS

Grays Harbor: 800-321-1924

Long Beach: 360-642-2400

Montesano: 360-249-5522

Ocean Shores: 360-289-2451

Port Townsend: 360-385-2722

Raymond: 360-942-5419

Sequim/Dungeness Valley: 800-737-8462

Westport/Grayland: 800-345-6223

OTHER RESOURCES

Grays Harbor Tourism: 800-621-9625

Hoh Visitor Center (west side, Olympic National Park): 360-374-6925

Hoodsport Ranger Station (east side, Olympic National Park): 360-877-5254

Makah Tribal Council: 360-645-2201

National Park Service/U.S. Forest Outdoor Information Center (Seattle) 206-470-4060

North Olympic Peninsula Visitor and Convention Bureau: 800-942-4042

Olympic National Park Visitor Center (north side): 360-452-0330

Port Angeles Visitors Center: 360-452-2363

Long Beach Peninsula Visitors Bureau: 800-451-2542

Index